Classical Confucian
Political Thought

Classical Confucian Political Thought

A New Interpretation

Loubna El Amine

PRINCETON UNIVERSITY PRESS
PRINCETON AND OXFORD

Copyright © 2015 by Princeton University Press

Published by Princeton University Press, 41 William Street,
Princeton, New Jersey 08540

In the United Kingdom: Princeton University Press, 6 Oxford Street,
Woodstock, Oxfordshire OX20 1TW

press.princeton.edu

Jacket Photograph: Ancient Chinese door knocker, located in
Temple of Confucius, Harbin City, Heilongjiang Province, China.
© aphotostory/Shutterstock

Library of Congress Cataloging-in-Publication Data

El Amine, Loubna, 1983-
Classical Confucian political thought : A new
interpretation / Loubna El Amine.
pages cm
Includes bibliographical references and index.
ISBN 978-0-691-16304-8 (hardcover : alk. paper)   1. Confucianism
and state.   2. Philosophy, Confucian.   3. Confucian ethics.
4. Political ethics.   I. Title.

BL1840.E5 2015

320.0931—dc23
2015000234

British Library Cataloging-in-Publication Data is available

This book has been composed in Palatino

Printed on acid-free paper. ∞

Printed in the United States of America

1 3 5 7 9 10 8 6 4 2

Contents

ﻌﻭ

Acknowledgments

There is an old Arabic saying, sometimes attributed to the Prophet Muhammad, that goes, "Seek knowledge, even in China." The idea of China as a faraway—the furthest away—land had not completely disappeared from the social imagination in the Arab world by the time I was an undergraduate. That I ended up writing a book on China's central intellectual tradition was the result of an unexpected journey that started with my professor and mentor at the American University of Beirut, Yahya Sadowski. He encouraged his students to think about the Arab world comparatively, often using East Asia as an example. When I started graduate studies at Indiana University, Bloomington, it was Robert Eno's class on Classical Chinese philosophy that introduced me to Confucianism, with which I have stayed since.

This book is based on my dissertation work at the Department of Politics at Princeton University and I cannot sufficiently express my gratitude to my advisors. Charles Beitz and Alan Patten encouraged this project from its inception, providing continuous help and meticulous feedback. Neither my background nor my research interests were typical, and they, and the Princeton political theory program more generally, were never anything but supportive. Willard Peterson openheartedly gave up much of his time to make sure that I was adequately versed in Chinese history. Stephen Angle's mentorship, both through the example of his own work in Chinese philosophy and through his tireless commentary on my chapters, was crucial. His characteristic generosity also extended to seeing me through the ups and downs of academic life.

I have received more feedback in the process of writing this book than I can adequately recognize here. I especially wish to thank Aaron Stalnaker and David Wong for reading and commenting on the whole manuscript. Stalnaker gave especially thorough feedback. Thanks are also due to three anonymous reviewers. I am grateful to Tongdong Bai, Daniel Bell, Joseph Chan, Jeffrey Isaac, Leigh Jenco, the late Iliya Harik, Martin Kern, Melissa Lane, Stephen Macedo, Michael Nylan, Kwong-loi Shun, Melissa Williams, and Yang Xiao for very helpful discussions and pointers along the way. For reading and commenting on particular chapters, I wish to thank Carlo Invernizzi Accetti, Karuna Mantena, Ryan Nichols, and Bernardo Zacka. Mick Hunter has always graciously answered all my questions and requests for help with early Chinese history and Classical Chinese grammar. Sandra Field and Geneviève Rousselière read various parts of the project at different stages and their feedback was particularly helpful, imbued as it was with precious friendship.

I have greatly benefited in working on this book from a two-year Mellon postdoctoral fellowship at the Whitney Humanities Center at Yale University. I have also received support from the Princeton University Center for Human Values, and the Princeton Institute for International and Regional Studies. Thanks are also due to Xu Xiangdong for the affiliation with Peking University during the fall of 2009. Last but not least, I wish to thank my new institutional home, the Department of Government at Georgetown University, as well as the Berkley Center for Religion, Peace & World Affairs, for their support.

My editor at Princeton University Press, Rob Tempio, appreciated my project from the first time I met him, and it has been a pleasure working with him since. I also wish to thank Nathan Carr, Ryan Mulligan, and the rest of the staff at PUP for their conscientious work on this book, as well as Maria DenBoer and Jingcai Ying for indexing and proofreading. Kevin Mazur read the whole book in its very last stage and prevented a few awkward locutions from making it into the final version. I am sure this would have been a better book had he had the chance to read it earlier.

I sometimes wonder, given the centrality of family to Confucian thought, whether I would have been drawn to it in the same way I was, ten years ago, had I not grown up in a happy family. My brothers Mehdi and Ramzy both react to the world with a healthy dose of humor and *bon sens*, gently tugging at me when I get too tied up in the throes of academia. My parents are both academics; we were raised amongst books, and dinner conversations at home always involved intellectual, political, and ethical issues. But seriousness was also balanced with light-heartedness, and combined with a freedom for each of us to choose our own way in the world. This book is dedicated to my parents who made it all possible.

Note on Translations and Transliterations

Unless otherwise indicated, I have quoted from Confucius, *The Analects*, trans. D. C. Lau (London: Penguin, 1979) for all translations from the *Analects*. I have also consulted Confucius, *Confucius: Analects with Selections from Traditional Commentaries*, trans. Edward Slingerland (Indianapolis: Hackett, 2003). Chapter and section numbers follow Lau. For the *Mencius*, I have quoted, unless otherwise indicated, from Mencius, *Mencius*, trans. D. C. Lau (rev. ed.; London: Penguin, 2003), and consulted Mencius, *Mengzi: With Selections from Traditional Commentaries*, trans. Bryan Van Norden (Indianapolis: Hackett, 2008). Chapter and section numbers follow Lau. For the *Xunzi*, I have quoted, unless otherwise indicated, from Xunzi, *Xunzi: A Translation and Study of the Complete Works*, 3 vols., trans. John Knoblock (Stanford: Stanford University Press, 1988–94), and consulted Xunzi, *Xunzi: Basic Writings*, trans. Burton Watson (New York: Columbia University Press, 2003). Chapter and section numbers follow Knoblock.

I have adopted the Hanyu Pinyin system for the romanization of Chinese characters throughout except for proper names that are predominantly romanized according to the Wade-Giles system in English-language texts.

Classical Confucian
Political Thought

Prologue

༄

Confucianism has become popular again in recent years. With the failure of communism as a state ideology, the Chinese government has been turning more and more to long-vilified Confucius for inspiration. The motto of a "harmonious society" (*hexie shehui* 和谐社会), strewn on banners throughout Beijing in preparation for the 2008 Olympics, was meant to signal the Confucian renaissance of the country. More recently, China's president, Xi Jinping, has been known to reference Confucius and other Chinese Classical thinkers in his speeches. The government also projects its reinvented identity worldwide, exporting cultural centers, known as Confucius Institutes, to countries around the world. This revival of Confucianism is not, however, limited to the political level; it also pervades contemporary social life in China.[1]

On the other hand, Confucianism has also witnessed a resurgence in Western and Chinese academia, fueled by post–Cold War debates about the compatibility between non-Western traditions and liberal democracy, and more specifically by the debate that became known as the "East Asian Challenge to Human Rights."[2] It has also benefited from increasing interest in political theory and in philosophy in non-Western traditions, which has led to the emergence of subfields like comparative philosophy and comparative political theory.

---

[1] See Daniel Bell, *China's New Confucianism: Politics and Everyday Life in a Changing Society* (Princeton: Princeton University Press, 2008).

[2] See, for example, Joanne R. Bauer and Daniel A. Bell, *The East Asian Challenge for Human Rights* (Cambridge: Cambridge University Press, 1999); William Theodore de Bary and Tu Weiming, eds., *Confucianism and Human Rights* (New York: Columbia University Press, 1998); and Kwong-loi Shun and David B. Wong, eds., *Confucian Ethics: A Comparative Study of Self, Autonomy, and Community* (Cambridge: Cambridge University Press, 2004).

Inspired by these two trends, this book investigates Classical Confucian political thought: its conception of government, of the relationship between ruler and ruled, of the methods of ruling, and of the obligations of individuals toward the political community. In other words, the book does for Classical Confucian thinkers what political theorists have long done for thinkers from the Western tradition, from Plato to Nietzsche.

Ethics and Politics in Classical Confucianism

Confucianism might not at first appear as the most likely candidate for a project that is motivated by an interest in non-Western conceptions of politics, for its wisdom has usually been understood to be of a moral or spiritual rather than political nature. This is not especially surprising insofar as the Classical Confucian texts, the *Analects*, the *Mencius*, and the *Xunzi*, include many sayings that express the Confucian masters' judgment about a person's conduct in society. To illustrate, the first entry in the *Analects* goes as follows: "The Master said: 'Is it not a pleasure, having learned something, to try it out at due intervals? Is it not a joy to have friends come from afar? Is it not gentlemanly not to take offence when others fail to appreciate your abilities?' "[3] Social relationships are indeed central to the early Confucian texts. The latter are full of guidelines about how to treat parents, siblings, neighbors, friends, and superiors. Anecdotes about the proper relationship between parents and sons especially abound. Mencius, for example, relates the story of Shun who persisted in his obedience to his parents despite their cruelty toward him. As the story goes, Shun's parents once asked him to fix the roof of the storehouse and then set fire to it while he was repairing it. On another occasion, they forced him down the well and then covered the well with him inside. Nevertheless, Shun remained unwavering in his respect for them, an accomplishment that, recognized by the extant emperor, was to earn him the position of next emperor.[4]

The preponderance of anecdotes about social relationships should not, however, mask the fact that the anecdotes relating to government are also plentiful, easily constituting half of the content of the texts. The *Mencius* begins with a presumed encounter between Mencius

[3] *Analects* 1.1.
[4] *Mencius* 5A.2.

himself and King Hui of Liang in which Mencius encourages the king to give up concern for profit in favor of *ren* 仁 and rightness (*yi* 義).[5] The *Xunzi* includes chapters on the regulations of kings, on enriching and strengthening the state, on the duties of ministers, and on military affairs, among others. In fact, it is precisely the intriguing question of the relationship between its ethical and political components that makes Confucianism an interesting case to study. To return to the story of Shun, we can glean already from the anecdote reported above the intertwining of ethics and politics, for it reveals the importance not only of filial piety per se, but also of filiality in a good ruler, which Shun was to become.

As Benjamin Schwartz has argued, one should think of the Confucian texts as working along two dimensions: an ethical dimension concerned with "self-development" (*xiu shen* 修身, *xiu ji* 修己) and a political dimension concerned with the "ordering of society" (*zhi guo* 治國) and the "pacification of the world" (*ping tianxia* 平天下).

The relationship between the two is fraught with a certain tension, indicated by Schwartz's use of the concept of "polarity" to characterize it.[6] Schwartz has also argued that the concept of the *Dao* (道)—the Way—in the *Analects*, refers, in its most expansive meaning, to the whole sociopolitical order. This usage includes the different social and political roles to be performed—starting in the family—and the rituals governing the performance of these roles. On the other hand, the *Dao* also "emphatically" refers to the "inner" moral life of the individual. Schwartz contends that "a central problematique of the *Analects* involves the relation between the two."[7]

In much of the recent literature on Confucianism, the relationship between ethics and politics in early Confucianism has been presented

[5] *Mencius* 1A.1. A wide controversy surrounds the translation of *ren* into English. Stephen Angle translates it as "humaneness," Hsiao Kung-chuan as well as D. C. Lau as "benevolence," Edward Slingerland as "goodness," Roger Ames and Henry Rosemont as "authoritative conduct," while others, like Benjamin Schwartz, prefer to leave it untranslated. I follow Schwartz in leaving it untranslated. I will return to the meaning of *ren* in Chapter 4. *Yi* (rightness) differs from *ren* in that *ren* indicates an internal disposition to relate to others in a reciprocal way, while *yi* denotes the application of external principles of proper behavior to given circumstances.

[6] See Benjamin Schwartz, "Some Polarities in Confucian Thought," in *Confucianism in Action*, ed. David Nivison and Arthur F. Wright (Stanford: Stanford University Press, 1959), 52. The other two polarities that Schwartz identifies in Confucianism are "knowledge versus action" and the "inner versus outer realms."

[7] Benjamin Schwartz, *The World of Thought in Ancient China* (Cambridge, MA: Harvard University Press, 1985), 62.

as a one-sided relationship where politics is wholly dependent on ethics, thus failing to capture the tension between the two. Indeed, prominent writers on Chinese political thought, including Joseph Needham,[8] Hsiao Kung-chuan,[9] Fung Yu-lan,[10] D. C. Lau, and Herbert Fingarette, have assumed that Confucian politics is the logical conclusion of Confucian ethics and that the second is therefore more important than the first. Thus Lau writes that "Mencius' political philosophy . . . is not only consistent with his moral philosophy but is derived from it. Ancient Chinese thinkers all looked upon politics as a branch of morals."[11] Sor-hoon Tan contends that "the early Confucians themselves subordinated politics to ethics."[12] Heiner Roetz has argued that Confucian politics is "subordinated to a moral goal," which is "the cultivation of man . . . his moral elevation."[13] Similarly, in an introductory book on Chinese philosophy, JeeLoo Liu writes that "Confucians believe that morality is an indispensable element in politics: the ideal ruler should be a sage king; the ideal function of government is to morally transform its people."[14] Paul Goldin also contends that "the only legitimate purpose of [Confucian] government" is to bring about "moral transformation in the populace."[15] Kwong-loi Shun argues that Confucius and Mencius "regarded the transformative power of a cultivated person as the ideal basis for government."[16]

[8] Needham argues that "in early Confucianism there was no distinction between ethics and politics." See Joseph Needham, *Science and Civilization in China*, vol. 2 (Cambridge: Cambridge University Press, 1956), 9.

[9] Hsiao compares Confucius to Plato, arguing that they both value ethics over politics. See Hsiao Kung-chuan, *A History of Chinese Political Thought*, trans. Frederick Mote (Princeton: Princeton University Press, 1979), 113.

[10] When discussing Confucius's thought, Fung does not discuss any of his political ideas. See Fung Yu-lan, *History of Chinese Philosophy*, trans. Derk Bodde (Princeton: Princeton University Press, 1952), 43–75.

[11] D. C. Lau, introduction to *Mencius*, xxxviii.

[12] Sor-hoon Tan, "Democracy in Confucianism," *Philosophy Compass* 7, no. 5 (2012): 295.

[13] Heiner Roetz, *Confucian Ethics of the Axial Age: A Reconstruction under the Aspect of the Breakthrough toward Postconventional Thinking* (New York: State University of New York Press, 1993), 77.

[14] JeeLoo Liu, *An Introduction to Chinese Philosophy: From Ancient Philosophy to Chinese Buddhism* (Oxford: Wiley-Blackwell, 2006), 187.

[15] Paul Goldin, *Confucianism* (Berkeley: University of California Press, 2011), 20.

[16] Kwong-loi Shun, "Mencius," in *The Stanford Encyclopedia of Philosophy (Winter 2010 Edition)*, ed. Edward N. Zalta, http://plato.stanford.edu/archives/win2010/entries /mencius/. May Sim writes that for Confucius, like for Aristotle, "the aim of government is to make people virtuous." See Sim, *Remastering Morals with Aristotle and Confucius* (Cambridge: Cambridge University Press, 2007), 167. Similarly, Shaohua Hu writes that "Confucian doctrine is less political theory than it is ethical teaching." See Hu, "Con-

Some commentators identify core Confucian virtues and then argue that the preferred Confucian political arrangement is the one that allows for the development of these for all members of society. For example, in Herbert Fingarette's short book, *Confucius: The Secular as Sacred* (1972), which set the tone for much of the contemporary philosophical reappraisal of Confucianism, the emphasis is on ceremonial ritual and its centrality to moral flourishing. Fingarette interprets Confucius's political vision as being aimed at propagating the same value of ceremonial ritual through an emphasis on cultural unity for the competing regional states of the day, on the grounds that culture is necessary for the development of ceremony.[17]

William Theodore de Bary has argued that the dependence of Confucian politics on ethics, specifically with relation to the idea of a "sage king," is "the trouble with Confucianism," "there from the start, to become both a perennial challenge and a dilemma that would torment it through history."[18] In a similar line of thought, Stephen Angle describes the "interdependence" between morality and politics as a "central tenet" of Confucianism, and as the main challenge in adapting Confucianism to a modern, democratic politics, given the weight it gives to the presence of a virtuous ruler on top of the political system, to the detriment of institutional constraints on the ruler's actions.[19]

Recent attempts to rethink Confucianism have thus centered on recasting core Confucian ethical values into a more democratic political vision than the one offered in the early texts. Angle's solution to the sage king problem rests on rethinking the implications of key Confucian ideas, such as the idea that each and every person can become virtuous, and the idea that virtue requires political involvement, to imagine a more inclusive form of politics.[20] David Hall and Roger

---

fucianism and Western Democracy," in *China and Democracy: The Prospect for a Democratic China*, ed. Suisheng Zhao (New York: Routledge, 2000), 66. Yang Guorong argues that Mencius's political thought has a tendency toward "a pan-moralist vision of political life." See Yang, "Mengzi and Democracy: Dual Implications," *Journal of Chinese Philosophy* 31, no. 1 (2004): 100.

[17] Herbert Fingarette, *Confucius: The Secular as Sacred* (Long Grove, IL: Waveland Press, 1972), 64.

[18] William Theodore de Bary, *The Trouble with Confucianism* (Cambridge, MA: Harvard University Press, 1996), 1.

[19] Stephen C. Angle, *Sagehood: The Contemporary Significance of Neo-Confucian Philosophy* (Oxford: Oxford University Press, 2009), 180, 193.

[20] Angle, *Sagehood*, 212–13. He develops this line of thought more fully in *Contemporary Confucian Political Philosophy: Toward Progressive Confucianism* (Cambridge: Polity, 2012). Similarly, Ranjoo Seodu Herr argues that Confucianism is compatible with democ-

Ames suggest, on the basis of "the unsuitability of the central tradition of rights-based liberalism for the Chinese situation," that essential Confucian tenets, like the emphasis on rites, "might well be translated into a communitarian form of democratic society."[21] Likewise, Sorhoon Tan takes her lead from core Confucian ideas like *ren* (仁) and rituals to offer a distinctive form of "Confucian Democracy" that combines Confucianism and the pragmatism of John Dewey and that builds on the idea that "ethical ends are political ends, and vice-versa, in early Confucianism."[22] Finally, Daniel Bell, while explicitly rejecting what he calls the "depoliticization" of the *Analects* (a reference to the approach of contemporary best-selling Chinese author Yu Dan, who focuses on the spiritual dimension of the text), also discusses the moral values advanced by the early Confucians more than he discusses their own political vision. Bell advocates the work of contemporary Chinese theorist Jiang Qing, who is interested in what he describes as "Political Confucianism,"[23] and whose proposals, such as a tricameral legislature (representing popular, sacred, and cultural legitimacy), owe more, as Bell says, to Jiang's "political imagination than to ancient texts."[24] Bell argues, however, that such imagination is precisely what is necessary in a forward-looking interpretation of core Confucian ideas, like hierarchy, ritual propriety, and merit that would yield a distinctively Confucian form of democracy. Jiang Qing is indeed one of many recent Chinese intellectuals, often referred to as the "New Confucians," grappling

racy by focusing on the Confucian notion of equality. Democracy follows, according to Herr, from the Confucian recognition of the equal potential of all for moral perfection. See Herr, "Confucian Democracy and Equality," *Asian Philosophy* 20, no. 3 (2010): 280. See also Chenyang Li, "Confucian Value and Democratic Value," *Journal of Value Inquiry* 31, no. 2 (1997), where Li, rejecting the argument that Mencius's conception of government is democratic, inquires about core Confucian values and their compatibility with core democratic values.

[21] David Hall and Roger Ames, *Democracy of the Dead: Dewey, Confucius, and the Hope for Democracy in China* (Chicago: Open Court, 1999), 13.

[22] Sor-hoon Tan, *Confucian Democracy: A Deweyan Reconstruction* (New York: State University of New York Press, 2004), 131.

[23] Jiang Qing favors the development of the Gongyang tradition, associated with the Han dynasty scholar Dong Zhongshu (179–104 BCE), who advocated Confucianism as an ideology for the Han imperial state, and later revived by Kang Youwei (1858–1927), in opposition to the Xinxing tradition, concerned with "self-cultivation." See Bell, *China's New Confucianism*, 176.

[24] Bell, *China's New Confucianism*, 180. For Jiang's proposals, see Jiang Qing, *A Confucian Constitutional Order: How China's Ancient Past Can Shape Its Political Future* (Princeton: Princeton University Press, 2013).

with the question of the relationship between ethics and politics in their attempt to offer a vision of Confucianism for the modern world. As David Elstein puts it, "Almost all modern Ruist [Confucian] thinkers see a tension between the ethical and political sides of Ruism and make a choice about which is more important."[25]

The tendency to favor a set of core Confucian moral values can arguably be understood as a reaction to the critique of Confucianism by modernization enthusiasts, both Chinese and Western. Indeed, in the late nineteenth and early twentieth centuries, various Chinese reformers called for the repudiation of Confucianism and the establishment of constitutionalism, democratic freedoms, and individual rights. In the middle of the century, the Chinese communists attacked Confucianism for its patriarchal conception of the family, its hierarchical leanings, its relegation of the least educated to the lowest rung of society, and its promotion of hypocrisy on the part of the ruler toward the masses.[26] To counter these charges, it was felt necessary to elicit the best in Confucianism, and build upon it a modern politics. This was the strategy pursued in the interlude between the May Fourth Movement and the Cultural Revolution, when disillusionment with Western ideals encouraged the reevaluation of Confucianism through a turn toward "the interpretation of Confucius' ethical concepts."[27] It is this same approach that has been pursued since the 1970s. As the eminent Chinese American historian Yu Ying-shih puts it, "In the West today we are more inclined to see Confucianism as a way of life involving faith and spiritual values," in contradistinction to "a crude but once dominant notion that Confucianism was no more than a political ideology that functioned to legitimate imperial authority."[28]

[25] David Elstein, *Democracy in Contemporary Confucian Philosophy* (New York: Routledge, 2015), 23. Elstein discusses this tension in the thought of Xu Fuguan (69–74), Mou Zongsan (49–52), Lee Ming-huei (98–100), and Jiang Qing (146.) On Mou Zongsan, see also Angle, *Contemporary Confucian Political Philosophy*, 24–35.

[26] Kam Louie, *Critiques of Confucius in Contemporary China* (New York: St. Martin's, 1980), 7, 105.

[27] Louie, *Critiques of Confucius in Contemporary China*, 177.

[28] From the introduction to Hoyt Tillman, *Confucian Discourse and Chu Hsi's Ascendancy* (Honolulu: University of Hawaii Press, 1992), ix. Yu also argues that "if we trust Confucius' *Analects*, then the sage's original vision was focused decidedly more on personal cultivation and family life than on the governing of the state. Or, we may say, Confucius was primarily concerned with moral order and only secondarily with political order." From de Bary et al., roundtable discussion on the *Trouble with Confucianism*, *China Review International* 1, no. 1 (Spring 1994): 27–28, quoted in Angle, *Sagehood*, 190.

Thomas Metzger also describes Chinese intellectuals of the 1970s and 1980s as "sifting through the impure ore of their past to extract a 'spirit' of morality which could serve for the future."[29]

Another reason why Confucian politics is relegated to a secondary status in comparison to Confucian ethics can be traced to the great Confucian commentator, Zhu Xi (1130–1200). At the risk of overgeneralization, it might be contended that, until the twentieth century when efforts to look at Confucianism afresh multiplied, most Chinese interpreters after Zhu Xi read Confucianism through the lens of moral self-cultivation. Zhu Xi is considered the most influential proponent of what is now known as Neo-Confucianism, characterized by a concern with the development of the inner self. Zhu Xi was in fact so influential that his selection and commentary on four Classical texts (the *Analects*, the *Mencius*, the *Great Learning*, and the *Doctrine of the Mean*),[30] known as the "Four Books," became the canon for learning and formed the foundation of the curriculum for the Chinese imperial civil examination system used from the fourteenth century until 1905. In recent attempts to present Confucianism to the modern world, Zhu Xi's influence is still felt. For example, William Theodore de Bary and Tu Wei-ming have contributed much to Confucian scholarship by unearthing a "liberal" strand in Confucianism based on its concern with the individual's inner life. Thus, in *The Liberal Tradition in China* (1983), de Bary illuminates what he considers Confucius's reformist creed and the "vitality," "creativity," "critical temper," strong individualism, voluntarism, and concern with self-development characteristic of the Neo-Confucianism of the Song period (960–1279 CE).[31] Similarly, in *Confucian Thought: Selfhood as Creative Transformation* (1985), Tu showcases Confucian authors and ideas that exhibit a concern with self-realization.[32]

Zhu Xi's ascendancy has overshadowed alternative interpretations of Confucianism. For example, consider the interpretation offered by

---

[29] Thomas Metzger, *Escape from Predicament: Neo-Confucianism and China's Evolving Political Culture* (New York: Columbia University Press, 1986), 7.

[30] The *Xunzi* was excluded because of Xunzi's argument that human nature is bad. According to Paul Goldin, Xunzi's decline in favor started in the Eastern Han, but quickened during the Tang and Song, reaching its climax with Zhu Xi, "who declared that Xunzi's philosophy resembled that of non-Confucians [statecraft/Legalist thinkers] such as Shen Buhai . . . and Shang Yang . . . and that he was indirectly responsible for the notorious disasters of the Qin dynasty." See Goldin, *Confucianism*, 67–68.

[31] William Theodore de Bary, *The Liberal Tradition in China* (New York: Columbia University Press, 1983), 8–9.

[32] Tu Wei-ming, *Confucian Thought: Selfhood as Creative Transformation* (Albany: State University of New York Press, 1985).

Chen Liang (1143–94), a contemporary of Zhu Xi. Chen and Zhu lived in a dwindling Chinese empire, at the time threatened by the Jurchens from the north. In the face of the crisis, Chen favored the turn within Confucianism toward a utilitarian ethics focused on social and political effects over Zhu Xi's "morality of personal virtue."[33] This involved Chen in emancipating Confucian concepts "from the confines of current [Song Dynasty] usage," for example, in recasting in positive light the category of rulers known as hegemons (*ba*),[34] and in glossing the idea of the golden age of antiquity when sage kings ruled as a useful myth rather than an actual historical reality.[35] Chen Liang remained a much less well-known figure in Chinese history than Zhu Xi but is tellingly associated with the Confucian school known as "statecraft," or more literally, "ordering the world" (*jing shi* 經世). This school of thought was concerned with administrative matters (flood control, the provision of grain, etc.) and political matters (the prerogatives of the ruler, power politics, etc.), and rebuked the emphasis on abstract ethical and metaphysical issues characteristic of mainstream Confucianism.[36]

The Thesis of This Book

My argument in this book is that the approach to politics offered in the Classical Confucian texts does not follow from Confucian ethics in any straightforward manner. This argument can be said to be orthogonal to the debate on the contemporary application of Confucianism: by showing that the Confucian political vision is not necessarily one of a sage king seeking the moral edification of his people, I raise some doubts about the accusation of the conflation of ethics and politics in Classical Confucianism and therefore about this being "the trouble with Confucianism." However, how Confucianism can be tailored to the modern world is not otherwise the concern of this book. Rather, my aim is to

---

[33] Hoyt Cleveland Tillman, *Utilitarian Confucianism: Ch'en Liang's Challenge to Chu Hsi* (Cambridge, MA: Harvard University Press, 1982), 133.

[34] More on hegemons in Chapter 1.

[35] Tillman, *Utilitarian Confucianism*, 135–36.

[36] See William Theodore de Bary, ed., *Sources of Chinese Tradition* (New York: Columbia University Press, 2000), 155–215. William T. Rowe explores the tension between moralism and practical management in the thought of the Chinese official Chen Hongmou (1696–1771) in *Saving the World: Chen Hongmou and Elite Consciousness in Eighteenth-Century China* (Stanford: Stanford University Press, 2001). I thank Leigh Jenco for this reference and for directing me to the statecraft writings.

reconstruct the political vision offered in the early Confucian texts through a close interpretation of them.

With this goal in mind, I take the political discussions in the Classical Confucian texts as my starting point.[37] In other words, instead of considering the discussions of rulers, ministers, political exemplars, rituals, and regulations as secondary or antiquated, I take them to be central to understanding early Confucian political theory, and Confucianism more generally. By emphasizing aspects that interpreters have mostly pointed to only in passing, and deemphasizing areas that have received much more attention, the approach I take will reveal a "pattern" underlying Confucian political thought that differs from the conclusions drawn by the ethics-first approach. My approach will thus not so much yield a radically different interpretation of Confucian political thought as much as a reconfiguration that, I argue, better accounts for the textual evidence.

More specifically, I contend that what commentators miss by adopting the ethics-first approach, and what my own reconfiguration reveals, is the Confucian concern with political order (zhi 治). Indeed, on my view, Confucian political philosophy is motivated by the same problem that Sheldon Wolin identifies as central to Western political philosophy, namely, the problem of how "to render politics compatible with the requirements of order," that is, "how to reconcile the conflict created by competition under conditions of scarcity with the demands of public tranquility."[38] I argue that the success of political rule in Confucianism is judged by its own standard, distinct from the standards the Confucians use for the assessment of individual life.[39] The standard in politics

---

[37] In *Envisioning Eternal Empire*, Yuri Pines also takes as a starting point his "wish to reverse the loss of interest in the political sphere of pre-imperial Chinese intellectual history in the West during the last twenty years." See Pines, *Envisioning Eternal Empire: Chinese Political Thought of the Warring States Era* (Honolulu: University of Hawaii Press, 2009), 6–7.

[38] Sheldon Wolin, *Politics and Vision: Continuity and Innovation in Western Political Thought*, expanded ed. (Princeton: Princeton University Press, 2004), 10–11.

[39] Similarly, Xu Fuguan identifies two distinct standards in Classical Confucianism: a standard for self-cultivation centered on virtue, and a standard for politics centered on people's livelihood (*renmin de ziran shengming* 人民的自然生命), that is, their material well-being. See Xu Fuguan, *Xueshu yu zhengzhi zhi jian* 學術與政治之間 [Between academia and politics] (Taizhong: Zhongyang shuju, 1957), 178–79. See also Angle, *Sagehood*, 191; Honghe Liu, *Confucianism in the Eyes of a Confucian Liberal: Hsu Fu-Kuan's Critical Examination of the Confucian Political Tradition* (New York: Peter Lang, 2001), 72–82.

is therefore not virtue (the moral edification of the people), but rather the establishment and maintenance of political order.

While I elaborate on the idea of political order in the chapters that follow, I should clarify here my claim about the relationship between ethics and politics in early Confucianism. One could read my endeavor in this book through the lens of ideal versus nonideal theory, and thus take this book as highlighting the nonideal parts of the Confucian political vision to complement the ideal theory aspects (the need for a sage king and the importance of the moral edification of the people) that other commentators have focused on. This is not, however, how I understand it. My argument in this book actually pushes back against the idea that the early Confucians offer an ideal political theory at all, if what is meant by the latter is a political theory that directly follows upon their moral theory. A comparison with Aristotle might be instructive here.

Like the early Confucians, Aristotle is often read as proposing a politics that is a conceptual development of his ethics. Richard Kraut has argued, for example, that "Aristotle conceives of the [*Nicomachean*] *Ethics* and *Politics* as following a logical progression" in that the latter provides "the further detail that allows his examination of human well-being [undertaken in the *Ethics*] to be put into practice."[40] On a closer look at Aristotle's *Politics*, however, it appears that the evaluation of political regimes is not always based on whether or not they allow for human flourishing for all. Instead, Aristotle often seems concerned with stability (as opposed to well-being and the excellences) in his judgment about different kinds of political arrangements.[41] Based on this revisionist reading, one might think of Aristotle's *Politics* as operating according to the two registers of ideal and nonideal theory: in the first, elaborated in Books VII and VIII, ethical ideas are embodied in the life of the community; in the second, implicit in Books III to VI, concerns about stability render the assessment of different constitutions relative to environmental, historical, and other contingent conditions.

The early Confucians, on the other hand, do not offer the corresponding ideal vision at all; they never delineate a society where all

---

[40] Richard Kraut, *Aristotle: Political Philosophy* (Oxford: Oxford University Press, 2002), 4.

[41] For example, in his argument in favor of a middle-class constitution. See *Politics* 1295a5–45.

members are engaged in a life of virtue, pursuing reciprocal relationships of care and trust, and coming together in a harmonious society, merit-based and ritual-centered, allowing all to flourish. In his new book, Joseph Chan uses the distinction between ideal and nonideal theory to argue that the "ideal ends" of Confucian political thought include "the flourishing of human virtues" and "a grand ideal of social harmony"[42] (whereas a "Confucian nonideal political theory" would treat the former as a "regulative ideal"[43] while being more sensitive to "the constraints of reality").[44] To illustrate the ideal ends, however, Chan refers to a chapter in *The Classic of Rites* whose "Confucian authenticity," he writes, "has been disputed in the history of Chinese thought" because it contains Daoist elements.[45] Chan adds that the "general consensus today" is that the ideal of "Grand Union" (and of "Small Tranquillity") offered in the chapter is "basically no different from the early Confucian masters' understanding of ideal politics and society."[46] In this book, I ask if it is in fact the case that the Confucian political ideal amounts to "the flourishing of human virtues" and hence whether it is not actually what Chan describes as "nonideal political theory" that is key to Classical Confucianism.[47]

My reading of the early Confucian political vision actually suggests more similarities to the Platonic vision in *The Republic* than to Aristotle's political theory. For there is no expectation in Plato's ideal state that anyone other than the philosopher-king and the guardians more generally will attain high virtue; what is expected instead is justice (where each member of society will perform the task they are most fit

[42] Joseph Chan, *Confucian Perfectionism: A Political Philosophy for Modern Times* (Princeton: Princeton University Press, 2014), 2.

[43] Chan, *Confucian Perfectionism*, 5.

[44] Chan, *Confucian Perfectionism*, 1. What Chan proposes to do in his own book is to offer a Confucian nonideal political theory that would be compatible with contemporary circumstances, or what he calls "the reality of modernity" (4). He also argues that the early Confucians were "keenly aware of the fact that their ideal . . . was unlikely to be realized in their times" (3).

[45] Chan, *Confucian Perfectionism*, 6.

[46] Chan, *Confucian Perfectionism*, 6.

[47] Similarly, while Eirik Harris favors understanding Xunzi's thought as comprising both an ideal and a nonideal theory, his discussion and the accompanying textual evidence concern the latter, not the former. The evidence that Harris adduces for Xunzi's ideal theory is his statement that anyone can become a sage like Yu (*Xunzi* 23.5a). I will show in Chapter 1 why this statement is actually in tension with the Confucian political vision. See Eirik Lang Harris, "The Role of Virtue in Xunzi's Political Philosophy," *Dao* 12 (2013): 93–110, 94.

at performing)[48] upon which follow harmony and order.[49] The analogy between the philosopher-king and a ship's captain also suggests that the goal is survival, security, and stability (preventing the ship from going off track, or even sinking).[50] On my reading, the political vision of the early Confucians is geared in the same way toward an encompassing political order in which not everyone is required or expected to develop the cardinal virtues.

This conclusion is more surprising in the case of the early Confucians than in the case of Plato because the former do emphasize the potential for all members of society to become virtuous, while Plato is clear that only a few can ever become philosophers. Yet, though the Confucian case is less obvious than the Platonic case, it is neither mysterious nor contradictory. On my interpretation, Confucian political theory does not follow upon Confucian ethics in the way recent interpreters propose because it is attuned to the material world in a particular way. To unpack this attunement, I will address three questions: the extent to which Confucian political thought is sensitive to empirical facts, whether it points toward an end-state or merely to a transitional phase, and finally whether and how it deals with the problem of noncompliance.[51]

The first question is the extent to which a theory is sensitive to "facts" or "reality." It is difficult to answer this question without also asking the one that it begs, namely: *what* facts? On my view, the early Confucians were mostly sensitive to what might be described as sociological facts (enduring but not unchanging), for example the level of technological development in society, the state of the economy, and the broad socioeconomic makeup of society. This largely explains, as I will argue in Chapter 1, why they do not expect most people to become virtuous.[52]

The Confucians are also sensitive to more specific political circumstances around them, such as the continual threat of interstate war during their time. This explains the distinction I will draw in the first three

<hr>

[48] Plato, *The Republic*, 433b.

[49] Plato, *The Republic*, 430e.

[50] Plato, *The Republic*, 488a–e. For an argument in this vein, see G. R. F. Ferrari's introduction to *The Republic* (Cambridge: Cambridge University Press, 2011), xxvi.

[51] These questions are drawn from Laura Valentini's "Ideal vs. Non-ideal Theory: A Conceptual Map," *Philosophy Compass* 7, no. 9 (2012): 654–64.

[52] As Benjamin Schwartz argues, "we find in China the clear development of a 'sociological' approach to the lives of the masses." See Schwartz, *World of Thought in Ancient China*, 105.

chapters of this book between two levels of political order: On a basic level, political order means the absence of chaos, produced through the fulfillment of the basic security and welfare needs of the common people. The Confucians recognize a political society that fulfills this level of order as acceptable, and rulers who, like hegemons, help achieve this level of order win Confucians' approbation. On the other hand, in its more exalted, and thus more durable, form, order is not merely the absence of disorder. It is harmony. Harmony (*he* 和) is not a concept that the early Confucians use much, but it is useful for my purposes here because it is a normative standard that signals high-level coordination among different segments of society. A harmonious society is achieved through the maintenance of a system of rituals (*li* 禮) that all members of society abide by. While they show a preference for the second level of order, the early Confucians, because of their sensitivity to political circumstances, also accept the first level of order when conditions such as internal political disturbances and interstate wars do not permit more.

The second question that the debate around ideal and nonideal theory raises is the question of "End-State" versus "Transitional Theory."[53] One might argue that the political order I describe in this book is only a transition stage toward a fully virtuous society. Yet there is no textual material suggesting that the early Confucians saw the matter in this way. On my reading, political order for these thinkers is not a means to an end; it is an end in itself. This is of course related to the question of their sensitivity to sociological facts, in the sense that it is due to the Confucian understanding of the socioeconomic makeup of society that the end of a fully virtuous society is not conceived of at all. On the other hand, the basic level of order just described could be considered as a transition toward the higher, ritual-centered level. Neither, however, is centrally geared toward a fully virtuous society.

The third and final question relating to the distinction between ideal and nonideal theory is the question of how the early Confucians deal with the problem of compliance:[54] what should individuals do under unfavorable conditions, such as a breakdown of political order, or in the face of a bad ruler? Since the Confucians deal with real-life cases, they do not shy away from this question; I reconstruct their view with regard to it in Chapter 5.

---

[53] Valentini, "Ideal vs. Non-ideal Theory," 660.
[54] Valentini, "Ideal vs. Non-ideal Theory," 650.

Given their sensitivity to sociological (and political) facts, and their recognition of the problem of compliance under adverse conditions, one might take the preceding discussion to suggest that early Confucian political theory is an instance of nonideal theory as such (without a corresponding ideal theory). Whether this is a helpful description at all depends on whether one finds the idea of a nonideal theory helpful in the first place. I should note here that the preceding is not meant to suggest that the Confucians were practical (as opposed to theoretical), or that the early Confucian texts, as is sometimes suggested, should be read as advice to kings. One would indeed be hard-pressed to describe the Confucian vision I will describe in the chapters that follow as "practical" in any meaningful sense, and it is in no way tailored to suit the ears of rulers (more on this in Chapter 1). My contention is that the early Confucian political vision is both theoretical and nonideal through and through.

The question remains: what does the preceding discussion show us about the relationship between ethics and politics in early Confucianism? I said above that the Confucian political standard of order is distinct from the Confucian ethical standard of virtue. To the extent that the political standard is a normative standard, it is difficult to insist that it has nothing to do with morality. This would be true of any vision of politics which is not based on brute force.[55] But it is true less trivially for the Confucians insofar as, for example, the distinction between the basic and exalted levels of order I mentioned above hinges on the development of civic-like qualities in the people in the latter. Furthermore, as I will argue in Chapter 4, the early Confucians find virtue on the part of the ruler to be important for the establishment of a durable political order. All of this suggests that the realm of politics is not completely independent from the realm of ethics. Yet, what is crucial for my argument is the idea that political order, not moral edification, is the end, and that political order is an end in itself, not a means toward virtue. A virtuous ruler is important because he knows what policies to pursue to achieve long-lasting political order, not because he governs through the force of his example to promote virtue in society.

[55] I thus disagree with Harris both in seeing the "Legalist" Han Feizi's position as totally devoid of morality (since his support for the use of consistent, transparent, and universal regulations can be said to partake of a certain kind of political ethic, even if it is geared toward the maintenance of the state, or even just the ruler) and in seeing Xunzi's vision as moralistic in the way he suggests (since, as I will argue in Chapter 3, rituals are not necessarily coeval with virtue). See Harris, "Role of Virtue."

The qualities to be developed by the common people, like honesty and industriousness, are neither preparatory ground for central Confucian virtues like rightness and wisdom, nor a diluted version of the latter. Whether they should still be described as "moral" turns on what is exactly meant by "moral." In other words, what is important for my purposes in this book is to show that Confucian political theory is not just an application of Confucian morality, at least not in any direct way.[56]

Let me address here, finally, a worry. The worry is that my argument in this book is an imposition on the early Confucians, that it is foreign to their self-understanding. They did not after all talk about political standards being separate from ethical standards. They did not even separate their ethical and their political discussions in the first place. The worry is legitimate, but it actually applies to all interpretations of early Confucianism, not mine alone. The early Confucians do not explicitly say that politics follows from ethics either. Indeed, the early Confucian texts, except perhaps for the *Xunzi*, do not offer "meta" discussions about any topic. They might even be seen as uninterested in argument at all.[57] This is related to the nature of the texts themselves, which I turn to in what follows. Suffice it to say here that the challenge is to propose a theory that makes the best sense of their manifold and sometimes disparate statements, at the acknowledged risk of reading too much into these.

Historical Background

Having outlined, in broad brushstrokes, the thesis of my book, it remains for me to relate it to the historical context in which Confucianism arose. Confucian thought is usually associated with the Spring and Autumn period (770–476 BCE) and the Warring States period (475–221 BCE), which together constitute the reign of the Eastern Zhou dynasty. The Zhou dynasty was the longest lived dynasty in Chinese history,

[56] In an article on Xunzi's conception of hegemons, Sungmoon Kim uses the expression "political morality" to describe the former. See Kim, "Between Good and Evil: Xunzi's Reinterpretation of the Hegemonic Rule as Decent Governance," *Dao* 12 (2013): 84. Speaking of the Confucian position on war, Tongdong Bai describes it as "realistic utopia." See Bai, "The Political Philosophy of China," in *The Routledge Companion to Social and Political Philosophy*, ed. Gerald F. Gaus and Fred D'Agostino (New York: Routledge, 2013), 185. Both these expressions, as well as ideas like "political virtue" and "civic virtue," capture elements of the Confucian political project as I present it in this book.

[57] Or so argues Robert Eno, who prefers to see them as masters of ritual and dance. See Eno, *The Confucian Creation of Heaven: Philosophy and the Defense of Ritual Mastery* (New York: State University of New York Press, 1990), 2–3.

but its glory is concentrated in the first half of its tenure, known as the Western Zhou (1045–770 BCE). As Edward Shaughnessy writes, "Throughout China's long history, the Western Zhou has served as its guiding paradigm for governmental, intellectual, and social developments."[58] The Western Zhou was also "the largest geopolitical unity ever achieved by a single power" until the reunification of the Chinese world by the Qin emperor in 221 BCE.[59] It stretched around the Yellow River, in the northeastern part of modern China.

The Zhou king ruled on the basis of what was known as the "Mandate of Heaven" (tianming 天命). Possibly one of the earliest references to this notion can be found in the "Great Proclamation" chapter of the Classic of Documents (more on the Five Classics below), which relates the story of the first succession crisis of the Zhou reign. As the story goes, two years after conquering the Shang dynasty, the Zhou leader King Wu died. Precedent had it that King Wu's son, Song (later known as King Cheng), was to succeed, as sons had succeeded their fathers for the preceding two generations. However, King Wu's younger brother, eventually known as the Duke of Zhou, announced that Song was too young to rule and that he would therefore act as his regent. King Wu's more senior brothers were not convinced. From their posts in the east, they rebelled against the supposed usurpation. A civil war followed, which the Duke of Zhou and King Cheng won.[60] The chapter in the Classic of Documents presents the debate between King Cheng and his advisers that preceded the former's attack on his uncles. King Cheng undertook the usual turtle shell divination to ascertain whether the signs concerning the attack were auspicious. They were. However, his advisers admonished him against such a difficult task. King Cheng insisted on his decision. Crucially, he read the divination signals as a sign from Heaven. What he said was that Heaven had assisted King Wen (father of King Wu and founder of the Zhou dynasty) and conferred its mandate upon the Zhou to rule. This was the first mention of the notion of the Mandate of Heaven in Chinese history.[61]

On the administrative level, in contrast to the preceding Shang dynasty, which was, according to Feng Li, an "aggregation of self-

[58] Edward Shaughnessy, "Western Zhou History" in The Cambridge History of Ancient China: From the Origins of Civilization to 221 BC, ed. Michael Loewe and Edward Shaughnessy (Cambridge: Cambridge University Press, 1999), 292.

[59] Feng Li, Landscape and Power in Early China (New York: Cambridge University Press, 2006), 2.

[60] Shaughnessy, "Western Zhou History," 311.

[61] Shaughnessy, "Western Zhou History," 314.

governing communities,"[62] the Zhou extended the reach of the central government, especially over the vast terrain to the east of the capital, by appointing princes of the royal family as local rulers. As Li writes, "These numerous states, bound to the Zhou royal court through a unified ancestral cult and by their need of royal support to survive in the new environment, formed the macro-geopolitical structure of the Western Zhou state."[63] Li argues against the common description of this system of Zhou rule as feudal.[64] The local Zhou states were both more independent and less independent than traditional European fiefs. On the one hand, each of the regional states "constituted an autonomous geopolitical entity located in a specific area, and was equipped with a small but complete government that enjoyed the combined rights of civil administration, legal punishment, and military authority."[65] On the other hand, the relationship between the Zhou king and the local state rulers was "much closer and more dictatorial" than the contractual relation between feudal lord and vassal. Central political authority was maintained through the "Lineage Law," which ensured the submission of "minor lines" to the "primary lines" of royal descent, through the installment by the royal court of the office of "Overseers of the States" in the regional states, and through the visits to the royal court that regional rulers were mandated to perform upon assuming office.[66]

As successful as it was, the Western Zhou dynasty eventually started to lose power, spurring both the new geopolitical realities and the nostalgia for the Zhou that defined Confucianism. The Western Zhou's weakening can be attributed to three factors: first, the increasing pressure and threats exerted by outside powers, like the Xianyun in the northwest and the Huaiyi in the southeast; second, the dissolution of blood ties, cultural commonalities, and, most important, political control between the central court and the regional states; and third, the weakness caused by the continual grants of landed property as a favor from the Zhou king to the aristocrats at the central court.[67] Since the

---

[62] Li, *Landscape and Power in Early China*, 2.

[63] Li, *Landscape and Power in Early China*, 2.

[64] Throughout the book, I will thus refer as "regional rulers" to what is commonly translated as "feudal lords" (*zhuhou* 諸侯). Similarly, I use "ruler" instead of "lord" (*jun* 君, *zhu* 主). I have kept however, the appellation "Duke" as in "Duke of Zhou" in line with common usage.

[65] Li, *Landscape and Power in Early China*, 111.

[66] Li, *Landscape and Power in Early China*, 112–14.

[67] Li, *Landscape and Power in Early China*, 139–40.

Zhou could no longer maintain their capital in the west, they moved east around 770 BCE. This move was accompanied by an eastward move of aristocratic lineages, like the Zheng and the Guo, who established their own states in the east. The move severely diminished the authority of the Zhou court, which became, in the words of Cho-yun Hsu, "virtually a government in exile,"[68] and concomitantly increased the power of regional rulers, who then competed among themselves for hegemony over the Eastern plain, inaugurating a "new era of interstate military conflict."[69] This era lasted until 221 BCE, when the ruler of the state of Qin succeeded at reunification and called himself emperor. The Qin's reign was short-lived, but it was the precursor to consecutive reigns of imperial dynasties that ruled China until 1911.

The period of the Eastern Zhou (770–221 BCE) is, as I said above, usually divided into the Spring and Autumn and Warring States periods, and it witnessed an increasing intensification of interstate conflict. The rise of territorial, centralized states out of a long period of war is sometimes compared to the rise of the modern European nation-states out of the Thirty Years' War, whereby in both cases "the state made war and war made the state."[70] Victoria Tin-bor Hui argues that "ancient China developed the art of war and the markers of territorial sovereignty light years before Western practices."[71] These markers included a "centralized authority with bureaucratized administration, monopolized coercion, and nationalized taxation."[72] Hui shows how the various states of the period pursued "self-strengthening reforms," including "universal military conscription," maintaining among themselves a balance of power that was stable for a long time but was ultimately broken by Qin's success in pursuing "the most comprehensive self-strengthening reforms and the most ruthless strategies and tactics."[73]

Despite the fierce competition of the Warring States period (or perhaps because of it), the period witnessed such intellectual ferment that it became known as the "age of the philosophers." Before examining

---

[68] Hsu, "The Spring and Autumn Period," in Loewe and Shaughnessy, *Cambridge History of Ancient China*, 551.

[69] Li, *Landscape and Power in Early China*, 277.

[70] Charles Tilly, *The Formation of National States in Western Europe* (Princeton: Princeton University Press, 1975), 73, cited in John Keay, *China: A History* (London: Harper, 2008), 74.

[71] Victoria Tin-bor Hui, *War and State Formation in Ancient China and Early Modern Europe* (Cambridge: Cambridge University Press, 2005), 5.

[72] Hui, *War and State Formation*, 6.

[73] Hui, *War and State Formation*, 35.

the social basis of scholarship during this period, it should be noted that, as Martin Kern argues, "even within the limited social group of ancient practitioners of textual knowledge, the particular circle that Western scholarship usually calls the 'philosophers' was a rather small minority."[74] Kern points to, on the one hand, the link between textual and ritual practice during this period,[75] since texts were usually inscribed on animal bones, turtle shells, bamboo slips, and, most lavishly, bronze ware, all of which were also used in ritual practices. That said, the disentangling of texts from ritual practices is not necessarily an alien imposition on the Chinese tradition. As Kern declares, "For the longer time of Chinese studies, *and partly following choices by the Chinese tradition in reflecting upon itself*, much of the culture of the Zhou dynasty and the early empire has been discussed in terms of intellectual history."[76] On the other hand, Kern's point is that "philosophy" in the early period was very much entangled with other kinds of textual practices. The early Chinese philosophical works thus greatly make use of what became known as the "Five Classics," attributed in the Chinese tradition to the Spring and Autumn period (and often to Confucius himself), but canonized only during the Han dynasty, in 136 BCE.[77] These include the *Classic of Documents* (*Shujing* 書經), which comprises presumed speeches and edicts of early rulers, the *Classic of Changes* (*Yijing* 易經), a divination manual, the *Classic of Poetry* (*Shijing* 詩經), comprising a collection of poems and hymns, the *Classic of Rites* (*Liji* 禮記), which includes an account of ancient rites and court ceremonies, and the *Spring and Autumn Annals* (*Chunqiu* 春秋), relating events in the state of Lu. Indeed, these Five Classics, as well as the essential commentaries on them, such as the *Zuozhuan* commentary on the *Annals*, formed a large part of the world of textual knowledge of early China, and thus the world with which the Confucians, as well as the Daoists, the Legalists, the Mohists, and other philosophers of the early period, were versed and which they contributed to. And vice versa: for example, in his study of the *Zuozhuan*, David Schaberg shows how the historiographical project of the commentary partakes of the same normative Confucian project as philosophical texts such as

[74] Martin Kern, ed., *Text and Ritual in Early China* (Seattle: University of Washington Press, 2005), viii.

[75] Kern, *Text and Ritual in Early China*, xi.

[76] Kern, *Text and Ritual in Early China*, viii, emphasis added.

[77] For an account of the origins, nature, and importance of the Five Classics, see Michael Nylan, *The Five "Confucian" Classics* (New Haven: Yale University Press, 2001).

the *Analects*, the *Mencius*, and the *Xunzi*, exhibiting similar aims and rhetorical devices.[78]

My focus in this book will be primarily on the philosophers, who offered new visions of life and society for a rapidly changing world. Indeed, it was during the breakdown of authority triggered by the fall of the Western Zhou that "schools" emerged, taking advantage, as Mark Edward Lewis argues, from the opening up of new avenues for social advancement as the prerogatives of birth that had defined the Zhou hierarchical system weakened.[79] Yuri Pines describes the world of the Warring States as "a huge market of talent, in which a gifted person could seek employment at any of the competing courts."[80] The emerging schools consisted of a master and his followers, and sometimes took their names from the master. Although their Latinized name, "Confucians," draws on the name of Confucius (*Kongfuzi*), the Confucians were actually known as *ru* 儒, a term used for ritual practitioners. This meant, to return to the point just made, that the early Confucians "were part of a broader social grouping of men who did not invariably devote themselves to the transmission of texts."[81]

Lewis explains that scholarship during the Warring States period emerged outside of government courts, but recruitment by competing rulers also meant that scholars entered the governmental sphere. The accession to political circles became significant in the fourth century when it is thought that the rulers of the states of Wei and Qi provided stipends for scholars to lure them to their own courts. In Qi, scholars are said to have gathered near the Ji gate of the capital city, hence the provenance of the much cited "Jixia Academy." Despite his acknowledgment that the specific nature of the Jixia Academy cannot be ascertained and its importance can be exaggerated, Lewis argues that "it marks a significant development. For the first time on record a state began to act as patron of scholarship out of the apparent conviction

---

[78] David Schaberg, *A Patterned Past: Form and Thought in Early Chinese Historiography* (Cambridge, MA: Harvard University Asia Center, 2001), 50–56.

[79] Mark Edward Lewis, *Writing and Authority in Early China* (New York: State University of New York Press, 1999), 53. For the argument against the idea that "academies" or "schools" existed in early China, see Michael Nylan, "Toward an Archaeology of Writing: Text, Ritual, and the Culture of Public Display in the Classical Period (475 B.C.E.–220 C.E.)," in Kern, *Text and Ritual in Early China*, 4.

[80] Pines, *Envisioning Eternal Empire*, 160.

[81] Lewis, *Writing and Authority in Early China*, 57. See also Eno, *Confucian Creation of Heaven*, 31 and Mark Csikszentmihalyi, *Material Virtue: Ethics and the Body in Early China* (Leiden: Brill, 2004), 15–20.

that this was a proper function of the state or as a means of increasing its prestige."[82]

It is likely, however, that the scholars maintained a certain distance from the state and were able to move between government and society, thus securing for themselves a position that could not be abolished with the disappearance of the local courts upon the Qin unification.[83] Schaberg makes a similar point, arguing that the protagonists of his own work, namely the historiographers, "separated themselves from a tendentiously characterized ruling class and identified themselves with a ministerial class depicted as steadfastly conservative, prescient, and eloquent."[84]

The tension in the scholars' relationship to government can be gleaned from what we know of the three early Confucians who will be the subject of this book. Kongzi 孔子, better known as Confucius (the Latinized version of his name adopted by Jesuit missionaries to China in the seventeenth century), is said to have lived during the Spring and Autumn period. He held minor positions in the state of Lu where he was born in 551 BCE, was then presumably promoted to a junior position, where some disagreement must have arisen to force him to travel to other states, first to Qi, after which he returned to Lu, and then left again for Wei, Song, Chen, and Cai, hoping to be employed by one of their rulers. His quest proved unsuccessful, and he is said to have died in his native state of Lu around 479 BCE.[85] The text attributed to Confucius, known in the West as the *Analects* ("Collected Sayings"), poses great difficulties for contextualization given the amount of controversy surrounding its composition. What we are certain of is that Confucius himself did not write any of it, and that whatever his disciples recorded

---

[82] Lewis, "Warring States Political History," in Loewe and Shaughnessy, *Cambridge History of Ancient China*, 643.

[83] Lewis, "Warring States Political History," 643. Yuri Pines disagrees with Lewis on this point, arguing that "scholars and other *shi* [men of service] who were patronized by a ruler or by a powerful courtier may have been independent of an individual court, for they could shift their allegiances to a different one, but they were not independent of the system of power relations that I call 'the state.' Not only was the ruler's patronage a direct extension of his power as the de jure owner of the state, but even the so-called private courts, famous for their support of *shi*, were largely entangled in the state-ordered web of power." See Pines, *Envisioning Eternal Empire*, 138. To the extent that my purpose here is to highlight the ability of scholars to move from one court to another (as opposed to move out of the state system altogether), the disagreement between Lewis and Pines is not crucial to it.

[84] Schaberg, *Patterned Past*, 259.

[85] Lau, trans., *Confucius: The Analects*, 161–94.

of his sayings—as is usually believed they did—was heavily edited by the imperial scholars of the Han dynasty. The received text that has been used for the longest period of time was compiled during the Eastern Han, edited by He Yan (190–249 CE).[86] He Yan used the chief commentaries of Zhang Yu (d. 5 BCE) and Zheng Xuan (127–200 CE). D. C. Lau divides the text into three strata, the third of which, consisting of the last five books, he considers a later addition to the text.[87] Others have gone further in questioning the consistency and dating of the *Analects*. In *The Original Analects*, E. Bruce Brooks and A. Taeko Brooks contend that the received text is in fact "*a series of texts* of different date," some of which "may go back to the historical Confucius," but many of which "were added in the next two centuries by his successors."[88] More recently, Mick Hunter has argued that the *Analects* was actually put together in the second century BCE, and is thus not so much a creation of the Warring States period as a product of imperial choices taken centuries later.[89] Edward Slingerland, on the other hand, argues that "it is highly unlikely that any stratum of the *Analects* was composed after the early fourth century B.C.E.," based on the idea that the text does not allude to the sophisticated controversies of Mencius's and Xunzi's times.[90] In any case, there can be no real solution to the problem of situating the *Analects* until scholars agree on its dating.[91] The only way out of this problem for my purposes in this book is to interpret the *Analects* in conjunction with the *Mencius* and the *Xunzi*, both of which present themselves as building upon Confucius's project, while their own origins are less controversial than the *Analects'* (though not uncontroversial). Granting that the question of authorship in the *Analects* is complicated, I refer throughout the book to Confucius saying this or that because most of the passages in the *Analects* start with "The Master said . . ." (*zi yue* 子曰).

Mencius (Mengzi 孟子) was born in the state of Zou around 372 BCE and, like Confucius before him, traveled to a few states, including Liang and Qi, offering his consultancy services. He is said to have re-

---

[86] See Lau, trans., *Confucius: The Analects*, 221 and Slingerland, trans., *Confucius: Analects*, xiii–xiv.

[87] Lau, trans., *Confucius: The Analects*, 233.

[88] E. Bruce Brooks and A. Taeko Brooks, *The Original Analects: Sayings of Confucius and His Successors* (New York: Columbia University Press, 1998), 1.

[89] Mick Hunter, "Sayings of Confucius: Deselected" (PhD diss., Princeton University, 2012).

[90] See Slingerland, trans., *Confucius: Analects*, xv.

[91] I have greatly learned about this problem of dating from Mick Hunter.

tired from public life in his old age, dying in 289 BCE. The text of the *Mencius* is likely a compilation of his disciples' (possibly verbatim) notes from his lectures. The version of the text we have today is an edition by the Han scholar Zhao Qi (d. 201 CE).[92] D. C. Lau argues that the *Mencius* is one of the best preserved texts from the Warring States period.[93]

Xunzi (荀子) was a native of the state of Zhao, probably born around 312 BCE. He is thought to have traveled to the states of Qi and Qin, then to Chu, where he held a position as a magistrate and where, though he eventually lost this position, he remained and died sometime around 221 BCE (late enough to witness the Qin imperial unification). The text of the *Xunzi* is less well preserved than the *Mencius*, but parts of it were probably written by Xunzi himself, while other parts were added later.[94] The division into thematic chapters is also thought to be a sign of later editing: the Han librarian Liu Xiang produced a collection of thirty-two chapters toward the end of the first century BCE; the order we have today was the creation of ninth-century commentator Yang Liang.[95] Since the bulk of the work was probably composed by or during the time of Xunzi, we can use the material it offers with more confidence than the *Analects*.

Given that the three texts do not mention events relating to, or coming after, the Qin unification, we can presume that their content mostly emerged during the Warring States period, but was later edited by the officials of the Han dynasty. Even, however, if there is no mark of actual additions by the Han officials (meaning additions that mention the Qin or Han dynasty), the latter could still have had a great impact on the content of the texts (especially the *Analects*) by deciding, among a corpus of recorded material that they had access to, what to keep in and what to keep out for the purpose of creating authoritative versions of the texts. They also provided the order and titles of the chapters that we have today (the original records were usually inscribed on thin

[92] Again, this is the version that Lau translates.

[93] Lau, trans., *Mencius*, 185.

[94] As Masayuki Sato argues, even those who regard the *Xunzi* as a "well-integrated work despite its miscellaneous and inconsistent guise" still argue that the last six chapters were added later by Xunzi's disciples. See Sato, *The Confucian Quest for Order: The Origin and Formation of the Political Thought of Xun Zi* (Leiden: Brill, 2003), 38. Robert Eno argues that the *Xunzi* should be considered the "collective work" of the "Xunzi school" rather than the work of one individual. See Eno, *Confucian Creation of Heaven*, 136.

[95] Dan Robins, "Xunzi," in The *Stanford Encyclopedia of Philosophy*, ed. Edward N. Zelta, http://plato.stanford.edu/archives/fall2008/entries/xunzi/.

bamboo slips, bundles of which were assembled with the use of a cord that often decayed with time, jumbling the original organization). One conclusion that one could draw from this is that the texts as the Han officials packaged them presented in their eyes a favorable, or at least not unfavorable, vision for the Han imperial agenda. This is different from arguing, as Yuri Pines does, that we find in early Confucianism, or early Chinese political thought more generally, the seeds of the imperial, monarchical culture that was to last in China until the early twentieth century.[96] My suggestion is merely that the Confucian political project was probably appealing to a new dynasty that was aiming to bring some order into a previously tumultuous realm. Whether the order it and consequent dynasties did bring about was actually "Confucian" in nature is a separate question.

In fact, one could actually argue that Confucian political thought was more aligned with the new state-centered politics of the Warring States period than with the politics of empire (despite its potential appeal to the latter). Indeed, I contend that the adulation of the Zhou dynasty notwithstanding, the Confucians offered a new politics that they took to be more responsive than the decaying Zhou system to the social and political transformations that were under way in their day, particularly the rise of the common people as an important political player. For, in the Zhou political system, the common people were far removed from the king. Their only contact was with the regional rulers responsible for their territory, and thus many layers of princely hierarchy separated them from the center of Zhou power. In the states emerging from the fall of the Western Zhou, as Mark Edward Lewis's account above reveals, the relationship between the ruler and the common people was much more direct, and also reciprocal. The ruler now needed his people: they formed the bulwark of his army and the producers of his realm. Indeed, the rise of taxes on production, which replaced labor services, signaled at least a "tacit recognition" of the peasants' right to use the land; in other words, a recognition of "ownership, or at least tenure of land."[97] As Hsu argues, in parallel with the rise of sovereign states out of the previous "feudal" order, the people were also gradually arising as "subjects" of the new sovereign states, a process only finalized during the Warring States period.[98]

---

[96] Pines, *Envisioning Eternal Empire*, 1–2.
[97] Hsu, "Spring and Autumn Period," 577.
[98] Hsu, "Spring and Autumn Period," 577.

Concomitant with the rise of the common people as an important political player, and as the Zhou weakened and was replaced by a multiplicity of smaller states each with its own ruler, a crisis of legitimacy ensued: the question inevitably arose as to who now enjoyed the Mandate of Heaven. The Zhou was able to maintain the mandate by tying it to the supreme position in a complex lineage order where status was obtained through hereditary succession. But as the Zhou received threats from outside, and as many of the regional rulers it appointed grew autonomous, the royal order could no longer work as a basis of authority. Indeed, now that the scene was populated by many a contender to the supreme position of ruler over the expansive territory that had previously been the Zhou's, new standards had to be devised to decide who was a legitimate ruler and who was not. As Tongdong Bai puts it, "a new social glue had to be discovered or invented for both the ruling class and the society as a whole."[99] The Confucians offered such new standards by linking legitimacy to the fulfillment of the needs of the common people. As I will show in Chapter 2, the Confucians recommended specific measures, centered on the welfare of the people, for forging a complementary relationship between the ruler and his new subjects.

Chapter Outline

The central argument of this book is that the Confucian political vision does not flow in a straightforward manner from Confucian ethics, and that political order is the central motivating principle of Confucian political thought. Within this larger argument, I make a series of smaller ones. I show for example that political order can be understood as having two variants: a basic level of order, where the political standard is largely separate from the Confucian ethical core, discussed in Chapters 1 and 2, and reemerging in Chapters 4 and 5, and a higher level of order, involving an overlap, though not a complete one, between ethics and politics in the Confucian vision of a harmonious society, explored in Chapter 3, but also touched upon in Chapters 4, 5, and 6. I take up the democratic interpretation of early Confucianism in Chapter 1. In Chapter 6, I discuss the relationship between Heaven and politics in the early Confucian texts. Finally, though I largely treat the three early Confucian texts as a single group in this book, key distinctions between

[99] Bai, "Political Philosophy of China," 183.

Mencius and Xunzi are discussed in Chapters 3 and 4. More generally, Chapters 3, and especially 4, focus mostly on Xunzi, while Chapters 5 and 6 focus more on the *Analects* and the *Mencius*.

The breakdown of the book, chapter by chapter, is as follows:

In Chapter 1, I explore the relationship between ruler and ruled that the Confucians advocated for the new territorial states. I argue against two common interpretations of this relationship: the virtue-centered view that presents Confucian government as aiming at the inculcation of virtue in the citizenry, and the (proto-)democratic view that highlights the people's role in the choice and removal of the ruler. I show instead that the underlying motif of Confucian political thought is, as I mentioned above, a concern with political order and that this order is produced, in its basic level, by forging a complementary relation between the ruler and the common people. I fulfill two further aims in Chapter 1: First, I elicit the qualities expected of the common people and show that they are qualities pertaining to orderliness, not full-fledged virtues. Second, I discuss the Confucian distinction between kings and hegemons, arguing that hegemons, though lacking in virtue, are somewhat accepted by the early Confucians because they are successful at establishing a minimal level of order.

While Chapter 1 outlines different elements in the early Confucian texts that reveal a concern with political order, Chapters 2 and 3 focus on methods of ruling, that is, the means for achieving political order. In Chapter 2, I discuss policies relating to security and the use of penal force, welfare and general economic measures, and merit and the methods used for appointment to public office. I argue that the fulfillment of these policies achieves a basic level of political order, and that they do not operate through the exemplary power of the virtue of the ruler, but rather through the regulation of the "basic structure" of society (the penal code, the procedures for promotion, the taxation system, the use of the commons, etc.).

Though the Confucians accept a society that achieves the basic level of order outlined in Chapters 1 and 2, as when a society is ruled by a hegemon, they prefer a society that produces a more exalted level of order. This higher level is achieved by means of rituals, which operate as an institutional mechanism for the regulation of society. This is the topic of Chapter 3. The chapter also explores the differences between Mencius and Xunzi on the question of human nature and its relationship to the use of rituals: Mencius is more optimistic about the ability of people to develop morally in a spontaneous way, and allows for a

bigger role for the emulative example of the ruler, while Xunzi emphasizes more strongly the importance of rituals.

In Chapter 4, I discuss the division of labor between ruler and ministers needed to maintain the Confucian vision of an orderly society, in
both its basic and exalted versions. I show the importance of ministers
in the Confucian vision of government, especially for Xunzi, who made
ministers responsible for the day-to-day business of government. I also
revisit the question of the role of virtuous rulership and show how my
interpretation of Confucian political thought can make sense of the
Confucian preference for a virtuous ruler despite the fact that the aim
of government, on my account, is order, not virtue.

Chapter 5 argues that involvement in politics is necessary for the
full development of virtue. The chapter is conceived from the perspective of the scholarly-official elite who, as I mentioned above, were co-
opted by the governments of different states but also tried to maintain
their distinctive place, resisting subservience to the rulers. I first present the case for the Confucian view that a person cannot become fully
virtuous in isolation from politics. I then argue against the contention
that the Confucians adopted a purist approach, rejecting any involvement in political regimes that they deemed corrupt. Instead, I suggest
that they advocated involvement in politics based on a consequentialist logic: involvement is permitted, even advisable, insofar as it can
bring about political order.

In Chapter 6, I explore the role of Heaven (*tian* 天) in the Confucian
political vision. I show how the resort to Heaven provides legitimacy
for Confucians' political pursuits by supporting some pursuits, like the
achievement and promotion of merit, and political engagement more
generally, but also by shielding political actors from responsibility for
events beyond their control.

CHAPTER 1

Ruler and Ruled

ᕽᗠᏌ

How should we describe the relationship between ruler and ruled in Confucian political thought? How is it best to understand the aims of Confucian government? The literature on early Confucianism largely involves two related sets of claims pertaining to these questions. On the one hand, it is argued, as I mentioned in the prologue, that Confucian government aims at the development of virtue in the populace. On the other hand, the concern with the people's well-being, physical and moral, is also used to argue for (proto-)democratic tendencies in early Confucianism. One large, interpretive problem burdens both sets of claims: the portrayal of the common people. Indeed, this portrayal suggests both that they are unlikely to become virtuous and that their role in choosing the ruler, or in having him removed from the throne, does not properly indicate consent.

This chapter sets the stage for the overarching thesis of the book by showing how the interpretive difficulties with the claims just mentioned can be solved by replacing the language of virtue and the language of democracy with the language of political order. What is meant by political order here, as will become clearer in what follows, is a simple idea: the administration of people who live together in a given territory for the sake of security and cooperation. I argue therefore, with Heiner Roetz, that "in general, the Confucians legitimize political rule as a precondition of a safe, peaceful, and civilized living together of men."[1] This explains why, as I argue in the third part of this chapter, they countenance, even at points approve of, hegemons.

---

[1] Roetz, *Confucian Ethics of the Axial Age*, 91. Roetz also adds, however, that Confucian

A concern with political order is usually recognized of Xunzi,[2] but it is precisely because of this recognition that commentators set him apart from his predecessors, Confucius and Mencius, who are thought to be concerned only with virtue in government. Although there is no denying the differences in the thought of the three Confucian thinkers, my aim in this chapter, and the book more generally, is to emphasize the similarities.[3]

The chapter proceeds as follows: I show, in the first section, that the qualities expected of the common people are not full-fledged Confucian virtues, but qualities pertaining to orderliness. I contend that the low level of expectations from the common people arises from viewing them as a "mass," as part of a perspective on politics that focuses on social groups, rather than on distinct individuals. In the second section, I show that the significance of the common people is not so much in choosing or removing a ruler, but in signaling the ruler's ability to maintain order. They so signal not by expressing individualized opinions, but by their physical movement, again as a "mass," away from, or in the direction of, the ruler. In the last part of the chapter, I turn to the Confucian discussion of hegemons, and I show that, contrary to received wisdom, the Confucians countenance hegemons because of the latter's ability to maintain political order.

The Virtue Argument

On the reading of early Confucianism presented in the prologue, in which Confucian politics is read through the lens of Confucian ethics, the aim of Confucian government is, as Hsiao Kung-chuan puts it, to make the common people "noble and virtuous in character and deed." In other words, its end is "transformation through teaching."[4] Schwartz

---

government has a moral purpose, relating to the cultivation of virtue. I argue in this chapter that this additional claim is misleading.

[2] Sato thus cites approvingly the argument of Chen Daqi, who takes Xunzi's ultimate purpose to be the attainment of order. See Sato, *Confucian Quest for Order*, 13.

[3] Sato also emphasizes the continuity in the thought of Mencius and Xunzi, though for historical, rather than theoretical, reasons: he argues that they are both part of the intellectual lineage of the Jixia Academy. See Sato, *Confucian Quest for Order*, 164. And though he argues, citing the famous Classical historian Sima Qian, that the Jixia Academy was concerned with "matters of order and disorder" (*zhiluan zhi shi* 治亂之事) (69–70), his goal is not to show that Mencius was concerned with order as well (he describes the concern with order as "post-Mencian" [120]), but that Xunzi was as concerned with morality as Mencius was (25, 427).

[4] Hsiao, *History of Chinese Political Thought*, 110.

draws a comparison between the Confucians and Plato and Aristotle, arguing that, like the early Greeks, Confucius views the political community as an ethical society aimed at promoting morality.[5] This explains, according to him, why it is the virtuous who are supposed to rule, and why providing for the welfare of the common people, a theme I will return to in the next chapter, is important: they can be hindered by adverse circumstances from achieving moral education.[6] Schwartz cites Mencius on this: "Nowadays, the means laid down for the people are sufficient neither for the care of parents nor for the support of wife and children. In good years life is always hard, while in bad years there is no way of escaping death. Thus simply to survive takes more energy than the people have. What time can they spare for learning about rites and [rightness] (*yi* 義)?"[7]

The thought that Confucians view political life as geared toward promoting virtue in the common people appears to be the logical continuation of their emphasis on virtue, and the idea that all persons are equally capable of becoming virtuous: told that he was being spied on with the purpose of seeing whether he was the same as everyone else, Mencius retorts, "In what way should I be different from other people? Even [sage kings] Yao and Shun were the same as anyone else."[8] Xunzi also believes that any person can become a Yu, Yu being the third sage king of antiquity, since, according to him, it is possible for all men to understand and to be able to practice *ren*, rightness, and regulations (*fa* 法).[9]

There also appears to be direct evidence in the Confucian texts for the view that Confucian government aims at the moral improvement of the common people. Consider, for example, Confucius's response to the question put to him by Ji Kangzi, one of the heads of the Ji family of the state of Lu, about the best way to govern. Confucius says, "To govern (*zheng* 政) is to correct (*zheng* 正). If you set an example by being correct, who would dare to remain incorrect?"[10] The same Ji Kangzi asks for Confucius's advice about getting rid of thieves. Confucius answers, "If you yourself were not a man of desires, no one would steal

---

[5] Schwartz, *World of Thought in Ancient China*, 96–97. While this is a common reading of the early Greeks, I argued in the prologue that an alternative reading is also possible.

[6] Schwartz, *World of Thought in Ancient China*, 105.

[7] *Mencius* 1A.7.

[8] *Mencius* 4B.32. See also *Mencius* 2A.8 and 6A.6.

[9] *Xunzi* 23.5a.

[10] *Analects* 12.17.

even if stealing carried a reward."[11] When asked by Ji Kangzi again about how to inculcate in the common people the virtues of reverence (*jing* 敬), of dutifulness (*zhong* 忠), and of enthusiasm (*quan* 勸), Confucius answers, "Rule over them with dignity and they will be reverent; treat them with kindness and they will do their best; raise the good and instruct those who are backward and they will be imbued with enthusiasm."[12] When asked by Zilu about government, he responds, "Encourage the people to work hard by setting an example yourself."[13]

All of these passages indicate that it is possible for the ruler, by providing for the people, setting himself as a model (of correctness and lack of desires), treating the people with dignity and kindness, and promoting the worthy, to encourage the people toward moral reform. But what is also clear, and no less significant, about these passages and other similar ones is that they reveal that the qualities expected of the common people are not the cardinal Confucian virtues of *ren* 仁, rightness (*yi* 義), and wisdom (*zhi* 智)[14] that Confucius expects of himself and his disciples. In fact, I could only find two examples (in the *Mencius*) that associate the common people with one of these virtues.[15]

---

[11] *Analects* 12.18.

[12] *Analects* 2.20.

[13] *Analects* 13.1.

[14] I will argue in Chapter 3 that the common people are encouraged to abide by ritual propriety (*li* 禮), but that they do not necessarily internalize the importance of ritual propriety in the way that a Confucian gentleman does.

[15] The first is the rhetorical question quoted above in which Mencius wonders how the people can fail to learn about the rites and rightness if they are provided for. The second is *Mencius* 7A.23: "When sages rule the world (*zhi tianxia* 治天下), they make grain be as plentiful as water and fire. When the people (*min* 民) have as much grain as they have water and fire, how can they fail to be *ren*?" (quoted from Van Norden). Two passages in the *Analects* are less obvious: *Analects* 1.9: "When funerals and sacrifices are properly undertaken, the virtue of the common people will incline towards fullness (*hou* 厚)" and *Analects* 15.35: "*Ren* is more vital to the common people than even fire and water. In the case of fire and water, I have seen men die by stepping on them, but I have never seen any man die by stepping on *ren*." In the first, it is not clear what virtue inclining toward fullness means, and in the second, it could plausibly be argued that it is vital for the people to have a *ren* ruler, rather than be *ren* themselves. Similarly, *Analects* 8.2 can be read as suggesting that the common people will be stirred by (those who are) *ren* or toward (those who are) *ren*, as opposed to being stirred to (becoming) *ren* themselves. Other potential evidence for the claim that the common people are expected to become virtuous is even less convincing: In *Mencius* 7A.13, people under the rule of a king (as opposed to a hegemon) are said to move toward goodness (*shan* 善), but this is not the same as *ren* per se, especially since they are said to do so "without realizing" it. In 4A.3, Mencius says that an ordinary man (*shuren* 庶人) should be *ren* in order to preserve his limbs, but here Mencius is not talking about the people taken as a mass—which is what I am concerned with—but as individuals. Finally, in 4A.20, Mencius says that "if a ruler is

That high virtue is not expected of the common people should not actually be surprising if one considers Confucius's view of the common people's intellectual abilities, expressed in his statement that "the common people can be made to follow it [i.e., the Confucian Way], but they cannot be made to understand (*zhi* 知) it."[16] Similarly, Mencius says that the multitude (*zhong* 眾) do not realize (*zhu* 著) what it is they practice, do not examine (*cha* 察) what they repeatedly do, and do not understand (*zhi* 知) the path they follow all their lives.[17] For Xunzi, the virtue of the common people merely consists in following custom, treasuring material possessions, and nurturing their lives.[18]

Even Hsiao admits that some people cannot actually be educated, and these "probably are not a minority," hence the Confucians' inevitable resort to punishment at times.[19] For Yuri Pines, the reason why the Confucians' concern for fulfilling people's needs and reaching their hearts did not result in an institutionalized form of political participation from below (more on this in the next section) is due to the identification of commoners with petty men (*xiaoren* 小人).[20] He cites in this regard Mencius's approval of the common saying: "There are those who use their minds and there are those who use their muscles. The former rule (*zhi* 治); the latter are ruled."[21]

I suggest, based on the preceding, that people's dispositions are indeed meant to be improved by Confucian government, but that such improvement does not amount to the full-fledged pursuit of virtuousness. Instead, it is more accurate to see the dispositions sought for the common people (to refrain from stealing, to work hard, and to be "correct") as dispositions relating to orderliness, rather than virtuousness. The qualities expected of the common people can be elicited in statements that establish the effect virtuous rulership has on the former,

---

ren, no one will fail to be *ren*." The interpretive problem with this passage is that it is not clear whether "no one" here refers to the ministers serving the ruler, or to everyone in the realm.

[16] *Analects* 8.9, quoted from Slingerland. Slingerland argues that early commentators, like Zhang Ping, read this statement as pertaining to rule by force only. In other words, the claim would be that those who rule by force cannot allow the people to understand their plans for fear they would evade them. See Slingerland, trans., *Confucius: Analects*, 81. It is unclear what the evidence for this reading is, especially since, as I contend, this statement is consistent with others made to the same effect by the early Confucians.

[17] *Mencius* 7A.5.

[18] *Xunzi* 8.7.

[19] Hsiao, *History of Chinese Political Thought*, 114.

[20] See Pines, *Envisioning Eternal Empire*, 209–11.

[21] *Mencius* 3A.4.

and that reveal that there is in fact no expectation of a one-to-one correspondence between the virtue of the ruler and the qualities attained by the people. Thus Confucius argues, "When those above are given to the observance of the rites, the common people will be easy to command."[22] Infuriated by Fan Chi's questions about growing crops, he answers, "When those above love the rites, none of the common people will dare to be irreverent (*bujing* 不敬); when they love what is right, none of the common people will dare to be insubordinate (*bufu* 不服); when they love trustworthiness, none of the common people will dare to be insincere (*buyongqing* 不用情). In this way, the common people from the four quarters will come with their children strapped to their backs. What need is there to talk about growing crops?"[23] Ritual propriety, rightness, and trustworthiness are thus matched with obedience and reverence, subordination, and sincerity, respectively. The latter set of qualities is also emphasized by Mencius and Xunzi. Thus Mencius contends that if the people are not provided for in times of plenty, then in times of need, when the ruler needs them to fight on his behalf, they could refuse to do so.[24] Xunzi says that the common people should be filial, respect their elders, be honest and diligent, and not dare to be indolent or haughty.[25]

In short, the qualities expected of the common people are qualities like reverence, subordination, honesty, diligence, and correctness. There is no talk here of *ren*, rightness, or wisdom. What is at stake, then, in statements to the effect that the people should learn about rites and duties,[26] or that the ruler should teach (*jiao* 教) and instruct (*hui* 誨) them,[27] is not a full-blown moral education, but instruction in qualities favorable to an orderly society. One can even understand the idea of "reform" in Confucius's famous statement that the goal of government should not be merely to keep people out of trouble, but also to encourage them to have a sense of shame (*chi* 恥) and to reform (*ge* 格) themselves, to simply mean the acquisition of the qualities listed above.[28] Indeed, Schwartz recognizes this when he argues that the people are to be educated "to live up to the moral norms which should

---

[22] *Analects* 14.41.
[23] *Analects* 13.4.
[24] *Mencius* 1B.12.
[25] *Xunzi* 4.7.
[26] *Mencius* 1A.7. See above.
[27] *Xunzi* 19.10.
[28] *Analects* 2.3.

govern their lives within their families and communities. This does not mean that they must achieve the highest levels of knowledge or achieve the highest realization of *ren*."[29]

But if this is true, then what should we make of the tension between the Confucians' insistence that anyone can become virtuous and the reluctance to describe the common people as being able to do so?[30] To deal with this tension, David Hall and Roger Ames argue for "a perhaps blurred yet significant contrast between the amorphous, indeterminate mass of peasants (*min* 民), in themselves having little by way of distinguishing character or structure, and particular persons (*ren* 人)."[31] The depiction of the common people as an "amorphous, indeterminate mass," I contend, stems from the Confucians' adoption of what can be called an "external" or "sociological" point of view, which looks at society as a whole, thus considering social groups, rather than individuals, as units of analysis. This perspective can be contrasted with an "internal" or "individual-oriented" one that looks at moral development from the standpoint of each and every (socially embedded)[32] individual. From the internal point of view, the theoretical possibility of becoming virtuous is emphasized because the Confucians do not believe that endowments of birth are different between individuals. In their position within society as a whole, however, individuals are part of social groups with distinguishing lifestyles. The common people, as Hall and Ames point out, were mostly peasants, and were thus engaged in daily manual labor. As such, they did not enjoy the leisure needed to invest their time in the mental and social activities required for moral perfection. Instead, they devoted their days to communal agricultural practices, and their worries were naturally related to their livelihood, which accounts for the passivity and lack of differentiation with which they are described.

This does not mean that individual peasants cannot, in theory, break out of their social group;[33] it just means that they are, as a matter of fact, unlikely to be able to do so. This is indeed how I understand Mencius's claim in 1A.7: as opposed to taking it as conditional—if the common

[29] Schwartz, *World of Thought in Ancient China*, 108.

[30] I thank Stephen Angle for pressing me on this question.

[31] David Hall and Roger Ames, *Thinking through Confucius* (New York: State University of New York Press, 1987), 139.

[32] Social relationships are crucial to the Confucian understanding of personhood and the self. Confucians do not conceive of individuals in isolation from society.

[33] As Shun did. See Chapter 2.

people lack constant means, then they lack constant hearts—I take it as descriptive—the common people lack constant means, therefore they lack constant hearts (in contradistinction to men of service [*shi* 士] who have constant hearts without necessarily having constant means).[34] Whether the common people would have constant hearts if they had constant means is in some sense beside the point, since it is not envisaged by Mencius or the early Confucians; as I argued in the prologue, the lens of an ideal theory in which hypothetical scenarios are envisioned is not the most obvious way to approach early Confucian political thought.

To reiterate my argument, the obstacle to the common people's moral and intellectual cultivation arises not from their ascriptive qualities, or their pedigree at birth, but from the social demands of the material life associated with the social group into which they are born. In other words, their limitation is not inborn but socially and economically imposed.[35] There is therefore no contradiction between the Confucians' insistence on equal potential among all human beings, and their recognition that the common people, from the standpoint of their status as peasants, are unlikely to develop their potential for virtue.[36] It is indeed telling that the only two anecdotes in which Mencius does associate the common people with *ren* and rightness are aimed at un-

[34] Because they have the leisure to learn and practice being virtuous, which enables them to reach this high stage of internal sufficiency. The *shi* started out as a warrior class but, as time passed, became mostly a bureaucratic class responsible for ritual and administrative functions, and were hence largely recruited on the basis of learning. See Cho-yun Hsu, *Ancient China in Transition: An Analysis of Social Mobility, 722–222 B.C.* (Stanford: Stanford University Press, 1965), 8. See also Donald Munro, *The Concept of Man in Early China* (Stanford: Stanford University Press, 1969), 10.

[35] Hall and Ames argue that what makes someone move from the group of *min* 民 to become individualized *ren* 人 is not the privilege of being born into an elite class, but the "personal cultivation and socialization that renders him particular," and they describe this move as "cultural." See Hall and Ames, *Thinking through Confucius*, 139. My contention, however, is that the conditions needed for this "cultural" move to occur are socioeconomic. My interpretation of the Confucian view of peasants is akin to the one that Jill Frank reads in Aristotle, which recognizes the effects of the activities they are devoted to in life on the development of persons' capacities and thus on their political status. See Jill Frank, "Citizens, Slaves, and Foreigners: Aristotle on Human Nature," *American Political Science Review* 98, no. 1 (February 2004): 91–104.

[36] Schwartz argues, in relation to Mencius, that what is needed to fulfill people's equal potential for goodness are the right circumstances (basically, ones in which basic needs are met), which are ensured by a virtuous elite. See Schwartz, *World of Thought in Ancient China*, 288. My contention is that more than basic needs have to be met before the common people are able to achieve virtue: a social class of peasants would have to no longer exist, a possibility that the Confucians did not envision.

derscoring the importance of providing for them and ensuring their livelihood, exceptions that prove the rule that the emphasis should be on the latter, not the former.[37]

To conclude, I have argued in this section that the idea that Confucian government aims at instilling virtue in the common people is unsustainable because the early Confucians very rarely associate the common people, viewed as a group, with virtue. I have also shown that the qualities expected of, and encouraged in, the common people are qualities worthy of an orderly society. In the following section, I further my discussion of the conception of the people in early Confucian thought by elucidating their role in the choice and removal of a ruler.

The People—Continued
Succession to the Throne

In the previous section, I elicited the Confucian political perspective from which the common people are viewed as a social group of manual laborers and argued that, from this perspective, the common people are expected not to become virtuous, but to acquire qualities relating to political order. In this section, my aim is to continue the preceding discussion by showing that the portrayal of the people as "mass" carries over into the Confucian discussion of succession to the throne. This means, as I will argue in what follows, that the framework of political order allows for a more plausible interpretation of passages from the *Mencius* that have traditionally been analyzed according to whether or not they reveal democratic tendencies. I move from there to analyzing the view of political order revealed by these passages, which I will show is based on a particular notion of fittingness between ruler and ruled.

In the first relevant passage where Mencius discusses succession to the throne, he starts out repudiating the story from the *Analects* in which Emperor Yao, a sage king of antiquity, is said to have abdicated the throne to Shun, another sage of antiquity, seeing that the latter was worthy of it.[38] Mencius argues that "the Emperor cannot give the Em-

[37] See note 15. My argument thus follows Xu Fuguan's contention that rituals and rightness are concerned with people's lives (*shenghuo* 生活) and not *vice versa*. See Xu, *Zhongguo sixiang shi lunji* 中國思想史論集 [Collected essays on the history of Chinese thought] (1974; repr., Taibei: Taiwan xuesheng shuju, 1975), 135.

[38] See *Analects* 20.1. Yao, Shun, and Yu are paragons of virtue often cited by the early Confucians. They are supposed to have lived between 2500 and 2000 BCE, but are probably mythical. For a discussion of the framing and implications of the abdication story as

pire to another." Instead, "Heaven (*tian* 天) gave it to him."[39] He then explains how Heaven's choice is revealed: When Emperor Yao died, Shun, who had served Yao for twenty-eight years, left the empire in the hands of Yao's son and took leave. Nonetheless, "the [regional rulers] of the Empire coming to pay homage and those who were engaged in litigation went to Shun, not to Yao's son, and ballad singers sang the praises of Shun, not of Yao's son." Mencius takes this to be a sign that Heaven favored the appointment of Shun, rather than Yao's son. He adds that Heaven "sees with the eyes of its people" and that it "hears with the ears of its people."

Mencius then recounts a similar story of succession following the death of Shun.[40] Shun recommended Yu, and Yu also withdrew once the mourning period for Shun was over. Yet the people followed him just as they had followed Shun upon Yao's death, suggesting that Heaven favored Yu over Shun's son.

These accounts, however, should not suggest that Heaven, and the people, will always choose meritorious ministers to accede to the throne, for the story takes a different turn when Yu dies. Mencius explicitly argues against the idea that virtue declined once Yu favored being succeeded by his own son, instead of choosing a "good and wise" man to ascend the throne. He again directs responsibility to Heaven: If Heaven decides to give the throne to a good and wise man, this would be the right choice. But if it decides to give it to the extant son, then this would also be right. And it is the people who again indicate Heaven's choice in this case. Instead of following Yi, whom Yu had recommended, they went to Yu's son, Qi, instead: "Ballad singers sang the praises of Qi instead of Yi, saying, 'This is the son of our prince.'"[41]

The literature on the democratic pedigree of Confucianism is vast and varied, and actually mostly draws on the idea discussed in the pre-

---

it appears in different texts from the Warring States period, see Yuri Pines, "Disputers of Abdication: Zhanguo Egalitarianism and the Sovereign's Power," *T'oung Pao* 91, no. 4 (2005): 243–300. Pines points out that the abdication story was used by its supporters to justify the idea of the promotion of the worthy, which I will discuss in the next chapter.

[39] *Mencius* 5A.5. "Empire" is a somewhat anachronistic translation for *tianxia* (天下), which can more literally be translated as "all under Heaven." Its connotations are both cultural (referring to the world that is heir to the Zhou dynasty's cultural legacy) and political (referring to the world constituted by the many warring states and later unified under the Qin, which heralded the imperial structure). See Yuri Pines, "Changing Views of *Tianxia* in Pre-imperial Discourse," *Oriens Extremus* 43, nos. 1–2 (2002): 101–16. I also use "emperor" for *tianzi* 天子 (literally, the "son of Heaven").

[40] *Mencius* 5A.6.

[41] *Mencius* 5A.6.

vious section about the Confucian recognition of equal potential for virtue.[42] But the passages from the *Mencius* that I just summarized have also been used as evidence for the idea that the people have an influence, even if indirect, on the choice of the ruler. For example, although he does not equate this with democracy, Joseph Chan identifies in these passages the notion that "acceptance or consent of the people is necessary for the ruler's political legitimacy."[43]

To clarify if a notion of consent is at play here, and what it amounts to, answers to the following two questions are needed: First, what is, all things considered, Mencius's preferred mode of succession to the throne? And what is the common people's role in it? I submit that there is reason to argue that Mencius is in favor of hereditary succession. Although in his account of the transition of power from Yao to Shun to Yu to Qi, Mencius says that the accession of both virtuous ministers (Shun and Yu) and heirs (Qi) is acceptable, it is possible, as Pines does,[44] to read the cases of Shun and Yu as exceptional (instead of taking Qi's accession to be the exceptional one, as is more common to do). Indeed, it is not untypical of Mencius to provide ad hoc justifications for the actions of the sage kings of antiquity when these do not fit his teachings.[45] On my reading, then, Mencius dwells on the cases of Shun and Yu not because he takes merit-based accession to the throne to be the model to follow but, on the contrary, because these cases depart from his preferred option—hereditary succession—and thus require justification.

My admittedly controversial interpretation relies on a statement that Mencius appends to the accounts above, and in which he argues that, when a ruler obtains the throne through hereditary succession (*jishi* 繼世), he can be put aside by Heaven only "if he is like Jie or

[42] For example, see Brooke Ackerly, "Is Liberalism the Only Way toward Democracy? Confucianism and Democracy," *Political Theory* 33, no. 4 (August 2005): 547–76.

[43] Joseph Chan, "Democracy and Meritocracy: Toward a Confucian Perspective," *Journal of Chinese Philosophy* 34, no. 2 (2007): 186. A similar argument can also be found in Yang, "Mengzi and Democracy," 90; Enbao Wang and Regina F. Titunik, "Democracy in China: The Theory and Practice of *Minben*," in Zhao, *China and Democracy*, 78, and Tongdong Bai, "A Mencian Version of Limited Democracy," *Res Publica* 14 (2008): 27n14. The argument about popular sovereignty can be found in Hsiao, *History of Chinese Political Thought*, 158. On the other hand, Chan argues that "the people's consent" is not necessarily a sign of a democratic system, since a monarchical system could also be based on consent. He contends that, for it to be a sign of a democratic system and of democratic ideals like "popular sovereignty or political equality," consent has to be the product of adequate "*institutions* or *procedures*" for equal political participation (emphasis original) (186–87).

[44] Pines, "Disputers of Abdication," 277.

[45] See, for example, the defense of Shun in *Mencius* 4A.26, 5A.1, and 5A.2.

Zhou [Xin]," both tyrants.[46] This statement shows that Mencius is not against hereditary succession, but also that whatever benefit he sees in it is forfeited by the rise of a tyrant. The best way to interpret this benefit such that it fits both the rule and the exception is to see it as revolving around the avoidance of political turmoil: heredity as the default method of succession helps in the maintenance of orderly transitions to power. On the other hand, it can also produce heirs who bring havoc to the realm, which defies its own purpose (order), and thus justifies the exception that Mencius attaches to it. This interpretation is in line with Mencius's preference for emolument of ministers on the basis of heredity,[47] and with Hsiao's interpretation of this preference as ensuring a modicum of order and propriety in a time of free-for-all competition for power and public office.[48] Speaking of Confucius's own preference for the heredity principle,[49] Benjamin Schwartz argues that the reason for it stems from Confucius's belief that lineage is "the most potent base for social order and harmony," and that the overthrow of rulers by force is a recipe for chaos.[50] Something similar, I argue, would explain Mencius's preference for the hereditary succession of rulers.

Although there is no further textual evidence supporting my view, all alternative views (merit-based succession, popular choice, appoint-

[46] Mencius adds another qualification to the accounts above. He says that, in the case of a commoner (*pifu* 匹夫), virtue alone is not sufficient to win the empire, the emperor's recommendation is also necessary. "That is why," Mencius says, "Confucius never possessed the Empire." How does the need for the ruler's recommendation fit with my reading? Justin Tiwald takes the point about the need for the ruler's recommendation to be an extension of hereditary succession, presumably in that a departure from the latter can be made only through the approval of the ruler. See Justin Tiwald, "A Right of Rebellion in the *Mengzi*?," *Dao* 7, no. 3 (Fall 2008): 274. Pines considers the ruler's recommendation to be important for Mencius to moderate the implication of his discussion of the people's will in the stories of abdication. See Pines, "Disputers of Abdication," 280. The problem with these interpretations, as with all interpretations of Mencius's view on succession (including mine), is that there is not enough evidence to support any view definitively: in this case, Mencius mentions only the need for a recommendation in relation to Confucius. I therefore find it more likely, as I explain in what follows, that interruption of hereditary succession typically occurs when a very bad heir arises, which is signaled by the people, not the extant ruler.

[47] *Mencius* 3A.3.

[48] Hsiao, *History of Chinese Political Thought*, 176–77.

[49] Confucius shows a preference for hereditary prerogative when he argues against the usurpation, in the state of Lu, of royal ritual prerogatives (*Analects* 3.1), and against the attack on the state of Zhuanyu, whose rulers have a royal prerogative to preside over sacrifices to the eastern Meng mountains (*Analects* 16.1).

[50] Schwartz, *World of Thought in Ancient China*, 115–16.

ment by Heaven,[51] and appointment by the current ruler) also have slim backing, given that all Mencius says about succession is included in the three cases mentioned above, and in the corollary statements on which my interpretation has relied. I think Robert Eno is right when he argues that the relevant passages in the *Mencius* "have the effect of delegitimizing arbitrary cessions of thrones and supporting the institutional status quo," and when he describes Mencius's attitude as "institutional conservatism."[52] As to what the "institutional status quo" consists of, this is where I lean toward the hereditary succession view. As Pines notes, despite the fluctuations in his view, Mencius ultimately "did not present any practical alternative to the hereditary principle of rule."[53]

If my argument about Mencius's preference for hereditary accession to the throne is correct, then this would make Mencius's position close to Xunzi's: Although he is the most adamant defender of meritocracy among the early Confucians, Xunzi's meritocratic principles do not extend to the position of king.[54] He justifies the nonhereditary accession of Shun and Yu by arguing that, in the absence of a worthy descendant, the accession of a virtuous high-ranking minister to the throne does not cause significant interruption in government.[55] Mencius does not explicitly make the same argument about Shun's and Yu's rise to the throne (he merely cites Heaven's choice to justify it), but if it is true, as I argue, that he is concerned about interruption in government, then a similar concern could explain his purpose in recounting the story of the accessions of Shun and Yu.

---

[51] See, for example, Goldin, *Confucianism*, 62–63. I discuss the role of Heaven and argue that it is largely symbolic in Chapter 6. The view I offer in Chapter 6 will thus explain why I have not assigned Heaven any role in the choice of the ruler in interpreting the passages above.

[52] Eno, *Confucian Creation of Heaven*, 255n28.

[53] See Pines, *Envisioning Eternal Empire*, 76. Elstein also argues, citing Li, "Confucian Value and Democratic Value," that "neither Mengzi nor any other early Ruist [Confucian] challenged the principle of hereditary succession." See Elstein, *Democracy in Contemporary Confucian Philosophy*, 30.

[54] He thus says, "Although a man may be the descendant of commoners, if he has acquired learning, is upright in conduct, and can adhere to ritual principles, he should be promoted to the post of prime minister (*qingxiang* 卿相), [man of service] (*shi* 士), or [counselor] (*dafu* 大夫)." There is no mention here of his appointment to the position of king (*Xunzi* 9.1, quoted from Watson, 36).

[55] *Xunzi* 18.5b. Like Mencius, Xunzi argues that when a bad descendant like Jie or Zhou Xin ascends the throne, he cannot be said to legitimately rule, and therefore the fact that the throne is taken over by worthy contenders (Kings Tang and Wu, respectively) is no usurpation (*Xunzi* 18.2).

The question that remains is how to determine when a ruler is bad enough, when he counts as a tyrant, such that the interruption of hereditary succession for his removal is warranted. This is where, I argue, the common people come in. Xunzi argues that a bad ruler is one who gets deserted by the regional rulers and the people.[56] This is the flip side of the portrayal of the people, in the stories of succession relayed above, as being "content" (*an* 安) in the presence of a good ruler, going to him for litigation, and singing his praises. In both cases, the people act as a gauge of the worth of candidates: If they find the ruler worthy enough, they give him their support. If they do not, they abandon him, either literally or metaphorically, precipitating the unraveling of political order. As Masayuki Sato argues in relation to Mencius, what the latter saw as "the most urgent problem facing contemporary rulers was to stop people from fleeing from their countries."[57]

It is important to note that the common people act as passive,[58] rather than as active, political agents whose approval of the ruler, as Chan puts it, is more "automatic"[59] than deliberative.[60] Another way to describe the people's approval is as instinctual or emotional (rather than reflective); as William Theodore de Bary suggests, it is the peo-

---

[56] *Xunzi* 18.2.

[57] Sato, *Confucian Quest for Order*, 128. Sato distinguishes between this concern with stopping people from fleeing from the concern with avoiding popular revolts, associating the latter with a concern for order. On my view, the loyalty of the common people, represented in their willingness not to flee, is actually key to political order.

[58] See David Elstein, "Why Early Confucianism Cannot Generate Democracy," *Dao* 9 (2010): 436. Sungmoon Kim suggests that, while it is true that the common people are "passive . . . beneficiaries of the benevolent government," Mencius is not referring to them alone when he speaks of the people's approval of various candidates to the throne. In fact, as mentioned above, the regional rulers also pay homage to their preferred candidate. Kim argues that the regional rulers, along with "ministers of the noble families," are "active subjects" who confer legitimacy on the ruler. See Sungmoon Kim, "Confucian Constitutionalism: Mencius and Xunzi on Virtue, Ritual, and Royal Transmission," *Review of Politics*, no. 73 (2011): 382. This argument does not undermine, but rather buttresses, my contention in this section about the passive role of the common people. More generally, I agree with Kim about the importance of ministers in government. This will become clear in my discussion of hegemons below. The division of labor between a largely symbolic ruler and his competent and virtuous ministers is a key aspect of Confucian government that will be discussed in Chapter 4.

[59] Chan, "Democracy and Meritocracy," 187.

[60] A lonely but intriguing statement in *Analects* 16.2 says that when the Way prevails, ordinary people do not "discuss" (*yi* 議), presumably matters of government, since what precedes in the anecdote is about government. This statement fits with the rest of my interpretation if it is taken to mean that the people express resentment (rather than actually deliberate) when they are not well governed.

ple's "feelings" that matter.[61] D. C. Lau speaks of the common people exercising "moral judgment," but describes this judgment as possible even for "the most simple-minded," which suggests that he also views the people's response as spontaneous rather than deliberative.[62] These views are borne out by textual evidence. Thus Mencius portrays the common people as turning to a virtuous ruler like the grass bends to the wind,[63] or like "water flows downwards or as animals head for the wilds."[64] Xunzi says that people follow their superiors "just as, for example, an echo responds to the sound and as the shadow has the shape of the form."[65] In other words, the common people act, in Justin Tiwald's description, as a "barometer"[66] of the success of government, rather than as agents expressing significant political choice. A. C. Graham makes a similar argument: "the people should make themselves felt only by the shifts of support towards or away from an occupant or contender for the throne which are a test of who has the mandate of Heaven [i.e., legitimacy]."[67] This means that any identification of proto-democratic seeds in these passages, even if only a notion of consent, is potentially misleading. To the extent that what we have here is an account of legitimacy, it is one based not on a normative conception of "the people" expressing consent to authority, but rather on an almost organic notion of fittingness between ruler and ruled. Political order ensues from this fittingness.

It is true that the Confucians recognize the common people as an important part of political society, and it is also true that they assign them the significant role of deserting a bad ruler through which they can cause the breakdown of the almost organic order that keeps them together. But, as will become clearer below, the importance of the common people can be reduced to being part of a holistic conception of political order based on the complementarity of interests between ruler and ruled. Government is neither "of the people" nor "by the people," and it is also not "for the people" exclusively. Government aims at an orderly society, of which the common people are a—key—

---

[61] De Bary, *Trouble with Confucianism*, 21.

[62] Lau, introduction to *Mencius*, xli.

[63] *Analects* 12.19, *Mencius* 3A.2.

[64] *Mencius* 4A.9. See also 1A.6 and *Xunzi* 15.5.

[65] *Xunzi* 16.8. See also *Xunzi* 12.4.

[66] Tiwald, "Right of Rebellion," 272.

[67] A. C. Graham, *Disputers of the Tao: Philosophical Argument in Ancient China* (Chicago: Open Court, 1989), 116.

component. The ruler derives his authority from establishing political order, and not from fulfilling the needs or aspirations of the common people per se.

I will discuss in the next chapter the policies that the ruler has to pursue to win the loyalty of the common people and thus create order. Suffice it to say that these policies revolve around the satisfaction of people's welfare needs and the pursuit of consistent regulations regarding appointments to office and punishments for crimes. What I want to emphasize here is the nature of the conception of political order being presented. On the one hand, part of my underlying aim in this chapter, and in the book more generally, is to show that the Confucians share Thomas Hobbes's motivating concern with how to secure "order, protection, safety, trust, and the conditions of cooperation"—to answer what Bernard Williams calls "the 'first' political question."[68] On the other hand, the Confucian view of political order as I have presented it is very different from that of someone like Hobbes. The Confucian view, combining hereditary succession with a limited role for the common people, is far from being based on any notion of individual interest as Hobbes's is. For Hobbes, political order is achieved by a group of persons, concerned with their individual security, contracting among themselves to authorize a sovereign to govern them, thus escaping the inevitable state of war outside of government. For the early Confucians, the common people act as a "mass" rather than as a group of individuals with distinct interests. The legitimacy they confer upon the ruler is produced not by deliberative agreement, but by an instinctive and physical movement of approbation. Political order is held together not by a juridical notion of authorization, but by the physical proximity between ruler and ruled enabled by the complementarity of the interests of both (more on this below). Conversely, political order is lost when the people withhold approval of the ruler by going to another one; legitimacy can thus be withdrawn from the ruler, as it cannot be in Hobbes. This, however, should not mean that the Confucians allow for popular revolution. I will briefly reject arguments about popular revolution in the following subsection, then turn to a further clarification of my conception of political order, before concluding this part of the chapter.

---

[68] Bernard Williams, *In the Beginning Was the Deed: Realism and Moralism in Political Argument*, ed. Geoffrey Hawthorn (Princeton: Princeton University Press, 2008), 3.

Removing a Bad Ruler

I concluded the previous section by suggesting that the people express their disapproval of a bad ruler by disentangling themselves from the web of connections that bind them to him. It is difficult to see how this image could be squared with any notion of popular revolution. But the idea "that the people may justly overthrow a ruler who harms them" is sometimes imputed to the early Confucians, primarily to Mencius.[69] This interpretation emerges from combining two sets of passages in the *Mencius*: the passages cited above revolving around the people's role in the choice of the ruler, and another set of passages that suggest the permissibility of the removal of a bad king. Since I already discussed the first set of passages in the previous section, arguing that the people's role in the choice of the ruler is limited, I focus here on the second set of passages, and argue that the permissibility of overthrowing a bad ruler has no implications for the role of the common people in it.

Consider, then, two anecdotes in the *Mencius* that deal with the issue of the removal of a bad ruler. In one anecdote, Mencius asks King Xuan of Qi what he thinks should be done about a friend who, entrusted with the care of one's wife and children, leaves them to suffer from cold and starvation. The king answers that one should break with this friend. Then Mencius asks what should be done about the Marshal of Guards who cannot maintain order among his ranks. The king answers that he should be removed from his office. Finally, Mencius asks what should be done if the whole society is badly governed. "The King turned to his attendants and changed the subject."[70]

In the second story, it is the king himself who asks Mencius about the truth of what is told of King Tang banishing the tyrant Jie, and King Wu marching against the dictator Zhou Xin. When Mencius confirms, the king asks whether this means that regicide is permissible. Mencius's answer goes as follows: "A man who mutilates *ren* is a mutilator, while one who cripples rightness is a crippler. He who is both a mutilator and a crippler is a mere fellow (*yifu* 一夫). I have indeed heard of the punishment of the 'fellow Zhou,' but I have never heard of any regicide."[71] What these two anecdotes specify are the reasons that make

[69] See, for example, Chan, "Democracy and Meritocracy," 188. Xu Fuguan and Hsiao Kung-chuan also subscribe to this view. See Xu, *Zhongguo sixiang shi lunji*, 135; Hsiao, *History of Chinese Political Thought*, 157; and Hu, "Confucianism and Western Democracy," 59.

[70] *Mencius* 1B.6.

[71] *Mencius* 1B.8.

removing a ruler permissible: when a ruler fails to fulfill his obligations in governing his realm or, worse, is ruthless, he is no longer worthy, and his removal is allowed. But do they specify the holders of the prerogative to remove the king?[72] One hint we get from the second anecdote is that those who banished the tyrants Jie and Zhou are Kings Tang and Wu, both virtuous contenders to power. Indeed, Xunzi, who similarly argues that the overthrow of Jie and Zhou by Kings Tang and Wu is not tantamount to regicide (since to execute a tyrannical ruler is like executing a "solitary individual"), also emphasizes the virtuousness of Tang and Wu against the wretchedness of Jie and Zhou.[73] The necessity that worthies be the ones to remove the tyrant is also made clear in another anecdote in the *Mencius*, relating to Tai Jia, the son of Prince Tang, and Yi Yin, his virtuous minister:

> Gongsun Chou said, "Yi Yin banished Tai Jia to Tong, saying, 'I do not wish to be close to one who is intractable,' and the people were greatly pleased. When Tai Jia became good, Yi Yin restored him to the throne, and the people, once again, were pleased. When a prince is not good, is it permissible for a good and wise man who is his subject to banish him?"
>
> "It is permissible," said Mencius, "only if he had the motive of a Yi Yin; otherwise, it would be usurpation."[74]

The actual removal of a bad ruler is thus clearly restricted to the inner circle of highly ranked officials. The removal is legitimate when

[72] Pines identifies the holders of this prerogative in the following statement by Mencius: "Those who rise (*xing* 興) only when there is a King Wen are ordinary men. Outstanding [men of service] (*shi* 士) rise even without a King Wen" (7A.10). One can read *xing* 興 as meaning "to flourish" rather than "to rise," in which case this passage from the *Mencius* has no relevance to the issue of rebellion. Pines, *Envisioning Eternal Empire*, 72.

[73] *Xunzi* 18.2. Despite his recognition that only a few members of the elite can ever depose a ruler, and then only if he is extremely bad (like Jie and Zhou Xin), Pines still finds Mencius to be "almost a revolutionary." See Pines, *Envisioning Eternal Empire*, 72. On the other hand, although Xunzi justifies Tang's and Wu's overthrow of Jie and Zhou Xin just like Mencius does, Pines finds him to be almost conservative. He reads Xunzi's view as a post facto justification of Tang's and Wu's acts, but not an attempt like Mencius's to apply this principle of removing a bad ruler to "modern circumstances" (88). On my view, Mencius should not be seen as more forward-looking than Xunzi: Both Mencius and Xunzi wanted to leave the door open, if only so slightly, to legitimizing the removal of bad kings. But this is only a fleeting possibility, and the hereditary principle of kingly appointment, and of kingly immunity, is still the default principle for ordinary times.

[74] *Mencius* 7A.31.

the member of the elite responsible for it is virtuous,[75] because this is the only way to make certain that the removal is done for the right reason, that is, for the reason that the extant ruler fails to govern well. What the preceding passage also reveals again is that the common people's importance is restricted to signaling the appropriateness or lack thereof of a ruler's appointment, by merely showing outward signs of satisfaction or lack of satisfaction.

In short, the common people are not themselves the agents responsible for the removal of a bad ruler. There is no revolutionary impulse in Mencius, or early Confucianism more generally. Instead, just as the web-like relationship that I have described between ruler and ruled is formed gradually, as the ruler initiates policies to which the people respond favorably, so does it unravel through the gradual untangling of the common people from the web as they lose trust in the ruler. There are no contracts to be ended, no rights to be recovered, and thus no popular revolution to achieve such aims.

Ruler and Ruled

That the common people do not choose the ruler, and that they are largely portrayed as passive, should not imply the view that Confucian government aims at the benefit of the ruler alone. On my interpretation, the maintenance of political order benefits both parts of society, ruler and ruled, equally. As I explained in the prologue, the common people emerged as an object of political concern with the rise of the warring states of early China (ca. 771–221 BCE). The leaders of the newly independent states relied on the common people as a source of military and economic strength. For the common people to persevere in this role, the ruler had to provide them with political order by promoting welfare and security measures—to be discussed in the next chapter. In other words, both ruler and ruled would benefit from the establishment of political order.

---

[75] Justin Tiwald discusses the anecdote in 2B.8 where Mencius argues that though the invasion of Yan is justified in itself, not anyone is justified in leading it; only a Heaven-appointed official is (and the king of Qi, who invades Yan, is not one). He takes it to suggest that what is important about this person (who is justified in overthrowing the ruler) is not so much his qualifications, but his appointment. In other words, he emphasizes what he calls the "procedural" aspect of political authority. See Tiwald, "Right of Rebellion," 273. In line with what I argued above, I disagree that one should take literally the idea of appointment by Heaven. I take the claim that one is appointed by Heaven to be a claim about this person's qualifications.

My view is thus distinct from two available ones in the literature. On one—minority—interpretation, sometimes made about the *Mencius*, the Confucian conception of government is ultimately aimed at fulfilling the ruler's self-interest. On this reading, Mencius's advice to kings is motivated by what is profitable for the king personally. The point of ensuring the satisfaction of the people, for example, is for the king to protect his own, personal rule, as opposed to protecting political society as a whole.[76] The problem with this argument is that, if the ruler's self-interest is really what is at stake in these texts, it is hard to see why the Confucians are so insistent on explicitly discouraging it. For example, the first story we read in the *Mencius* illustrates Mencius's practice of convincing rulers not to care for profit:

> Mencius went to see King Hui of Liang. "You, Sir," said the King, "have come all this distance, thinking nothing of a thousand [leagues]. You must surely have some way of profiting my state."
> "Your Majesty," answered Mencius. "What is the point of mentioning the word 'profit' (*li* 利)? All that matters is that there should be *ren* and rightness (*yi* 義)."[77]

In another anecdote, Mencius is dismayed by Song Keng, who is eager to convince the kings of Qin and Chu to end their hostilities by showing them the "unprofitability" of war. As Mencius tells Song Keng, "Your purpose is lofty indeed but your slogan is wrong."[78] Xunzi's case against profit is also as straightforward as it is succinct: to put rightness (*yi* 義) before profit (*li* 利) is honorable; to put profit before rightness is disgraceful.[79] This is why "the [emperor] does not discuss quantities, [regional rulers] do not discuss benefit and harm, grand officers do not discuss success and failure, and [men of service] do not discuss commerce and merchandise."[80] It is true, of course, that ultimately the rejection of profit allows the king to maintain his rule, since, as Mencius suggests, it prevents discord with the people and the possibility of regicide on the part of officials. But though it might be true

[76] Thus Creel argues that, against conventional wisdom, Mencius actually advocates that the ruler adopt a utilitarian position, citing the encounter with King Hui of Liang. See Herrlee Glessner Creel, *Chinese Thought, from Confucius to Mao Tsê-Tung* (Chicago: University of Chicago Press, 1953), 86–87.

[77] *Mencius* 1A.1.

[78] *Mencius* 6B.4.

[79] *Xunzi* 4.6.

[80] *Xunzi* 27.63.

that the maintenance of political order is beneficial for the ruler, this does not mean it is beneficial to him alone.

On the second, more common view, which forms the ground for the proto-democratic view presented above, and which Chan, borrowing from Joseph Raz, calls the *"service conception of authority,"*[81] the common people are said to be the most important element in Confucian political theory, and the goal of the Confucian ruler is to satisfy their needs. This view is taken to be illustrated by Mencius's statement that the people are most important, followed by the altars of the earth and grain (the symbols of the state), while the ruler comes last,[82] and it is usually expressed by the idea of a *minben* (民本), a later notion that translates as the "people as the basis" of government.[83] The difference between my argument about political order and this view is revealed by my disagreement with the way some describe the mixed scenario that Mencius's account of the role of the people in government presents "as government for the people," perhaps "of the people," but not "by the people."[84] It is obvious from this description that interpreters struggle with understanding how the common people matter, without their importance translating into influence in government. The struggle is clear in Lau's following thought on Confucius: "Confucius may not have had too high an opinion of the intellectual and moral capacities of the common people, but it is emphatically not true that he played down their importance in the scheme of things. Perhaps, it is precisely because the people are incapable of securing their own welfare unaided that the ruler's supreme duty is to work on their behalf in bringing about what is good for them."[85]

The analogy that comes to mind here, which the Confucians themselves use, is to parents and children.[86] Mencius, indeed, suggests that the proper attitude for the ruler to assume toward his people is that of a parent: in various sections in which he propounds the need to ensure

[81] Chan, "Democracy and Meritocracy," 188, emphasis original.

[82] *Mencius* 7B.14.

[83] Tan, "Democracy in Confucianism," 295.

[84] See Hsiao, *History of Chinese Political Thought*, 161. Chenyang Li argues that it is "for the people" but neither "of the people" nor "by the people." See Li, "Confucian Value and Democratic Value," 185–86.

[85] Lau, introduction to the *Analects*, 36.

[86] The analogy actually predates these Confucian texts, as it can be found in the *Classic of Poetry* (*shijing* 詩經) and also in the *Classic of Rites* (*liji* 禮記). In other words, it is not an idea introduced by the Confucians, but one that they gave their own spin to. I thank Mick Hunter for alerting me to this.

the people's welfare, he reminds the ruler that not doing so is failing to satisfy his role as "father and mother to the people" (minfumu 民父母). The following is a characteristic passage where he confronts King Xuan of Qi: "There is fat meat in your kitchen and there are well-fed horses in your stables, yet the people look hungry and in the outskirts of cities men drop dead from starvation. This is to show animals the way to devour men. Even the devouring of animals by animals is repugnant to men. If, then, one who is father and mother to the people cannot, in ruling over them, avoid showing animals the way to devour men, wherein is he father and mother to the people?"[87] Besides providing for the people, for Mencius, acting as a parent also involves promoting the worthy to government.[88] As for Xunzi, he argues that superiors generally, and kings particularly, should treat their inferiors as if they were protecting a child.[89] The people will, in turn, treat their king as they would their own parent and will be willing to die for him.[90] Xunzi also echoes Mencius when he argues that if a ruler is good, promotes the worthy, and provides for the people's needs, then those even from distant lands will follow him, looking upon him as their father and mother.[91]

The parental analogy, however, is misleading since it would suggest, as Elstein points out, that at some point the people will stop being children and become the ruler's equals, that is, that the ruler's obligation toward them is only temporary, which is nowhere suggested in the early texts.[92] The parental analogy should thus be interpreted not with an emphasis on the status of the common people as children but rather on the way the ruler should relate to them. Thus Xunzi suggests that if he desires safety in governing, the ruler should govern fairly (pingzheng 平政) and love the people.[93] The ideal of fairness or evenhanded treatment can also be found elsewhere in the texts: in the Analects we are told that impartiality (gong 公) is the best way to win the people,[94] and Mencius is at pains to deny that Emperor Shun was partial to his

[87] Mencius 1A.4.
[88] Mencius 1B.7.
[89] Xunzi 11.9a, 11.12.
[90] Xunzi 11.12.
[91] Xunzi 9.26. Mencius 2A.5. See also Xunzi 15.1b.
[92] Elstein, "Why Early Confucianism Cannot Generate Democracy," 437. I thus disagree with Sim's argument that, in Confucianism, "political government is simply the father-son relationship writ-large." See Sim, Remastering Morals with Aristotle and Confucius, 166 (also 184–85). See also Li, "Confucian Value and Democratic Value," 185.
[93] Xunzi 9.4.
[94] Analects 20.1. See also Analects 7.31, where the governor is criticized for being partial in taking a wife from the same clan as his own.

own brother to the detriment of the common people.[95] Furthermore, the parental analogy can be seen to buttress the sense in which the ruler and the common people are inextricably tied to each other, as I have argued above, by suggesting that the ties between them are almost organic, rather than artificial, and that a relationship of mutual dependency prevails between them.

The parental analogy in the early Confucian texts thus need not necessarily be equated with a view that Confucian government is ultimately "for the people" in the way that parenthood or guardianship could be defined as aiming at the well-being of the children involved. On my view, in fact, there is no normative conception of "the people" as the aim of government. The aim of government is political order. It is for "the people" to the extent that they benefit from living in an orderly, secure, and productive society. What Mencius means, then, by his statement that the people are more important than the ruler is not that their well-being is the ultimate aim of Confucian government, for which the ruler is a mere means, but rather that they are developmentally (rather than normatively) more important than the ruler, that is, that no political order can obtain without their needs being satisfied first. This is made clear in Mencius's statement that winning all under Heaven requires winning the hearts of the people.[96]

To conclude, I have elucidated in this section the relationship between ruler and ruled as a way to further clarify the Confucian conception of political order. I have emphasized the complementary relationship between the two, suggesting that political order follows precisely from this complementarity. This view is set in contradistinction to two alternative views: one that argues that politics in Confucianism benefits the ruler primarily, and one that argues that Confucian government is "for the people."

Hegemons

In the last part of the chapter, I further illustrate and substantiate my contention that the central organizing motif of Confucian political thought is the concern with orderliness by showing how this concern explains the intriguing acceptance, even praise, that the early Confucians express for a subset of rulers who are far from virtuous.

---

[95] *Mencius* 5A.3.
[96] *Mencius* 4A.9.

Hegemon (*ba* 霸, literally "the senior one") was the title attributed to the statesmen who rose to prominence during the Spring and Autumn period (770–476 BCE). At that time, the Eastern Zhou king was king in name alone, and the Zhou realm had disintegrated into many independent states ruled by princely vassals of the preceding Western Zhou dynasty. Different states achieved dominance at various times. While the first state to do so was the state of Zheng, the first one to actually receive the title of hegemon was the state of Qi.[97] Ancient texts usually refer to "five hegemons" of the Spring and Autumn period.[98] These hegemons helped maintain a system of alliance among the states of the day, fending off attacks from "barbarians" at the borders, with the stated aim of preserving "the Zhou cultural and political order."[99] In reality, though, they contributed to the gradual dissolution of the Zhou order. The precarious system of alliance they established was not to last long: the alliance devolved into more open competition during the subsequent Warring States period. As mentioned before, it was only in 221 BCE that the ruler of Qin succeeded at conquering all of his adversaries and called himself emperor.

Because of their effectiveness in government, hegemons are usually associated with a school of thought now known as Legalism (*fajia* 法家), which consists of an amalgamation of texts on statecraft from the Warring States period.[100] Given the usual opposition between Legalism and Confucianism, hegemons are often thought to be anathema to the Confucians.[101] Against the view that for the Confucians the only contrast is between "kingliness and despotism,"[102] however, I show in what follows that there is a third meaningful class of rulers for the

[97] Hsu, "Spring and Autumn Period," 551–57.

[98] See, for example, *Mencius* 6B.7, 7A.30. These hegemons are thought to be Duke Huan of Qi, Duke Wen of Jin, King Zhuang of Chu, Duke Mu of Qin, and Duke Xiang of Song.

[99] Hsu, "Spring and Autumn Period," 566.

[100] One of these, the *Guanzi*, is actually named after Guan Zhong, the prime minister of Duke Huan of Qi (the first of the hegemons), and is presented as a collection of his thoughts on government, but the attribution is spurious.

[101] Bryan Van Norden, in his introduction to an abridged translation of the *Mengzi*, writes that "Confucians typically condemned them [i.e., hegemons] for usurping the authority of the Zhou King and ruling by force and guile rather than by Virtue." See Van Norden, trans., *The Essential Mengzi: Selected Passages with Traditional Commentary* (Indianapolis: Hackett, 2009), xvii. On the other hand, closer to my reading, Irene Bloom describes the Confucian account of the legitimacy of the hegemons' rule as "ambiguous." See Bloom, trans., *Mencius*, 6n19.

[102] Chan, *Source Book in Chinese Philosophy*, 64.

Confucians (less good than virtuous kings but better than despots) and that hegemons occupy it. Indeed, although hegemons' political effectiveness often came at the expense of virtuousness, the early Confucians countenanced, even praised, them. I contend that this approval stems from their ability to maintain political order at a time of chaos.

Before I proceed to discussing the early Confucians' view on hegemons, I should note that it is generally not the hegemons per se that the Confucians express praise for: except in Xunzi's case, the achievements of hegemons are mostly attributed to their ministers. For the purposes of this chapter, however, I am interested in the aims of government rather than in its internal division of functions. Therefore, the relevant unit of analysis is the mode of government pursued by hegemons. When I discuss "hegemons," it is thus in reference both to hegemons and to their ministers, that is, as a shorthand for hegemonic government more generally.

Consider, then, the state of Qi, the first to acquire the title of hegemon. Its ruler, Duke Huan, one of the "five hegemons" mentioned above, owes his ascent to power to his prime minister Guan Zhong.[103] It is these two figures who are mostly discussed in the Confucian texts. To start with Confucius, he disparagingly calls Guan Zhong a "vessel of small capacity" and wonders whether, if even Guan Zhong can be said to understand the rites, anyone does not.[104] Everything else he says about Guan Zhong, however, is positive. He recounts that Guan Zhong took over three hundred households from the fief of a certain Bo family, without the latter daring to complain, which presumably indicates the extent of Guan Zhong's popularity.[105] He also says that Guan Zhong was behind Duke Huan's ability to unite the regional rulers several times without resort to force.[106] Confucius adds, "Guan

---

[103] For the tensions in the historical records about Guan Zhong, see Sydney Rosen, "In Search of the Historical Kuan Chung," *Journal of Asian Studies* 35, no. 3 (May 1976): 431–40.

[104] *Analects* 3.22. Lau points out that a vessel is designed for "a specific purpose" and hence the fact that Guan Zhong is both a vessel and one of small capacity indicates his limited abilities. See Lau, *Analects*, 64n4.

[105] *Analects* 14.9. For this interpretation, see Hoyt Cleveland Tillman, "The Development of Tension between Virtue and Achievement in Early Confucianism: Attitudes toward Kuan Chung and Hegemon (*pa*), as Conceptual Symbols," *Philosophy East and West* 31, no. 1 (January 1981): 18.

[106] *Analects* 14.16. The sentence that concludes this last anecdote, however, is more controversial. Like Chinese commentators before them, those translating the text into English disagree on how to render the sentence *ru qi ren* 如其仁. D. C. Lau translates it as "Such was his benevolence [*ren*], such was his benevolence" (Ames and Rosemont also

Zhong helped Duke Huan to become the leader of the [regional rulers] and to save the Empire from collapse. To this day, the common people still enjoy the benefit of his acts. Had it not been for Guan Zhong, we might well be wearing our hair down and folding our robes to the left. Surely he was not like the common man or woman who, in their petty faithfulness, commit suicide in a ditch without anyone taking any notice."[107]

On a straightforward reading, the contrast that Confucius establishes is between Guan Zhong and petty commoners. But a more telling, albeit more conjectural, way to recast this contrast is as a contrast between Guan Zhong's actions and those of Zhao Hu, who served with Guan Zhong as minister to Prince Jiu of Qi. When the prince was murdered by his own brother, none other than Duke Huan, who then ascended the throne, Zhao Hu killed himself while Guan Zhong simply shifted allegiance to Duke Huan. However loyal Zhao's decision was, it was Guan Zhong's that had the more admirable consequence: as Confucius says, Guan Zhong saved Zhou civilization from complete breakdown (by helping Duke Huan win the authority that made him into a hegemon and thus allowed him to unite the states and repel outsiders).[108] Indeed, Benjamin Schwartz takes Confucius's defense of Guan Zhong to be motivated by the master's loyalty to the collapsing Zhou dynasty and his readiness to "do anything possible to prevent the further disintegration of its sacred authority."[109] But one can understand Confucius's loyalty to the Zhou to be more than a mere emotional attachment to the vestiges of the past. It is a principled commit-

---

adopt the "such was his *ren*" formulation). Edward Slingerland's translation, on the other hand, denotes criticism: "But as for his goodness [*ren*], as for his goodness. . . ." While earlier Chinese commentators adopted a position closer to Lau's, they took the claim to mean that Guan Zhong's actions merely had the appearance of *ren*, or had the consequence, but not the form, of *ren*. The latter is also Zhu Xi's position. See Tillman, "Development of Tension," 19. I lean toward this last interpretation for reasons that I will lay out in Chapter 4, when I revisit the question of virtuous rulership.

[107] *Analects* 14.17.

[108] Duke Huan is described favorably in *Analects* 14.15, where he is said to be correct (*zheng* 正), in comparison to Duke Wen of Jin, who is "crafty." Slingerland reports that a few Chinese commentators describe Duke Huan as having "dedicated himself to public duty at the expense of his own interests," which fits with the rest of the description of his and Guan Zhong's actions as I present them here. See Slingerland, trans., *Confucius: Analects*, 160.

[109] Schwartz, *World of Thought in Ancient China*, 110. Schwartz also writes, in relation to the depiction of Guan Zhong in the *Analects*, that he is judged, not on the basis of "pure ethics," but on the basis of an "ethics of political life which often involves the typical political choice between the greater and lesser evil" (109).

ment to the ideal of political order that the Zhou represented. In other words, Guan Zhong's praiseworthiness stems from his ability to maintain order in a time of chaos.[110]

Moving now to Mencius, he is also at points dismissive of Guan Zhong and Duke Huan. He is thus appalled when one of his disciples, Gongsun Chou, asks him whether, were he to get the chance to rule in the state of Qi, he would do as Guan Zhong did. Mencius cites Zeng Xi's claim that Guan Zhong's achievements were not important.[111] In another similar anecdote, when King Xuan of Qi asks Mencius about Duke Huan of Qi and Duke Wen of Jin (the second of the five hegemons), Mencius dismisses the question as one that Confucians were never keen on answering. He offers to speak instead of virtuous kings.[112]

Yet, like Confucius, Mencius is more ambivalent about Guan Zhong than is generally recognized,[113] since he describes him in a different passage as an accomplished statesman: indeed, Mencius cites Guan Zhong as part of a longer list of statesmen, which includes Shun, but also other less known ministers such as Jiao Ge, who was a worthy official at the court of the tyrant Zhou Xin,[114] and Boli Xi, who helped Duke Mu achieve political eminence.[115] The purpose of the list is to illustrate the lowly origins of all these statesmen, and Mencius argues that it is only when a person first suffers that he is then able to innovate.[116] The reference to Guan Zhong together with other worthy statesmen is noteworthy.

[110] Slingerland writes at one point that "Confucius admired his [Guan Zhong's] skill and achievements, but had doubts about his moral worthiness" (250). In his commentary on 3.22, however, he contends that despite Confucius's admiration for Guan Zhong, "at a deeper level he disapproves of his narrowly pragmatic approach and flouting of traditional norms and institutions" (27). But why should we think that the disapproval of Guan Zhong on the moral level is "deeper" than the approval of him on the political level? My argument is that the standards used to judge political action are simply different from (rather than less important than) the standards used to judge action from a strictly moral point of view.

[111] *Mencius* 2A.1.

[112] *Mencius* 1A.7.

[113] Kim writes that Mencius "berated" the hegemons "harshly," especially Duke Huan. See Kim, "Confucian Constitutionalism," 386. Though recognizing Confucius's ambivalence about hegemons, Schwartz also argues that Mencius has a "much more purist attitude towards the hegemonic system," that "he feels he can stand in final judgment on them," and that his is a "soaring and defiant idealism." See Schwartz, *World of Thought in Ancient China*, 286. See also Hsiao, *History of Chinese Political Thought*, 170 and Fung, *History of Chinese Philosophy*, 112.

[114] *Mencius* 2A.1.

[115] *Mencius* 5A.9.

[116] *Mencius* 6B.15.

That Guan Zhong is not an altogether bad minister, in Mencius's eyes, is further revealed in another anecdote from the *Mencius*. Mencius describes Guan Zhong as an example of a minister "who cannot be summoned" (*suo buzhao zhi chen* 所不召之臣), that is, a minister who is respected by his ruler. This is especially significant since Mencius refers to himself as one such minister: when Mencius receives a message from the king asking to see him, he refuses to go, justifying his refusal by arguing that

> a prince who is to achieve great things must have [officials] he does not summon. If he wants to consult them, he goes to them. If he does not honour virtue and delight in the Way in such a manner, he is not worthy of being helped towards the achievement of great things. . . . Today there are many states, all equal in size and virtue, none being able to dominate the others. This is simply because the rulers are given to employing those they can teach rather than those from whom they can learn.[117]

Mencius then mentions two examples of officials who cannot be summoned: Yi Yin (who served under Prince Tang) and Guan Zhong. Yi Yin is a paragon of virtue from antiquity.[118] Guan Zhong is thus being compared to Mencius himself and to Yi Yin. Based on the quote above, it is clear that what makes Guan Zhong worthy of such a comparison is that he helped his ruler (Duke Huan of Qi) toward "the achievement of great things" and toward gaining "dominance" over neighboring states. The achievements of Duke Huan, allowed by his sponsorship of Guan Zhong, are made explicit in yet another anecdote where Mencius describes Duke Huan as the leader who brought the regional rulers together on a fivefold pledge, revolving around filiality, merit, and the good treatment of neighbors.[119] In short, what Mencius's discussion of Guan Zhong and Duke Huan reveals is the implicit recognition that, however lacking in virtue Duke Huan of Qi was, his ability to unite the states of his day, and set up rules for their interaction and internal regulation, prevented conflict and anarchy from erupting. Duke Huan was able to do this only because he was willing to listen to the advice of Guan Zhong.[120]

[117] *Mencius* 2B.2.
[118] *Mencius* 5A.6. See also *Mencius* 7A.31.
[119] *Mencius* 6B.7. Kim also cites 7A.13, where Mencius says that people under the rule of a hegemon look happy, while under the rule of a king they look satisfied. See Kim, "Between Good and Evil," 78.
[120] In two anecdotes in the *Mencius*, Mencius is encouraged to take up an official post

Finally, Xunzi offers the most sustained discussion of hegemons among our three thinkers.[121] He suggests at first that hegemons only give the appearance of *ren*, but are actually only concerned with profit.[122] They do not care for instruction or culture (*wen* 文), but merely seek to master the tactics of war,[123] and their army is motivated only by a desire for rewards.[124] What better proof is there of hegemons' lust for power than the fact that Duke Huan, whom Xunzi considers the most successful of the five hegemons, started his career by killing his own brother and usurping the throne?[125] As for Guan Zhong, Xunzi describes him as nothing but a man from the fields not fit to become the counselor of a king.[126]

This depiction of hegemons shows that they are inferior to virtuous kings. On the other hand, Xunzi says that hegemons are better than rulers who merely rely on force. Indeed, he contends that the hegemon "opens up lands for cultivation, fills the granaries and sees that the people are provided with the goods they need. He is careful in selecting his officials and employs men of talent, leading them on with rewards and correcting them with punishments. He restores states that have perished, protects ruling lines that are in danger of dying out, guards the weak, and restrains the violent."[127] But if hegemons do all this, what makes them less worthy than virtuous kings? Xunzi says that the virtuous king extols rituals, while the hegemon is merely good at governing (*zheng* 政), which he argues is better than being merely good at collecting taxes.[128] Xunzi also says that the king seeks to establish rightness (*yi* 義) while the hegemon seeks to establish trust (*xin* 信).[129] This trust is obtained through consistent punishments and re-

---

with the argument that he can turn the ruler either into a king, or at least into a hegemon, suggesting that the latter possibility was not considered as anathema to Mencius (it would arguably not otherwise have been used in efforts to convince him). See *Mencius* 2A.2 and 3B.1.

[121] Though Xunzi is clearest in his support for hegemons among our three thinkers, some still argue that this support is not wholehearted. Thus Mark Edward Lewis argues that later essays in the *Xunzi* "grudgingly accept the practices of the Spring and Autumn hegemons when no true king exists." See Lewis, *Writing and Authority in Early China*, 66.

[122] *Xunzi* 7.1 and 9.8.

[123] *Xunzi* 7.1.

[124] *Xunzi* 15.1d.

[125] *Xunzi* 7.1.

[126] *Xunzi* 27.58.

[127] *Xunzi* 9.8, quoted from Watson, 42.

[128] *Xunzi* 9.5.

[129] *Xunzi* 11.1a. For Kim, trust is *"political morality* that a ruler in the pursuit of *badao* [the Way of a hegemon] must possess" (for example, the way Duke Huan trusted Guan

wards, avoiding deceiving the people, and honoring agreements with allies.[130] Xunzi's most repeated formulation of the difference between virtuous king and hegemon is that one who extols rituals and honors the worthy becomes a king, while one who stresses regulations (*fa* 法) and loves the people becomes a hegemon.[131]

As Hoyt Tillman suggests, Xunzi's systematic account of hegemons could be seen as distinct from the account of the historical hegemons (Duke Huan and Guan Zhong) who, though they were competent, did not necessarily fulfill all the responsibilities adumbrated by Xunzi above.[132] What Xunzi offers in the comparison between virtuous kings and hegemons is an idealized model of the latter, which can be seen as building upon the historical hegemons' achievements, to imagine what their principles of government should have been like. It should be clear from this account of idealized hegemons that their government aims at the production of an orderly society through the provision of grain, the use of consistent punishments, winning the trust of the people, and honoring agreements with allies.

In short, for our three Confucian thinkers, hegemonic rule is appreciated for its success in preventing the unraveling of the Chinese states amid turbulent times. It might be argued, however, that this success, and the praise that it induces, stems from the fact that hegemons provide the conditions necessary for the emergence of a society in which morality flourishes. Thus, according to Sor-hoon Tan, "hegemons' coercive authority is legitimate to the extent that it creates the external conditions for personal cultivation; its inadequacy lies in failing to foster the internal conditions for personal cultivation through transformative exemplification."[133] On my view, however, although it is true that personal cultivation; in principle requires adequate external conditions (such as basic subsistence), it is not necessarily true that the aim of establishing the latter is personal cultivation. Welfare, peace, and order

---

Zhong), but also what the hegemon seeks to obtain in his relationship to the people. See Kim, "Between Good and Evil," 84.

[130] *Xunzi* 11.1c.

[131] *Xunzi* 16.1, 17.9, and 27.1. Another formulation is that the king seeks to win the people, the hegemon seeks to win allies, while the ruler who relies on force seeks to win land (*Xunzi* 9.6).

[132] See Tillman, "Development of Tension," 23. Sumner B. Twiss and Jonathan Chan also argue that although Mencius and Xunzi at point criticize "the actual operation" of the system of hegemons, hegemons' role "as such might not be objectionable from the Confucian point of view." See Twiss and Chan, "The Classical Confucian Position on the Legitimate Use of Military Force," *Journal of Religious Ethics* 40, no. 3 (2012): 450, 453n7.

[133] Tan, *Confucian Democracy*, 196.

are goods in themselves and need not be justified through the fulfillment of "ethical" standards. Indeed, this is precisely what my discussion of hegemons is meant to show. To put it differently, my aim in this
chapter, and in this book as a whole, is to elicit a space between "ethical
politics" and "crass politics." Hegemons lie in this space.

Tan also offers a related but different argument to the effect that hegemons exemplify a modicum of moral virtues such that, if we conceive morality as a spectrum from least virtuous to most virtuous, hegemons would fall somewhere in the middle. She argues, for example,
that "Mencius' distinction between hegemony and true kingship does
not preclude the possibility of a developmental process connecting the
two."[134] She cites in this regard *Mencius* 2A.3, in which hegemons are
said to borrow from *ren*, and 7A.30, in which Mencius repeats the same
idea and then wonders that "if a man borrows a thing and keeps it long
enough, how can one be sure that it will not become truly his?" The
problem with this interpretation is that it suggests that the early Confucians, especially Confucius and Mencius, should have actually been
much more positive about the early hegemons, if the latter were indeed on the road to becoming *ren*. In fact, the rest of the textual evidence does not indicate that the qualities recommending hegemons are
a primitive form, or a diluted version, of the central Confucian virtues.
It is true that hegemons exhibit trustworthiness, which is an important
virtue for the Confucians.[135] They also exhibit, at least for Xunzi, love
for the people, which Xunzi takes to be a characteristic of hegemons
borrowed from kings.[136] But they do not exhibit the Confucian cardinal
virtues of *ren*, rightness, ritual propriety, and wisdom. Indeed, the
qualities that the three Confucians converge on in describing Guan
Zhong are qualities like resoluteness, courage, and effectiveness. These
qualities become moral only when they are associated with other moral
virtues. Thus, in the *Xunzi*, resoluteness is used to describe a worthy
person to whom the whole world yields,[137] a good minister,[138] and mo-

---

[134] Tan, *Confucian Democracy*, 197.

[135] Kim describes trust as a "civic virtue." See Kim, "Between Good and Evil," 85. I
agree with this description, which fits with my description of the qualities expected of
the common people as civic as well. But though it can be described as "virtue," the important point for my purposes here is that it is a political, not a moral, virtue. As I argue
in what follows, political virtues are not a diluted version of ethical ones, but form a distinct category.

[136] This explains why Xunzi says that hegemons enjoy a "mixed" form, while kings
possess the pure form of Confucian government. (*Xunzi* 16.6).

[137] *Xunzi* 6.10.

[138] *Xunzi* 13.4.

rality as such.[139] Courage (*yong* 勇) is also praised in the Confucian texts, yet the courageous person needs to also be versed in the rites in order to be counted as virtuous.[140] In fact, in the *Analects*, martial courage is rejected in favor of moral courage,[141] and Mencius makes a distinction between small and great valor: the first is the valor of common men, while the latter is the valor of virtuous men like King Wen.[142] In short, though trust, resoluteness, courage, and effectiveness can attach themselves to a moral person, they are not by themselves preparatory qualities for becoming moral. Guan Zhong is complimented for having them as such, and not for being on the path toward virtue. The spectrum view of virtue cannot thus account for the Confucian approval of hegemons.

This said, Tan is right to raise questions about the relationship between hegemons and virtuous kings specifically in the case of Mencius because Mencius, as I will show in Chapter 4, does suggest the importance of a *ren* (benevolent) government for the achievement of political order. Thus, to the extent that hegemons do promote political order (rather than because we expect the Confucians to favor moral government as such), one would expect them to partake of benevolent government. Based on the view I will offer in Chapter 4 on the relationship between *ren* and *ren* government (*renzheng* 仁政), however, I contend that hegemonic government, insofar as it promotes order, partakes of *ren* government, without hegemons necessarily partaking of *ren*.

To summarize, then, hegemons are countenanced, and at points praised, because they have historically succeeded, through the efforts of their leading ministers, at saving the Chinese world from all-out war by forming strong states and rules of engagement among these. Also, as an ideal type, at least in the way Xunzi presents them, hegemons provide the model of how a ruler succeeds at achieving political order

[139] *Xunzi* 30.4. Resoluteness (*gang* 剛) is mentioned three times in the *Analects* as something one should aspire to, but it is not clearly defined. See *Analects* 5.11, 13.27, and 17.8. In 5.11, it is associated with a lack of desires. In 17.8, it is said to need to be balanced by a love of learning.

[140] *Analects* 8.2, 14.12, and 17.24. In 17.8, the suggestion is that courage must be combined with learning.

[141] *Analects* 5.7, 8.10, 14.4, and 17.23.

[142] *Mencius* 1B.3. See also 2A.2. On the distinction between moral and nonmoral courage, see Xinyan Jiang, "Mengzi on Human Nature and Courage," in *Essays on the Moral Philosophy of Mengzi*, ed. Xiusheng Liu and Philip J. Ivanhoe (Indianapolis: Hackett, 2002), 143–62.

without necessarily showing qualities of virtue. In other words, hegemons model what an heir should do to maintain the throne.[143]

Conclusion

I have argued in this chapter that the aim of Confucian government is not primarily either to instill virtue in the common people or to represent their needs and interests, but rather to promote political order. I have elicited the concern with order in the qualities expected of the common people, in the preference for hereditary succession, and in the approval of hegemons. I have also shown that political order follows from a complementary relationship between ruler and ruled in which the common people express loyalty and allegiance to a ruler who satisfies their needs. I have not, however, specified what tasks and policies the ruler has to pursue to win the approval of the people. The chapter that follows explores this question.

---

[143] This said, historically speaking (rather than as an ideal type) hegemons, like Duke Huan of Qi, usurped hereditary prerogative to become rulers. When Mencius and especially Xunzi advocate hereditary succession, they are therefore implicitly criticizing hegemons for violating hereditary rule.

CHAPTER 2

Rules and Regulations

The identification of Confucian politics with Confucian ethics has led to the portrayal of Confucian politics as primarily centering on the presence of a sage king who rules by example. In the preceding chapter, I questioned this identification by showing that Confucian politics, unlike Confucian ethics, does not have as its primary purpose the development of virtue. I argued that the central motivating principle of Confucian politics is political order, and that rulers who are able to achieve a minimum level of order, are approved of, even if they are not virtuous. My aim in this chapter is to show that the Confucians offer specific policy suggestions for the achievement of order, giving lie to any charge of idealism.[1]

There are two terms in the Classical Chinese texts that point to politics (and that make up the modern Chinese term for it): *zheng* 政 and *zhi* 治. *Zheng* (政) refers to government, or regulations, or policies. *Zhi* (治), on the other hand, has a more normative connotation (although it also generally refers to government or rule): it points to the achievement of good government, or, more broadly, order. *Zhi* appears only a few times in the *Analects*, but it is frequently used in the *Mencius* and

---

[1] Sato presents Mencius as idealistic in trusting in the power of morality but argues that Xunzi is different. He indeed contends that it was the failure of moral argumentation as undertaken by Mencius and the Mohists that produced a "strong skepticism regarding the feasibility of morality as a tool for improving the current situation" and prompted the "more objective and analytical examination of socio-political mechanisms" of Xunzi and other members of the Jixia Academy. See Sato, *Confucian Quest for Order*, 109–10. I argue instead that both the *Mencius* and the *Xunzi*, as well as the *Analects*, show a concern with "socio-political mechanisms" for the regulation of society.

especially in the *Xunzi*, often in contrast with the word for chaotic or chaos: *luan* (亂).[2]

The question that this chapter attempts to answer concerns what successful *zheng* involves or, in other words, what governing should consist of such that the ruler manages to make his country *zhi*.[3] The answer to this question can already be elicited from the discussion of hegemons I offered at the end of the previous chapter, and can be divided into a threefold account. The first part relates to the use of force in foreign and domestic policy. In the second part of the chapter, I show the extent to which the Confucians emphasize the need for the ruler to provide for his people, then discuss some of the policies and economic assumptions that underlie these injunctions. In the third and final part, I discuss the Confucian commitment to the promotion of the worthy and their preference for appointment systems that track merit.

Security

The previous chapter revealed that a large part of hegemons' success stems from their ability to forge and lead sturdy alliances with neighboring states: Confucius praises Guan Zhong because he was able "to save the Empire from collapse" by helping Duke Huan bring together the regional rulers of the day. Similarly, Xunzi cites the ability to honor agreements with allies as one reason that makes hegemons successful at ruling. In both cases, the praise is directed at hegemons' ability to defend their states without resort to force, yet this is possible precisely because of hegemons' ability to exude power, that is, to threaten its use. This raises the question of the Confucian position on the use of force, which can be separated into its external and its internal dimensions.

Concerning the foreign policy dimension, Aaron Stalnaker argues in relation to Xunzi that he "seems to dismiss the utility of the strategic

---

[2] Sato cites forty-three examples of *zhi* and sixteen of *luan* in the *Mencius*, and shows that the two words are used as antonyms, though he adds that "at this juncture [i.e., during Mencius's time], the condition that is described by these two terms has not yet become an analytical object." On the other hand, he also argues that "the argument of Mencius was directed towards the restoration of an orderly state." See *Confucian Quest for Order*, 120–121.

[3] The third relevant term here is *fa* (法), which means model or standard (including of government), and which is also used to refer to government regulations or laws. Among the early Confucians, Xunzi uses the term the most and I discuss his use of it in Chapter 4.

tradition in ancient China," emphasizing instead that what is important in war is the "loyalty and devotion of one's troops" which, in turn,
relates to the "quality of leadership in a state."[4] Stalnaker refers this
emphasis to the context of the Warring States period which, as I discussed in the prologue, heightened the "need for loyal ministers and a
compliant populace" given that "competitors for their allegiance were
close at hand."[5] Stalnaker ties the quality of leadership, and hence the
ability to win the loyalty of one's subjects, to morality, arguing that
what defines good government, and thus military strength, is the practice of the Confucian virtues, including *ren*, rightness, and ritual propriety.[6] But as I have suggested in the preceding chapter, hegemons
are also able to win the loyalty of their subjects (by pursuing the policies to be discussed in what follows) and the trust of their allies (and
the fear of their enemies). The two are related: they win the loyalty of
their subjects by providing them with external security, but they are
also able to provide security because they can rely on such loyalty. In
other words, hegemons, as I argued in the previous chapter, occupy
the space between morality and reliance on military stratagems alone.
Stalnaker recognizes this, writing that hegemons achieve "moderate
stability," which is a "dramatic improvement" over the failed states of
Xunzi's time.[7]

There is, however, another side to the question of military power,
beyond its use for protecting one's state. As commentators have
pointed out, the early Confucians also accept, even praise, military
ventures aimed at helping people of neighboring countries.[8] Sumner
Twiss and Jonathan Chan have analyzed the criteria of legitimacy for
the launching, and operation, of these so-called punitive expeditions
(*zheng* 征), arguing that they involve, among others, bringing more
benefit than harm to the people involved (proportionality), and avoiding harm and abuse to innocent civilians, prisoners of war, and the ci-
vilian infrastructure. While Daniel Bell argues that "offensive war is
justified only if it is led by an actually or potentially virtuous ruler who
aims to punish oppressive rulers and bring about global peace,"[9] Twiss
and Chan contend that hegemons, to the extent that they promote

[4] See Aaron Stalnaker, "Xunzi's Moral Analysis of War and Some of Its Contemporary
Implications," *Journal of Military Ethics* 11, no. 2 (August 2012): 99. See also *Analects* 15.1.
[5] Stalnaker, "Xunzi's Moral Analysis of War," 99.
[6] Stalnaker, "Xunzi's Moral Analysis of War," 100.
[7] Stalnaker, "Xunzi's Moral Analysis of War," 102.
[8] See *Mencius* 1B.10, 1B.11, 3B.5, and 7B.4 and *Xunzi* 9.19a, 15.1f, 15.2, and 15.6a.
[9] See Daniel Bell, "Mencius on Just and Unjust War," in *Beyond Liberal Democracy: Po-*

order in their own states and earn the trust of their allies, are justified in pursuing such wars.[10] It remains the case, however, that the punitive expeditions offered as models by Mencius and Xunzi are led by the virtuous King Wu, Prince Tang, and the Duke of Zhou, and are never associated with hegemons. Though one could imagine a scenario, as Twiss and Chan do, of hegemons waging a war on a tyrant to save his subjects, it is not difficult to see why the Confucians do not actually offer such a scenario, given that the order achieved by hegemons is a limited—albeit stable—one, suggesting that hegemons would jeopardize both the people's loyalty and the state's resources through grand, risk-prone missions. Instead of spreading morality and global peace, hegemons promote stability through a federative system. As Stalnaker argues in relation to Xunzi, "despite Xunzi's basic tendency to prefer harmonious, integrated, universal government under as sagacious a ruler as possible," he also allows for a system whereby a "strong, reasonably well-run state that refused to attack others to gain territory" would exert "indirect economic and military pressure" to restrain other states' aggression.[11]

Zooming in now on the internal dimension, Xunzi's account of hegemons emphasizes their use of consistent punishments and rewards, raising the question of whether the Confucians countenanced this use more generally. It might be thought that the Confucians would reject the resort to punishments, at least in contrast with the Legalists, who are portrayed as in search of forceful policies and efficacious strategies to strengthen the ruler. In fact, the third-century BCE Han Feizi, the best-known representative of the Legalist school, jabs at the Confucians for solely relying on benevolence and rightness in government. This, according to him, will never get the people to conform. He offers the example of a young man of bad character. Try as they might, his parents and teachers are unable to change him. "But let the local magistrate send out government soldiers to enforce the law (*fa* 法) and search for evildoers, and then he is filled with terror, reforms his conduct, and changes his ways."[12]

---

litical Thinking for an East Asian Context (Princeton: Princeton University Press, 2006), 38–39.

[10] See Twiss and Chan, "Classical Confucian Position," 457–58, 470. See also Twiss and Chan, "Classical Confucianism, Punitive Expeditions, and Humanitarian Intervention," *Journal of Military Ethics* 11, no. 2 (August 2012): 81–96.

[11] Stalnaker, "Xunzi's Moral Analysis of War," 108.

[12] *Han Feizi* chap. 49, quoted from Han Feizi, *Basic Writings*. Translated by Burton Watson (New York, Columbia University Press, 2003), 104. Han Feizi argues that, in

Han Feizi's argument is, in some sense, as Eirik Harris contends, directed against a "Confucian straw man."[13] Xunzi's ruler (and on my view Mencius's as well) rules according to "ritual and proper social norms" rather than simply according to his moral judgment.[14] I will discuss rituals in the next chapter; the—related—point I want to make here, to the effect that the Confucians clearly did not think that the ruler as model and as educator was sufficient in government, is two-fold: The first point, to be discussed further in the next section, is that the Confucians advocate welfare policies as a first step toward improving the lives of the common people and thus making it less likely that they would be prone to crime. Put differently, welfare policies are the first step toward the acquisition of the qualities of orderliness that I described in the previous chapter. The second point to be emphasized here is that the Confucians also allow a role for punishments, even if only as a last resort. Thus, Confucius says, "In hearing litigation, I am no different from any other man. But if you insist on a difference, it is, perhaps, that I try to get the parties not to resort to litigation in the first place."[15] One can also find in the *Analects* the suggestion that the use of punishments is necessary so long as they fit the crime."[16] Xunzi offers a similar reasoning, arguing that punishments work only as long as they are strictly applied, but as soon as they are slightly relaxed, the people will inevitably return to being disobedient.[17] Xunzi considers their use to be appropriate only as a last resort, and even then, restricted to as few people as possible. One can take as an illustration of his vision his account of the ideal times of antiquity: "If there were any who did not follow commands, then and only then were punishments applied. Therefore, the rulers had only to punish one man and the whole world submitted."[18] Finally, Mencius says that the ruler should be sparing in

---

order for them to work, laws should be made consistent, public, and universal. The ruler is in principle exempted from their application, though in practice encouraged to follow them, to serve as a model for others.

[13] Eirik Lang Harris, "Constraining the Ruler: On Escaping Han Fei's Criticism of Confucian Virtue Politics," *Asian Philosophy* 23, no.1 (2013), 44.

[14] Harris, "Constraining the Ruler," 46.

[15] *Analects* 12.13.

[16] *Analects* 13.3.

[17] *Xunzi* 16.2.

[18] *Xunzi* 15.4, quoted from Watson, 76. See also 10.10 (suggesting that rewards and punishments are important, though not most important), 14.5, 14.9 (suggesting that benefiting the wayward is better than harming the worthy), 15.5, 16.2, 24.3, 25.18, 25.50, 27.64, and 28.3. *Xunzi* 18.3 suggests that punishments have to be harsh to engender order. It is in line with 15.4, where Xunzi suggests that the best way to apply punishments is to

his use of punishments,[19] and that punishing people after having neglected their needs (and thus allowed crime to happen) is to set a trap for the people.[20]

In short, as Xu Fuguan argues, though the early Confucians did not emphasize punishments, they did not oppose them either.[21] The Confucians' acceptance of punishments as a last resort indicates, as Hsiao contends, the recognition that there will always be people who will only be affected by the threat of force,[22] which buttresses my argument in the previous chapter that not everyone in society is expected to internalize virtue. The point remains, however, that though the early Confucians accept the use of punishments and penal laws, or at least assume their continuing existence, they clearly prefer other methods for ruling. As Confucius famously puts it, "Guide them by edicts (*zheng* 政), keep them in line with punishments, and the common people will stay out of trouble but will have no sense of shame. Guide them by virtue, keep them in line with the rites, and they will, besides having a sense of shame, reform themselves."[23]

Sungmoon Kim glosses the space opened by the Confucians between full reliance on penal laws and their complete rejection as "Confucian civility."[24] As I will argue in the next chapter, the Confucians favor the promotion of rituals and filiality as a way to hone humans' natural disposition to be sociable toward the creation of a sustainable political and civil order.

---

apply them harshly (such as using capital punishment), but only to one man, in order to provide a model for others and thus to avoid having to punish more people. In 28.2, Xunzi relates that when Confucius was a prime minister in Lu (temporarily), the first thing he did was execute Deputy Mao. His disciples ask him why this will not make him lose the support of the people, so Confucius goes into a defense of the propriety of his action based on the badness of Deputy Mao.

[19] *Mencius* 1A.5.

[20] *Mencius* 1A.7.

[21] Xu, *Zhongguo sixiang shi lunji*, 138. See also Sa Mengwu, *Zhongguo zhengzhi sixiang shi* 中國政治思想史 [The history of Chinese political thought] (Taibei: Sanmin shuju, 1969), 16, 45.

[22] Hsiao, *History of Chinese Political Thought*, 114. Sato also argues that "*fa* [law, regulation] was not incompatible with the promotion of moral politics as advocated by the early Confucians such as Mencius and Mohists." See Sato, *Confucian Quest for Order*, 145.

[23] *Analects* 2.3. Notice Lau's translation of *zheng* as "edicts" here. Slingerland uses "coercive regulations"; Arthur Waley uses "regulations" *simpliciter*. See Waley, trans., *The Analects* (New York: Knopf, 1938).

[24] Sungmoon Kim, "Virtue Politics and Political Leadership: A Confucian Rejoinder to Han Feizi," *Asian Philosophy* 22, no. 2 (2012): 185.

Welfare

In this section, I focus on Confucian policies that can be subsumed under the general category of "political economy." These were briefly mentioned in the discussion of hegemons in the previous chapter: Xunzi describes hegemons as providing lands for agriculture, stocking the state's granaries, and generally making sure that the people's welfare needs are satisfied. The discussion of economic policies in the early Confucian texts is worth dwelling on further because it is an area that has been largely ignored in the secondary literature on early Confucianism. What the literature does underscore is the Confucian emphasis on the need to provide for the common people, but there has not been sufficient attention to the exact policies favored by the Confucians for doing so.

A few words are first in order about the injunction to provide for the people, after which I turn to the policies meant to fulfill it: Rulers are enjoined not to overwork or overburden the people: "In guiding a state of a thousand chariots," Confucius says, "employ the labor of the common people only in the right seasons."[25] As a response to a bad harvest, You Ruo, a disciple of Confucius, advises Duke Ai to reduce taxes to one in ten (of agricultural output). Duke Ai retorts that the tax of two in ten is already insufficient for the government, how could a tax reduction help? You Ruo's reply suggests the intimate connection between the interest of the ruler and that of the common people. As he puts it, if the people have enough, the ruler cannot be said to be lacking, but if the people are in need, how could the ruler ever be content?[26]

Mencius develops You Ruo's argument by recasting the welfare requirement not so much as a matter of restricting expenditures or actively pursuing the state's enrichment, but rather a matter of sharing, thus again emphasizing the complementarity between ruler and ruled.[27] When King Xuan of Qi complains to Mencius that he has a park only forty leagues square but the people consider it big, Mencius

[25] *Analects* 1.5.

[26] *Analects* 12.9.

[27] *Mencius* 1A.2. Michael Nylan and Harrison Huang see in his emphasis on the ruler's sharing, rather than restricting, his pursuit of his desires, the importance for Mencius of pleasure, pleasure-seeking being preparatory ground for, rather than detrimental to, the achievement of human morality and the harmonization of society. See Nylan and Huang, "Mencius on Pleasure," in *Polishing the Chinese Mirror: Essays in Honor of Henry Rosemont*, ed. Marthe Chandler and Ronnie Littlejohn (La Salle, IL: Association of Chinese Philosophers of America and Open Court, 2007), 245–70.

advises the king to share his park with the people.[28] King Xuan of Qi is also encouraged to share his fondness for music,[29] money, and women with the people,[30] and King Hui of Liang to share his pond and terrace[31]. Duke Wen of Teng, for his part, is counseled to do his part in militarily defending the country alongside the people.[32] Finally, Xunzi emphasizes kindness (*hui* 惠) as the attitude that the government should espouse toward the people.[33] Kindness involves taking care of the "five incapacitated groups" (the dumb, deaf, crippled, limbless, and dwarfed),[34] but also more generally rearing (*zhang* 長) and nourishing (*yang* 養) the common people.[35]

While these injunctions are widely documented in the secondary literature (in order to show the importance the Confucians bestow on the common people), less attention has been given to the specific mechanisms meant to fulfill them. Benjamin Schwartz writes that "there were many . . . signs during [the Warring States] period of what we could call now development" and continues that "the crucial point is that they are not particularly germane to the concerns of the Master [i.e., Confucius]."[36] This, I think, is incorrect. I show in what follows that the Confucians were indeed concerned with issues of political economy, that is, issues of land expansion, population increase, taxation, agricultural production, and so on.

First, the early Confucians recognize simply that size (territory and population) matters for economic productivity. This is important to note because the Confucians, especially Mencius, suggest at points that virtue trumps all other means for establishing a successful government. For example, in 4A.7, Mencius argues that no one can be stronger than a ruler who models himself after King Wen (founder of the

---

[28] *Mencius* 1B.2.

[29] *Mencius* 1B.1.

[30] *Mencius* 1B.5.

[31] *Mencius* 1A.2.

[32] *Mencius* 1B.13. See also *Mencius* 1B.4: "The people will delight in the joy of him who delights in their joy, and will worry over the troubles of him who worries over their troubles. He who delights and worries on account of the Empire is certain to become a true King."

[33] *Xunzi* 9.4.

[34] *Xunzi* 9.1.

[35] *Xunzi* 6.8.

[36] Schwartz, *World of Thought in Ancient China*, 59. On the other hand, Erin Cline writes, "It is not the case . . . that the *Analects* simply does not show a concern with basic matters such as the distribution of food and taxation." See Cline, *Confucius, Rawls, and the Sense of Justice* (New York: Fordham University Press, 2013), 134.

Zhou dynasty), on account of his virtue, and not on account of the size of his state. As he says, "Against *ren* there can be no superiority in numbers."[37] Yet, turning to the first part of the anecdote, one can also find the suggestion that size does matter. There, Mencius claims that the success of those emulating the virtuous King Wen will be faster in coming for the rulers of large states than for the rulers of small states: seven years for the latter, and only five for the former. This is akin to his assessment of the state of Qi, in which he argues that it is easier for the ruler of Qi to become a true king than it was for King Wen, because Qi has a territory (*di* 地) exceeding that of the Zhou, the Xia, and the Shang, at their height. Qi has a concomitantly large population (*min* 民), supposedly evidenced by the fact that "you can hear roosters crow and dogs bark from one side of the state to the other."[38]

The evaluation of Qi echoes Confucius's exclamation, upon traveling by the state of Wei, "How numerous (*shu* 庶) the people of this state are!"[39] That this comment has a positive connotation is made clear in the follow-up question by Ran Qiu, who wonders what more can be done once the population is already numerous, suggesting that a numerous population is itself a goal to pursue. Commenting on this passage, Slingerland notes what I discussed in the prologue about the importance of population during this period, observing that "the main source of state wealth and strength were taxes on peasant agricultural production and levying of peasant armies." He also adds that the peasants were mobile, and could thus easily leave a given state if unsatisfied, hence the added keenness with which rulers tried to win them over.[40]

If, thus, a large population is important as a source of revenue and military strength, a large territory is important as the source of the physical space and the land resources needed to sustain a large population.[41] Moreover, as Mencius explains, "The territory of the [emperor] is a thousand [leagues] square. If it were not a thousand [leagues], it would be insufficient to entertain the various [regional rulers] at his court. The territory of each of the various [regional rulers] is a hundred

[37] *Mencius* 4A.7. Xunzi also emphasizes virtue over territory in 7.1, 8.10, 11.6. Yet in 14.2, Xunzi argues that it is the combination of territory and population on the one hand, and the Way on the other, that secures the foundations of a country.

[38] *Mencius* 2A.1.

[39] *Analects* 13.9, quoted from Slingerland.

[40] Slingerland, trans., *Confucius: Analects*, 143.

[41] Mencius thus argues that for a regional ruler (i.e., someone who is not—yet—king), there are three treasures: territory, people, and affairs of state (but not pearls and jade) (*Mencius* 7B.28).

[leagues] square. If it were not a hundred [leagues], it would be insufficient to preserve the practices of their ancestral temples."[42] In other words, a ruler needs a large territory to sustain the court ceremonies and the ancestral sacrifices worthy of a state of many dependents. This is the first indication of the tight relationship between the economic base and the complex workings of a ritual-centered political realm, which will be discussed in the next chapter.

Important as it is, however, territory is also the cause of a quintessential dilemma for statesmen. On the one hand, the strength of the state is dependent on the span of its territory and the size of its population. On the other hand, an increase in territory, by itself, does not compensate for the increase in mouths to feed, and sophisticated methods have to be devised for the extraction of resources and the administration of vast fields. This is an area that also concerns the early Confucians. Indeed, Mencius and Xunzi show, for example, a clear interest in the development of agriculture. The methods they espouse center on the avoidance of arbitrary interference in the spontaneous course of nature. For Mencius, the first step along the kingly way thus requires that the ruler "not interfere with the busy seasons in the fields," "not allow nets with too fine a mesh to be used in large ponds," and permit hatchets and axes to be used "only in the proper seasons."[43] Similarly, Xunzi's proposals involve encouraging farming and proscribing banditry,[44] regulating farming according to the appropriate seasons,[45] and closing and opening common territories (like mountains, forests, and lakes) according to seasons but imposing no taxes on their use.[46]

One specific farming arrangement espoused by Mencius is the so-called well-field system,[47] an idealized land tenure system of the Zhou requiring the division of public land among groups of eight families. Each family gets its own plot (all eight plots being equal), while the ninth plot is cultivated collectively, for the benefit of the regional ruler.[48] The importance of this system is its protection of the livelihood of the peasants, ensuring their mutual aid while also providing revenue for the ruler.[49]

[42] *Mencius* 6B.8, quoted from Van Norden.
[43] *Mencius* 1A.3.
[44] *Xunzi* 12.6.
[45] *Xunzi* 9.16b.
[46] *Xunzi* 9.13.
[47] *Mencius* 3A.3.
[48] Hsu, "Spring and Autumn Period," 576.
[49] Schwartz, *World of Thought in Ancient China*, 281.

The well-field system gave way, during the Warring States period, to a more consolidated form of land ownership by peasants. This transformation was not unnatural, as one can identify in the well-field system the orientation toward small-scale farming that was characteristic of the period and that was a natural precursor to land ownership.[50] Indeed, already in the *Xunzi*, and even in a few passages in the *Mencius* and in the *Analects*, we find a discussion of taxes on land output, a sign of development toward land ownership. Xunzi thus wants to make sure that the rate of taxation on land does not surpass one in ten,[51] which is also the rate favored by You Ruo, Confucius's disciple encountered earlier.[52] Mencius calls for a general decrease in all forms of taxation levied in grain and cloth, but also in labor.[53]

As for trade, both Mencius and Xunzi emphasize the freeing up of trade and exchange. Both want no taxes to be levied on borders and in markets so as to free the circulation of goods.[54] Mencius spells out the textbook version of the importance of trade: "If people cannot trade the surplus of the fruits of their labours to satisfy one another's needs, then the farmer will be left with surplus grain and the women with surplus cloth. If things are exchanged, you can feed the carpenter and the carriage-maker."[55] Xunzi's account takes Mencius's a step further, as he is specifically sensitive to what we call today "comparative advantage," arguing that each region should provide the goods that it specializes in producing (horses and dogs from the north, feathers and copper from the south, etc.).[56] Interestingly, despite their encouragement of trade, Mencius and Xunzi also want to regulate and limit the number of tradesmen.[57] To understand the source of the suspicion against merchants, the following passage from the *Mencius* is revealing: "In antiquity, the market was for the exchange of what one had for what one lacked. The authorities merely supervised it. There was, however, a despicable fellow who always looked for a vantage point and, going up on it, gazed into the distance to the left and to the right

---

[50] See Lewis, "Warring States Political History," 605.

[51] *Xunzi* 9.13.

[52] *Analects* 12.9.

[53] *Mencius* 1A.5, 3A.3, 7B.27. In 3A.3, the suggestion is that the best mode of taxation is that which increases taxes on agriculture in times of plenty and alleviates them in times of need.

[54] *Xunzi* 9.13, *Mencius* 1B.5 and 2A.5.

[55] *Mencius* 3B.4.

[56] *Xunzi* 9.14.

[57] *Xunzi* 10.4.

in order to secure for himself all the profit there was in the market. The people all thought him despicable, and, as a result, they taxed him. The taxing of traders began with this despicable fellow."[58] This account clarifies that merchants were suspected of abusing the workings of the market for their own, personal profit, hence the need to control them.

To summarize, it is crucial to remark on the nature of the Confucians' favored economic policies: from the preceding, it is clear that the ruler does not micromanage the economy, nor distribute resources directly to the people. Instead, he works on the "basic structure" itself (by regulating the commons, removing obstacles on trade, etc.), thus ensuring the appropriate functioning of the socioeconomic system such that it works to everyone's benefit.[59]

It is also important to note the link between these economic policies and the theme of political order developed in the previous chapter: the aim of these policies is to promote the state's productivity and thus provide for the common people's basic needs. Only when this is achieved can the ruler be successful at winning the loyalty of the common people and thus at maintaining political order.

Promoting the Worthy

Finally, the discussion of hegemons in the previous chapter underscored the importance of the promotion of the worthy for our three Confucians. The recognition of merit (in his treatment of Guan Zhong and in the fivefold pledge he sponsored among the states of the day)[60] is indeed a central reason behind Mencius's admiration for Duke Huan of Qi. The promotion of the worthy is also explicitly cited by Xunzi as a typical policy employed by hegemons. On the other hand, I also argued in Chapter 1 that the Confucians favored hereditary succession, at least under existing circumstances, as the least disruptive method for the appointment of the ruler. This preference actually only heightens the need for meritorious ministers in government.

---

[58] *Mencius* 2B.10.

[59] I borrow the term "basic structure" from John Rawls. See Rawls, *A Theory of Justice*, rev. ed. (Cambridge, MA: Harvard University Press, 1999). In *The Economic Principles of Confucius and His School* (New York, 1911), Chen Huan-chang describes the Confucian economic system as "*laissez-faire*," though he clarifies that he does not mean to suggest "that Confucianism leaves every thing wholly unregulated," but simply that its economic principles depend "upon the development of the natural course of things" (175).

[60] *Mencius* 6B.7.

Ministers gained a new importance in the politics of the Warring States. While under the Zhou positions were mostly distributed on the basis of descent, the states of the Warring States period relied on the recruitment of able men who could assist in the administration of the newly autonomous governments. Men of hitherto unknown origins were suddenly promoted to ministerial ranks, often becoming more famous than the rulers themselves. These developments prompted the thinkers of the Warring States period to advocate a new meritocratic politics and to propose standards for the assessment of merit.[61] The promotion of the worthy was indeed part of an almost universal discourse in early China. More specifically, the Confucians, Mohists (more on them in the next chapter), and Legalists all presented the promotion of the worthy as a political doctrine, meaning that they defended it for its contribution to success in governing, and not on grounds of moral desert per se. This is not to say that there was no sense that those to be promoted deserved it, for example that virtuous men for the Confucians deserved to become ministers or rulers, but the justification that they give for the promotion is not fairness to these individuals, but the good that it brings to society at large. Thus, in the *Analects*, Confucius proposes the promotion of the worthy as a response to Duke Ai's question about how to gain the allegiance of the people: "Raise the straight (*zhi* 直) and set them over the crooked (*wang* 枉) and the common people will submit (*fu* 服). Raise the crooked and set them over the straight and the common people will not submit."[62] In the same line of thought, Mencius says that "a state which fails to employ good and wise men will end by suffering annexation. How can it hope to suffer no more than a reduction in size?"[63] And Xunzi argues that failing to employ the wise results in the death of individuals and the destruction of coun-

---

[61] This commitment had a historical pedigree in early China, starting with the Duke of Zhou and more specifically with two chapters from the *Classic of Documents* presenting the debate between the Duke of Zhou and his half-brother, who disapproved of the former's takeover of power. Edward Shaughnessy, reconstructing the argument, presents it as the first instance of the "Minister-Monarch" debate in Chinese political philosophy. In Shaughnessy's reconstruction, the duke appeals to merit to justify his regency. Duke Shi of Shao, on the other hand, insists that it is only kings who receive the mandate, which is "freely given" to them rather than "earned," and they alone can thus be said to be the legitimate rulers. Whoever won the debate at the time, the Duke of Zhou was remembered by posterity not as a usurper, but as a man of exemplary merit. See Shaughnessy, "The Duke of Zhou's Retirement in the East and the Beginnings of the Minister-Monarch Debate in Chinese Political Philosophy," *Early China* 18 (1993): 41–72.

[62] *Analects* 2.19.

[63] *Mencius* 6B.6.

tries.[64] Mozi also echoes the political importance of merit by arguing that rulers often fail in their quest for "their provinces to be wealthy, their people to be numerous, and their jurisdiction to secure order," because they fail "to exalt the virtuous (*shang xian* 尚賢) and to employ the capable (*shi neng* 事能) in their government."[65] Similarly, Han Feizi counts as "portents of ruin" for a state the use of bribery as a means to accede to official posts and the absence of tests of merit in official appointments.[66]

One distinguishing trait of the Confucians' position on merit, however, is that, while it is true that they, like the Mohists and the Legalists, defend merit for its usefulness for government, they are also keen on exonerating lowliness of origins as such, on showing that humbleness of birth is no obstacle to moral and political worth. One would expect to find such an attempt in Mozi as well, given what historians conjecture of his origins: his unusual surname "Mo," which means ink, is thought to refer to the tattoos slaves and convicts had to wear on their faces. But Mozi's stiff writing style does not allow for straightforward expressions of sympathy with those of unlucky origins; the most we get from him is a hint of resentment in his wariness of the appointment of "the relations of the rulers, the rich without merit and the good-looking."[67] The case is much clearer for the Confucians. Their identification with the underdog is illustrated by Confucius's statement that he was ready to teach—where teaching involved preparation for public service to a large extent[68]—anyone who offered him no more than a "bundle of dried meat as a present."[69] As for Mencius, he says of himself that, just like Emperors Yao and Shun, he was "the same as anyone else,"[70] which is part of his general argument that anyone can become a sage and thus that anyone can be worthy of appointment to government.[71] Even revered Emperor Shun, Mencius re-

---

[64] *Xunzi* 32.6.

[65] *Mozi* bk. II, chap. VIII, 30, quoted from Mei. For all references to the *Mozi*, I have consulted Mozi, *Mozi: Basic Writings*, trans. Burton Watson (New York: Columbia University Press, 2003), Mozi, *The Ethical and Political Works of Motse*, trans. Yi-Pao Mei (London: Arthur Probsthain, 1929), and *The Mozi: A Complete Translation*, trans. and annotated by Ian Johnston (New York: Columbia University Press, 2010). The book, chapter, and page numbers follow Mei.

[66] See *Han Feizi* chap. 15 (points 7 and 16).

[67] See *Mozi* bk. II, chap. X, 50, quoted from Mei.

[68] See Chapter 5.

[69] *Analects* 7.7.

[70] *Mencius* 4B.32.

[71] Asked by King Xuan of Qi about kingly government, Mencius cites to him, by way

minds us, "rose from the fields."[72] He continues, "Fu Yue was raised to office from amongst the builders; Jiao Ge from amidst the fish and salt; Guan Zhong from the hands of the prison officer; Sunshu Ao from the sea and Boli Xi from the market."[73] Fu Yue and Jiao Ge are ministers from the Shang dynasty (1600–1046 BCE); Guan Zhong, Sunshu Ao, and Boli Xi from the Spring and Autumn period (770–476 BCE). Xunzi says of Fu Yue that he "looked like he had a fin emerging from his back"[74] and that Sunshu Ao "was bald with splotches of short hair, had a left leg that was too long, and was short enough to go under the upturning poles of a state carriage."[75] He describes Sunshu Ao as humble and as a "meritorious minister."[76] Of Jiao Ge, we have a brief mention in the *Mencius* where he is described as a worthy minister to the tyrant Zhou Xin.[77] Xunzi and Mencius concur that Boli Xi made Duke Mu powerful.[78] In short, all these were accomplished ministers regardless of their humble origins. As Mencius says, the list shows that Heaven tests humans' resolution before placing a great burden on them, shaking and waking and toughening and improving them.[79] Lowly origins are thus not an impediment, but rather a contributing factor, to political achievement. In the same general line of thought, Xunzi argues that a man should not be banned from office just because his father or brother had been executed for committing a crime. Criminality and virtuousness are not transferrable by blood,

---

of recommendation, the methods employed by King Wen, including among others, the fact that "descendants of officials received hereditary emolument (shilu 世祿)" (*Mencius* 1B.5). On another occasion, when asked by Duke Wen of Teng about government, Mencius says, clearly approvingly, that "hereditary emolument as a matter of fact is already practiced in Teng" (*Mencius* 3A.3). To the extent that these statements refer to emolument, rather than appointment, they do not contradict Mencius's emphasis on the promotion of the worthy.

[72] In *Mencius* 2A.8, Shun is said to have been "a farmer, a potter and a fisherman."

[73] *Mencius* 6B.15.

[74] *Xunzi* 5.1.

[75] *Xunzi* 5.1. We know all of this because Xunzi was interested in proving that virtue and physiognomy were not correlated (as some of his contemporaries believed).

[76] *Xunzi* 13.1, 32.4. I will return to this category of the "meritorious minister" in Chapter 4.

[77] *Mencius* 2A.1.

[78] *Mencius* 5A.9, *Xunzi* 25.10. Xunzi uses the character 伯 (bo), which can be understood to mean hegemon (ba 霸), in this case. Mencius, on the other hand, says that Boli Xi made Duke Mu "distinguished" (xian 顯), in the whole world. I will return to Boli Xi in Chapter 5.

[79] *Mencius* 6B.15. In the same line of thought, see *Mencius* 7A.18: "It is often through adversity that men acquire virtue, wisdom, skill and cleverness. . . ."

and one should be assessed according to his own worth, not according to the deeds of his family members.[80]

Another difference that sets the three schools of thought apart in their conception of merit concerns the definition of merit itself. For Han Feizi, for example, merit is intimately connected to the accomplishment of the task one is assigned to. This is well illustrated in his infamous anecdote about Marquis Zhao of Han: "Once in by-gone days, Marquis Zhao of Han was drunk and fell into a nap. The crown-keeper, seeing the ruler exposed to cold, put a coat over him. When the Marquis awoke, he was glad and asked the attendants, 'Who put more clothes on my body?' 'The crown-keeper did,' they replied. Then the Marquis found the coat-keeper guilty and put the crown-keeper to death. He punished the coat-keeper for the neglect of his duty, and the crown-keeper for the overriding of his post."[81]

As Han Fei puts its elsewhere, the rewards the ruler bestows are given for "meritorious services" and not for "any act of benevolence and [rightness]."[82] In other words, what matters, as Hsiao says in his discussion of the Legalists, is that the "actual performance correspond to the titles,"[83] not that the act be virtuous as such. One can glean in the Legalist position a developing notion of expertise.[84] The Mohists, on the other hand, were still operating with a notion of merit as all-around goodness. Mozi thus describes the men whom he wants the ruler to appoint as versed in morality (de 德), in rightness (yi 義), in wisdom (zhi 智), as well as in rhetoric (yantan 言談) and statecraft (daoshu 道術, literally the methods of the Dao).[85] The Confucians also define merit in terms of multifaceted goodness. For example, like the Mohists, they hold Yao's appointment of the sagely Shun as a precedent for exemplary appointment.[86] But the Confucians also add to this a direct attack on specific expertise (not to be found in the Mozi). Thus Confucius says that "the gentleman is not a vessel," which, according to Lau, means

[80] Xunzi 24.3.

[81] Han Feizi chap. 7, quoted from Han Feizi, The Complete Works of Han Fei Tzŭ: A Classic of Chinese Legalism, Volume 1, trans. W.K. Liao (London: Arthur Probsthain, 1939), 49.

[82] Han Feizi chap. 14, quoted from Liao, 129.

[83] Hsiao, History of Chinese Political Thought, 397–98.

[84] See Hsu's discussion of "New Administrative Expertise" in Hsu, Ancient China in Transition, 96–100.

[85] Mozi bk. II., chap VIII, 31.

[86] See Mozi bk. II, chap. VIII, 33, Analects 20.1, Mencius 3A.4, 4A.2, 5B.6, Xunzi 18.5a, 25.25, 25.28.

that he is not a specialist, since vessels are used for specific functions.[87] Confucius also mocks the emphasis on particular skills, like archery or farming.[88] Mencius and Xunzi similarly contrast such skills with those of Confucian gentlemen.[89] This said, just as they accept hegemons, the early Confucians do not necessarily expect praiseworthy ministers to exhibit the full gamut of Confucian virtues. This is clearest in Xunzi's distinction between "sagely" and "meritorious" ministers. I will elaborate on this point in Chapter 4.

In short, the Confucians, not unlike the Mohists and the Legalists, considered meritocratic appointment as an essential policy to be pursued by the ruler, ensuring the regulation of society and fostering the trust of the people by assigning official posts to the most worthy of them, regardless of origins. Furthermore, the Confucians discussed specific mechanics to assess candidates for ministerial posts. Mencius thus tells King Xuan of Qi that the decision to promote men of low origins "should not be taken lightly"; he elaborates on this word of caution as follows in 1B.7:

> When your close attendants all say of a man that he is good and wise, that is not enough; when the [counselors] all say the same, that is not enough; when [the people] (*guoren* 國人) all say so, then have the case investigated. If a man turns out to be good and wise, then and only then should he be given office. When your close attendants all say of a man that he is unsuitable, do not listen to them; when the [counselors] all say the same, do not listen to them; when [the people] (*guoren* 國人) all say so, then have the case investigated. If the man turns out to be unsuitable, then and only then should he be removed from office.

This passage is sometimes taken to indicate the democratic leanings of Mencius, since he grounds government appointments in the opinion of the people.[90] But it is easy to exaggerate the significance of Mencius's statement to this effect. For the statement mostly reads as an admonition to employ all means possible to verify the competence (or incompetence) of the candidates for office: the ruler needs to make sure that

---

[87] *Analects* 2.12. See chapter 1, note 104, of this volume. See also *Analects* 5.4.
[88] *Analects* 9.2, 13.4.
[89] *Mencius* 3A.4, *Xunzi* 11.1d.
[90] See, for example, Viren Murthy, "The Democratic Potential of Confucian *Minben* Thought," *Asian Philosophy* 10, no. 1 (2000): 37, and Bai, "Mencian Version of Limited Democracy," 27.

the maximum number of people approve of the candidates. Indeed, D. C. Lau simply translates *guoren* as "everyone,"[91] which suggests that, on his reading of the passage, what is stake is not so much a view about the importance of the people's opinions, but a view about the necessity of putting candidates through as many circles of examination as possible. This becomes even more evident as Mencius's counsel does not end there: he argues that once universal approval is secured, then investigation is appropriate. In other words, as Sa Mengwu argues, the ultimate decision is taken not by the people, but by worthy men on top.[92]

The above should show that Mencius envisions no "democratic" mode of appointment to government posts. Moreover, the idea that the people must be consulted about decisions on appointments to ministerial positions has no significant echo in the *Mencius*,[93] or anywhere else in the other Confucian texts.[94] On the other hand, the idea that the people's opinions are like signposts is akin to the idea explored in the preceding chapter of the people acting as a gauge of competence by inclining toward the competent ruler and moving away from the incompetent one. It is also echoed in the *Analects* where Zhong Gong, a steward to the Ji family, asks Confucius about the way to recognize men of talent. Confucius answers, "Promote those you do recognize. Do you suppose others will allow those you fail to recognize to be passed over?"[95] Again, the thought here is that the people around him will signal to the ruler the presence of competent men because, alone, he cannot survey the vast terrain of candidates available.

As for Xunzi, though it is true that he claims that the good ruler attracts worthy scholars merely by projecting his own virtue, just like light attracts locusts,[96] the rhetoric should not hide the fact that, for Xunzi too, the most important phase of selecting men to office is that of actually assessing their competence. Instead of developing the idea of

[91] The Chinese character typically translated as "the people," and referred to in the previous chapter, is 民. Pines, in contrast, translates *guoren* as "all the dwellers of the capital." Pines, *Envisioning Eternal Empire*, 51. Bai disagrees with the latter translation. See Bai, "Mencian Version of Limited Democracy," 27.

[92] Sa, *Zhongguo zhengzhi sixiang shi*, 36. See also David Elstein, "Why Early Confucianism Cannot Generate Democracy," *Dao* 9 (2010): 437.

[93] The closest we get to this idea is *Mencius* 1B.11, where it is said that its people should be consulted before the appointment of a ruler for the state of Yan is made. But this is also a lonely statement in the *Mencius*.

[94] Pines recognizes this. Pines, *Envisioning Eternal Empire*, 208.

[95] *Analects* 13.2.

[96] *Xunzi* 14.4.

other people's opinions as indicators of worthiness, however, Xunzi develops the "investigation" part of the inquiry. And a rigorous investigation it is for Xunzi. For its purpose is for the rulers to test the ability of ministers to respond well to situations of success and situations of adversity: "They alternately promote and dismiss them, transferring them from position to position so as to review their ability to respond to changing circumstances. They bestow ease and comfort on them so as to observe their capacity to avoid wayward and abandoned conduct. When ministers were exposed to the pleasures of music and women, to the privileges and benefits of power, to angry indignation and violent outbursts of fury, and to misfortune and adversity, the ruler observed their capacity not to depart from strict observance of their duties."[97] Xunzi continues that the distinction between those who have this ability and those who do not will be as stark as the distinction between black and white. Thus, just as the so-called Bole, master horseman, cannot be deceived about horses, so the gentleman cannot be deceived about men. Another important part of the selection method is the idea of impartiality in appointment: as mentioned above, Xunzi is against the ruler appointing his kin and favorites to office. As he puts it, "the intelligent ruler, when he has personal affection for a person, expresses these affections with gifts of gold, gems, pearls, and jade. But he does not express personal affection for others through appointment to office or by assignment of duties and responsibilities."[98]

Conclusion

My aim in this chapter has been to elicit and discuss three sets of policies that the Confucians recommend for regulating society, winning the loyalty of the common people, and thus achieving political order. I showed that the Confucians countenanced the use of strict but restricted punishments, if only as a last resort. I also argued that they advocated specific economic policies for ensuring the state's productivity, and thus producing the conditions necessary for the possibility of a well-contented populace. Finally, I elaborated on the Confucian commitment to merit as a basis for appointment to office. Crucially, these are all policies that rely on the regulation of institutions (the taxation system, the appointment system, tariffs, punishments, etc.), not on

[97] *Xunzi* 12.8c.
[98] *Xunzi* 12.9.

the exercise of virtue by the ruler per se. In other words, this aspect of Confucian political thought is largely independent of the Confucian concern with virtue and self-cultivation, and might indeed make Confucianism appear as much more similar to the hard-headed political realism of Legalism than is usually thought.[99] I suggested in the second part of the chapter, however, that the Confucians actually disagreed with the Legalists on the precise role and significance of punitive regulations in society. In the following chapter, I explain why the Confucians did not emphasize the former as much as the Legalists did, and what mechanism they ultimately favored for the regulation of society, when conditions permit, and above and beyond the basic policies described in this chapter.

[99] Louie argues that it was the anti-Confucius movement of the early 1970s that made much of the contrast (on all levels), between Legalists and Confucians. As he puts it, "The black-and white contrast between the Confucians and the Legalists was a new development." See Louie, *Critiques of Confucius in Contemporary China*, 104.

CHAPTER 3

A Harmonious Society

ᔄ

In the previous two chapters, I have argued that the early Confucians condone a simply ordered society where ruler and ruled are both contented and mutually support each other. It in this sense that political order is the foundational concept of Confucian political thought: it can be seen at play in the second-best option, defining the limits of what is normatively acceptable and what is not. As Xunzi says, when speaking of government and order (*zhengzhi* 政治), the gentleman "does not go below peace (*an* 安) and survival (*cun* 存)."[1] Political order, however, also operates to define and delimit the higher and better option. When conditions allow for it, the Confucians favor a more durable conception of order, which fosters not merely peace, but also what we might describe as "harmony," in society.

Although often associated with Confucianism, harmony (*he* 和), as mentioned in the prologue, is not actually a concept central to the early Confucian texts. I will use the word here, however, because its connotations in English and Chinese do capture what is distinctive about this level of political order: bottom-up coordination among different members of society.[2] This coordination rests on the development of the "civic" qualities I adumbrated in Chapter 1; the political and the ethical

---

[1] *Xunzi* 8.13.

[2] Harmony in the Chinese intellectual tradition is a rich philosophical concept that is beyond the scope of this chapter to attend to in its various manifestations; my concern is mainly to offer an account of the ideal vision of political order that helps distinguish it from the more basic one discussed in the preceding chapters. For a discussion of the Confucian concept of harmony that traces it back to the early texts, see Chenyang Li, *The*

do overlap at this level of political order. Importantly, however, they do not completely overlap: neither is everyone expected to become virtuous, nor does government rest on the transformative power of an exemplary ruler. Government operates, I argue, through a set of institutional mechanisms, primarily rituals.

At this level of order, differences between Mencius and Xunzi sharpen, and I point to them in this and the following chapter: Mencius, who believes that human nature should be left to its own devices to flourish, emphasizes the promotion of filiality through educational means, including the ruler's role as a model. Xunzi, on the other hand, believing that human nature should be groomed, emphasizes rituals in all their varieties and leaves a symbolic role for the ruler to play. In other words, the conventional view of Confucianism more closely reflects, in this dimension of their thought, Mencius's politics than Xunzi's, but even here, in Mencius's case, the educational role of the ruler and of government more generally has been exaggerated, as I suggested in the previous chapter, and will continue to show in this and the next chapter.

This chapter proceeds as follows: In the first part, I locate the Confucian position within the political debates of early China, showing why they favored rituals and filiality over economic frugality and impartiality as mechanisms to regulate society. In the second part, I elaborate on the political importance of rituals, underscoring their role in clarifying everyone's position in society, thus avoiding competition over scare resources. Since Xunzi offers the most sustained conception of rituals, I will reverse the chronological order of presentation and focus on him first, and then conclude this second part of the chapter by explaining why Xunzi's view of human nature led him to emphasize rituals more strongly than Mencius does. The third part presents Mencius's view, which focuses on a subset of ritual propriety, namely filiality, as the springboard from which political dispositions like loyalty, diligence, and sincerity flow. As will become clear below, both Mencius's and Xunzi's positions can be found in rudimentary form in the *Analects*, while the latter does not advance a single, consistent view of government. The *Analects* will therefore not be discussed independently, but will be used to further illustrate both Xunzi's and Mencius's positions.

Confucian Philosophy of Harmony (New York: Routledge, 2014); on the Neo-Confucian conception of harmony, see Angle, *Sagehood*, 61–76.

The Case against the Mohists

Before working out the nature of the complex conception of political order espoused by the early Confucians, it is helpful to understand what other contemporary philosophical ideas about the regulation of society were prevalent and why the Confucians rejected these. This approach helps locate the Confucian political vision within the philosophical debates of the time, while elucidating the reasoning behind their adoption of their vision rather than another.

First, consider frugality in government expenditures as a way to confine the use of the resources of the state to the fulfillment of people's welfare needs. Frugality was the motto of Mozi (ca. 470–391 BCE), the originator of the fleeting school of thought in early China now known as Mohism. Like the Confucians, Mozi was worried about the chaotic state of his times, but he identified the source of the problem not only in corruption and greed, but also in the conflicting values and attitudes espoused in society. His solution was thus to find a universal principle for judging actions that everyone could agree to, and that was to be that actions should be judged according to the benefit (*li* 利) they bring to society.[3]

Consequently, Mozi argues that the government should spend only on what is beneficial for the people. He makes an analogy to clothing: the point of making clothes is to keep warm in winter and cool in summer. To add decorative elements is of no utility, and should therefore be avoided.[4] The idea, then, is that governmental expenditures are to be countenanced only when they bring benefit to the people.[5] Particular emphasis is laid on repudiating the need for elaborate funerals; Mozi proposes to judge the arguments for and against elaborate funerals by evaluating the latter on four counts (within the broader emphasis on utility): whether they enrich the poor, increase the population, remove danger, and regulate disorder.[6] He then suggests that elaborate funerals cannot but require great expenditures: for a regional ruler, they require several layers of coffins, jewels to ornament the deceased,

---

[3] For this interpretation of Mohist thought, see Chris Fraser, "Mohism," in *The Stanford Encyclopedia of Philosophy (Summer 2010 Edition)*, ed. Edward N. Zalta, http://plato.stanford.edu/archives/sum2010/entries/mohism/.

[4] *Mozi* bk. VI, chap. XX, 117.

[5] *Mozi* bk. VI, chap. XXI, 122.

[6] *Mozi* bk. VI, chap. XXV, 123.

and carts and horses to fill the grave.[7] Elaborate funerals also require extended mourning periods during which the mourners are to retire from their official positions, their fields, or their handicrafts, and during which their health dwindles and they become emaciated—a required sign of grief—thus wasting revenue and labor force for the state.[8] In short, elaborate funerals make the poor poorer, and by making people weak, obstruct population growth, produce disorder, and undercut the state's defenses. The conclusion is that they should not be undertaken.

It is hard not to read Mozi's analysis as a rebuke to practices favored by the ritual masters, the *ru* 儒, from whose midst Confucius arose, and who sought to preserve the ritual vestiges of a fast-disappearing Zhou world. This said, Confucius himself, in the *Analects*, is actually keen on stressing modesty in ritual. He thus argues that "with the rites, it is better to err on the side of frugality than on the side of extravagance; in mourning, it is better to err on the side of grief than on the side of formality."[9] Confucius appears to be worried about the same extravagant practices that annoyed Mozi. However, Confucius and Mozi were not totally in agreement on the importance of frugality. For example, Confucius praised former Emperor Yu not only for being modest in his daily clothes but also for "sparing no splendor in his robes and caps on sacrificial occasions."[10] The thought is probably that different standards for judging wastefulness apply in public ceremonies and in daily life; in other words, ornamentation might be necessary in public functions even if not in mundane ones. So not all extravagance is equally wasteful—a recognition not to be found in the *Mozi*. Though this thought is not repeated elsewhere in the *Analects*, it finds echo in the *Mencius* and the *Xunzi*.

Unlike Confucius, Mencius does not emphasize the need for simplicity in daily life: in his encounters with King Xuan of Qi, as mentioned in the previous chapter, Mencius never called on the king to slash his indulgence in money, women, and popular music; the point was merely to share his enjoyment of them with the people.[11] On the other hand, Mencius unsurprisingly agrees with Confucius on the ne-

---

[7] *Mozi* bk. VI, chap. XXV, 125.
[8] *Mozi* bk. VI, chap. XXV, 126.
[9] *Analects* 3.4. See also *Analects* 3.20 and 7.36.
[10] *Analects* 8.21.
[11] See *Mencius* 1B.1, 1B.2, 1B.5.

cessity of ceremonial spending. This can be gleaned in the following anecdote in which he shows resistance to Bo Gui's wish to lower taxes to one in twenty (his preference is for one in ten):

> Bo Gui said, "How would it be if I were to reduce taxation to one part out of twenty?"
>
> Mencius replied, "Your Way is that of a primitive tribe like Mo. Could a state with ten thousand households make do with a single potter?"
>
> Bo Gui replied, "It could not. There would not be enough pottery."
>
> Mencius continued, "The Mo do not grow all of the five types of domesticated grain but only grow hog millet. They have no cities, no large buildings, no temples and no ritual sacrifices. They have no [regional rulers], hence no silk gifts or ceremonial banquets. They have no official position, either. Hence, taxing one part out of twenty is sufficient.
>
> "But if one dwells in the Middle Kingdom, how could it be appropriate to abandon the human relationships and do without gentlemen? If one has few potters, one may not have a state. How much less so if one has no gentlemen! If someone wants to make the Way (of taxation) lighter than that of Yao and Shun, this is to be more or less the Mo tribe. If someone wants to make the Way heavier than that of Yao and Shun, this is to be more or less Tyrant Jie."[12]

In other words, while heavily taxing people is tantamount to acting toward them like a tyrant, taxing them lightly is akin to following the rudimentary ways of primitive tribes. For the amount of taxation is not only to be measured by the welfare needs of the people: resources are also needed to ensure that official decorum is observed in the treatment of regional rulers, the performance of sacrifices, and so on. Mencius does not consider ceremonial banquets to be wasteful, as Mozi would have. On the contrary, rituals and gifts and temples and banquets are all considered vital to the flourishing of the state.

As for Xunzi, his case for lavishness in public life is spelled out in the clearest possible terms. For Xunzi, there is no better way to ensure the obedience of the people than to cause them to be in awe of the ruler's sumptuousness:

---

[12] *Mencius* 6B.10, quoted from Van Norden.

Hence, it is necessary that the great bell be struck, the sounding drums be beaten, the reed pipes and shawms be blown, and the zithers and lutes be strummed in order that their ears be filled. It is necessary that jade be carved and polished, metals be incised and inlaid, and fabrics be embroidered with the white and black axe emblem, the azure and black notched stripe, the azure and crimson stripe, and the white and crimson blazon in order to fill their eyes. It is necessary that they be provided with the meat of pastured and fattened animals, with rice and millet, with the Five Tastes, and with aromas and bouquets in order that their mouths be filled. Only when this has been done will the population multiply, officeholders become ample, all be influenced by commendations and incentives, and all be made to stand in awe of the penalties and punishments in order to keep their minds on constant guard.[13]

Xunzi's vision of funerals is also elaborate, but it falls short of the extravagance criticized by Mozi. For example, Xunzi wants the carriage to be buried with the dead, but not the horses. The carriage itself is also not wholly included: "its metal and leather fittings, reins and harnesses, are not included, to make clear that it is not intended for use."[14] Note that the reason he does not favor more elaborate burials is not primarily about frugality but, as he says, the idea is to emphasize the form of the articles buried, as opposed to their use, as befits the treatment of the dead.

Xunzi's defense of public display is also accompanied by a direct attack on Mozi's concern with the restriction of expenditure. In fact, for Xunzi, Mozi's concern with "moderation in expenditures" works counterproductively to cause poverty: having to put up with coarse clothing and bad food, "with only hardship and grief when music and joy have been condemned," the people will feel deprived. When they are deprived, they will not have an incentive to work. This will result in "a decreasing population, a diminishing number of officeholders, and the elevation of toilsome and bitter efforts, with each member of the Hundred Clans having equal responsibilities and tasks and equivalent efforts and toils. In such a situation, there is no awe of authority; and where there is no awe, penalties will not work."[15]

[13] *Xunzi* 10.9.
[14] *Xunzi* 19.7a.
[15] *Xunzi* 10.8.

In short, the three Confucians agree to a large extent that frugality is not only inessential to government, but also detrimental to it. Some of the reasoning for their position is already apparent, and it involves the importance of public ceremony for a civilized state, in terms of both the aura it creates and the incentives it inspires in its participants. I will further develop these points below; for now the task is to demarcate the boundary between Confucianism and its opponents. I thus now turn to a second solution to political turmoil espoused by the Mohists and rebuffed by the Confucians, namely the idea of impartiality.

The Mohists are famous for their notion of *jian'ai* 兼愛, commonly translated as "universal love," but which could also be rendered as "impartial care" or "inclusive care."[16] As mentioned above, Mozi identifies the source of the political mayhem of his day in the conflicting values and attitudes people espouse in society, a consequence of which is the absence of mutual love (*xiang'ai* 相愛). He thus portrays a world in which fathers and sons work at cross-purposes; younger brothers and older brothers do not care for each other; ministers cheat their rulers and rulers mistreat their ministers; regional rulers worry only about their own states, freely attacking those of others, and so on. Suppose then, as Mozi proposes, that mutual care is the norm everywhere in the world, that is, that people care for others as much as they care for themselves. Were this to be the case, says Mozi, no son will remain unfilial, no minister will be disrespectful, and people will generally care for each other. Even more, what place will there be for thieves in a society where everyone treats others' families as one's own, and what place for war in a world where everyone regards the countries of others as one's own?[17]

Its usefulness for society, then, is again what recommends the notion of impartial care. Mozi answers objections to this notion, for example as to its impossibility/impracticability, by citing presumed historical precedent, and suggesting that the people are often made to do more difficult things than loving others equally, such as sacrificing their own lives in war.[18] He also argues, as is clear from his description above of a world in which impartial care rules, that impartial care is actually in agreement with filiality: taking care of a friend's parents like one's own guarantees that the friend will reciprocate when needed, thus ensuring that one's parents are cared for by others.

[16] The latter is the translation favored by Fraser. See Fraser, "Mohism."
[17] *Mozi* bk. IV, chap. XIV, 82.
[18] *Mozi* bk. IV, chap. XV, 83.

Mozi's notion of impartial care swings uneasily between its two poles: care and impartiality. The text sometimes shifts from impartiality to care *tout court*, as when Mozi applies impartial care to the ruler, arguing that it is more beneficial for the ruler to care for his people than not to, for if he does, the people will, in turn, stand by the ruler in times of need.[19] Filiality is also defended at points to such an extent that it suggests that Mozi should be more willing to allow preference to one's own family than he seems to do.[20] This said, what matters for my purposes here is that these subtleties were lost on the Confucian opponents of the Mohists, who took the notion of "impartial care" at face value, as can be seen in Mencius's vehement condemnation of it: defending himself against the charge that he is "fond of disputation," Mencius shifts the blame to those whom he takes to be responsible for the confusion of the times. He cites in this regard Yang Zhu, who advocated a philosophy of extreme egoism, and Mozi with his notion of impartial care. Mencius says that Yang Zhu's motto of everyone for himself amounts to the denial of one's prince, presumably because it entails that subjects will be unwilling to fight for their ruler. As for Mozi's notion of impartial care, Mencius insists that it amounts to a denial of one's father. He concludes that "to ignore one's father on the one hand, and one's prince on the other, is to be no different from the beasts."[21]

In other words, the crux of Mencius's response to Mozi lies in his belief that the notion of impartial care is unnatural. This is different from the argument that impartial care is impractical or beyond human means: Mencius would likely not have accused Mozi of being an instigator of disorder if he merely found his ideas to be unachievable. Mencius's fear of the impact of Mozi's ideas is rather based on his belief that adopting these constitutes a clear attack on the basis of humanity and the thread that holds human society together. In one anecdote where Mencius confronts Yi Zhi, a Mohist disciple, Mencius identifies the source of the mistake in Mohist thinking in the fact that the Mohists give "two roots" for things when Heaven gave them only one.[22] Mencius's statement can be interpreted to mean that the Mohists saw two sources for human action: the heart (which tells one to love one's parents) and philosophical doctrine (which tells one to love everyone

---

[19] *Mozi* bk. IV, chap. VIII, 91.
[20] For a discussion of these problems, see Fraser, "Mohism."
[21] *Mencius* 3B.9.
[22] *Mencius* 3A.5.

equally) or, to put it simply, emotion and reason.[23] Contrary to this Mohist duality, Mencius believes, as we will see below, that the obligation to care for strangers has the same source (but a different form) as the obligation one has toward one's own parents. Filiality is the basis of all concern for others.

Xunzi's criticism of Mozi combines Mozi's economy of expenditures and his doctrine of impartial care as a single target for attack. Xunzi condemns Mozi, as well as the fellow philosopher Song Xing, for focusing on merit, utility, and frugality while ignoring "distinctions of rank" (*chadeng* 差等). The charge against Mozi is perplexing, since Mozi's focus on merit, discussed in the previous chapter, naturally leads him to recognize, and encourage, gradations of rank and status: he thus says that the virtuous must be rewarded in three ways: they must enjoy high rank, receive a large salary, and have their orders be obeyed.[24] To make sense of Xunzi's accusation, consider the rest of the section: Xunzi continues that Mozi and Song Xing "are unwilling to admit that there are differences that must be explained and that there must be social distance between the [ruler] and his subjects."[25] To get a sense of the differences that Xunzi has in mind, we can turn to his description of how the ancient kings established the proper patterns to organize society: "On the one hand, they decorated the worthy and good so as to clarify differences of nobility and baseness. On the other hand, they decorated the young and old so as to make clear [the difference between near (*qin* 親) and distant (*shu* 疏)]."[26] Since the differences between noble and base are actually highlighted in Mozi's system, Xunzi's accusation is presumably motivated, like Mencius's, by Mozi's disregard of distinctions between the near and far. The reason why Xunzi's target of accusation is not specified in this way might potentially be explained by the close connection Xunzi finds between the vertical distinctions (the more meritorious, the higher the rank) and horizontal distinctions (the closer the relationship, the more privileged the treatment). Since both types of distinction are central to the vision of ritual order he recommends and which I will discuss below, the destruction of even one of the two presumably collapses the whole.

[23] See David Nivison, "Two Roots or One?," in *The Ways of Confucianism: Investigations in Chinese Philosophy*, ed. Bryan Van Norden (La Salle, IL: Open Court, 1996), 134.

[24] *Mozi* bk. II, chap. VIII, 32–3.

[25] *Xunzi* 6.4.

[26] *Xunzi* 12.6.

The Mohists and the Confucians thus disagreed fundamentally on human nature and human government: the former favored a return to the most basic of human needs and the most common denominator in human ties. The Confucians found them to misunderstand both the nature of humans (their preference for the near and dear) and the foundation of government (the need for public display). The vision of government offered by Mencius and Xunzi is inflected to a large extent by this disagreement.

The question that arises from all of the preceding is as to the nature of the methods favored by the Confucians. If, for the Confucians, the regulation of society is not achieved primarily through the tightening of expenditures and the fostering of impartiality among the people (or through the application of laws and punishments, as I argued in the previous chapter), then how is it achieved? In the responses given by the Confucians to their Mohist rivals, and in the charges leveled by the Legalists against the Confucians,[27] we can glean the outline of a Confucian theory of political order: it is a theory that accepts partiality to the near and dear, that recognizes the importance of public display, and that takes it to be possible to regulate people without the constant use of force. The motivating idea behind this theory, as I will show, is that human inclinations and emotions must be tapped into—rather than opposed—in the construction of a durable society. This co-optation of prevalent human tendencies can be described as a kind of "optimism" in the possibility of a harmonious society, despite the fact that virtue education is not open for all.

Rituals

Rituals (*li* 禮) were not in any way an invention of the Confucians; they were in fact one of the central pillars of Zhou rule.[28] They included marriage rituals, mourning rituals, court rituals, such as rites for investiture and the distribution of titles, and rites surrounding divination and ancestor worship. Ancestral temples were indeed the site of many communal rituals: they hosted, for example, capping ceremonies for

[27] See Chapter 2.
[28] Edward Shaughnessy argues that as the Zhou developed more complex structures of government, rituals also transformed from intimate affairs using small sets of vessels to more elaborate performances, using much bigger sets, and having a much more public character, including an audience witnessing their performance. See Shaughnessy, "Western Zhou History," 332.

coming-of-age men.[29] There is some indication that activities at these temples were not exclusive to noble families but were activities that commoners also engaged in.[30] This is evidenced by the fact that the amount of revenue devoted to offerings in local shrines and village altars "corresponded to more than half the annual budget for one member of a [peasant] family."[31] Sacrificial routines at temples had clear nonspiritual social purposes. As Hsu and Linduff explain, "The services at ancestor temples, held several times a year, were not to pay homage to awesome spirits who existed beyond the human world. Rather, they were thought to be communal gatherings for both the deceased and the living. The brethren and the cousins, both close and remote, came there to reassure each other of their kinship bonds."[32] This is the dimension of rituals that I will focus on in what follows.

Though the Confucians did not invent rituals, these became associated with them. For what they did was to broaden rituals further to include all sorts of daily performances by all sorts of individuals.[33] In the tenth book of the *Analects*, for example, we learn in minute detail how Confucius behaved and dressed, and what he ate and said, on different occasions.[34] I will mention more examples in what follows. In general, the rituals described by the Confucians function as socially prescribed, and publicly visible, patterns of behavior repeated through the generations, which achieve two main, related, social goals: First, they help individuals deal with the major events of life by offering clear guidelines of behavior.[35] Second, and related, they ensure the regulation of society through the regulation of individuals' behavior. I am more concerned here with the latter of these goals, but the role of rituals in social regulation cannot be clarified without explaining first how rituals affect the behavior of individuals.

[29] See Cho-yun Hsu and Katheryn M. Linduff, *Western Chou Civilization* (New Haven: Yale University Press, 1988), 374 and Hsu, *Ancient China in Transition*, 19.

[30] See Roel Sterckx, "The Economics of Religion in Warring States and Early Imperial China," in *Early Chinese Religion: Part One: Shang through Han (1250 BC–220 AD)*, ed. John Lagerwey and Marc Kalinowski (Leiden: Brill, 2009), 860.

[31] Sterckx, "Economics of Religion," 851.

[32] Hsu and Linduff, *Western Chou Civilization*, 376.

[33] See Michael Ing, *The Dysfunction of Ritual in Early Confucianism* (Oxford: Oxford University Press, 2012), 20.

[34] It should be noted however, as Michael Ing points out, that Confucius's actions in Book 10 are not explicitly identified as *li*. See Ing, *Dysfunction of Ritual*, 23n17.

[35] For a more "tragic" reading of Confucian rituals that emphasizes the likelihood of failure and the concomitant anxieties failure produces, see Michael Ing's discussion of the *Liji* (the *Classic of Rites*) in *Dysfunction of Ritual*.

The main example here is mourning rites.[36] On the one hand, mourning is the time when one expresses one's utmost devotion to one's parents. In the words of Master Zeng, one of Confucius's disciples, "I have heard from the Master that, even when a person has not yet been able to exert himself to the fullest, he will necessarily do so when it comes to mourning his own parents."[37] On the other hand, mourning rituals set standards for the appropriate amount both of emotional outpouring and of material spending to honor the deceased. Thus, Confucius himself is reprimanded by his disciples, upon the death of his favorite disciple Yan Hui, for wailing beyond proper bounds.[38] Confucius is also saddened by the fact that the other disciples gave Yan Hui, against their teacher's wish, an inappropriate burial. He laments, "Hui looked upon me as a father, and yet in this case I was unable to treat him as a son."[39] The problem with the burials given for Yan Hui was that they were too lavish for someone of his modest social status. Similarly, two different anecdotes in the *Mencius* are devoted to justifying Mencius against the charge that he violated ritual obligations by providing a more lavish coffin for his mother than for his father. In the first anecdote, the justification is based on the higher social status (counselor) Mencius enjoyed at the time of his mother's death;[40] in the second, the argument is that fine wood for coffins is permitted to all segments of the population and that Mencius was simply unable to afford it when his father died.[41]

Xunzi argues that rituals "will cause anyone born to the world to consider the long view of things and think of the consequences [of their actions], thereby protecting a myriad of generations."[42] The idea is that rituals promote the tendency people have to forgo short-term pleasures for long-term ones. Xunzi describes this tendency in the following way:

> Now in real life, though a man knows how to raise chickens, dogs, pigs, and swine as well as oxen and sheep, when he eats he dares not have wine and meat. Though he has surplus knife- and spade-shaped coins and stores in cellars and storehouses, he does not presume to dress in silk. Though the miser has treasures depos-

---

[36] *Mencius* 4B.13, 7A.46, 7B.33, *Xunzi* 27.20.
[37] *Analects* 19.17, quoted from Slingerland.
[38] *Analects* 11.10.
[39] *Analects* 11.11, quoted from Slingerland.
[40] *Mencius* 1B.16.
[41] *Mencius* 2B.7.
[42] *Xunzi* 4.11.

ited in boxes and trunks, he does not travel by horse and carriage. Why is this? Not that men do not desire to do this, but because, considering the long view of things and thinking of the consequences of their actions, they are apprehensive that they may lack means adequate to perpetuate their wealth. In this way, they, too, moderate what they expend and control what they desire, harvesting, gathering, hoarding, and storing up goods in order to perpetuate their wealth.[43]

How do rituals promote this tendency? One way to see how rituals can make people "take the long view of things" is to consider the way in which mourning rituals, in regulating the mourning period for example, permit people to restrict their grief with an eye to their various social duties and obligations. Sacrificial rituals (the *Analects* speaks of ancestor worship,[44] the *di* sacrifice [a sort of ancestor worship],[45] ceremonial dances outside ancestral halls,[46] and the sacrifice to the sacred Mount Tai),[47] on the other hand, involve literally sacrificing objects of momentary gratification (like meat) for future happiness. Rituals concerning eating,[48] drinking,[49] hunting,[50] and contacts between the sexes,[51] are also meant to restrict indulgence in short-term pleasures.

In short, rituals offer people the safety of tried, shared, and socially guaranteed guidelines for action, providing them with an incentive to forgo quick gratification, and freeing them from the burden of deciding what to do in the face of new circumstances. In fact, this is precisely what distinguishes the ritual behavior of the sages from that of others: the sage, while conforming to rituals, also transcends them, in that, understanding their rationale, he knows when they should be followed and when they can be bent. The average person, on the other hand, merely conforms to ritual. As Tiwald argues in relation to Xunzi's thought, the sage is a moral expert and moral experts are rare; most of us in society engage in ritual practices "whose grounds or basis we cannot see for ourselves."[52]

[43] *Xunzi* 4.11.
[44] *Analects* 2.24.
[45] *Analects* 3.10, 3.11.
[46] *Analects* 3.1.
[47] *Analects* 3.6.
[48] *Analects* 10.8; *Mencius* 6B.1, 7A.46.
[49] *Analects* 10.13.
[50] *Xunzi* 27.26.
[51] *Mencius* 4A.17.
[52] Justin Tiwald, "Xunzi on Moral Expertise," *Dao* 11 (2012): 284.

As mentioned above, I am more concerned here with the institutional setup, rather than the personal compass, afforded by rituals, and with the way in which social regulation is achieved through the regulation of the average person's desires rather than through the ethical mastery achieved by sages (in fact, a line of thought that has been building up so far in this book, and which I will return to more explicitly in Chapter 4, is that having sages rule society is not strictly necessary, precisely since governing involves institutions and mechanisms, not simply moral power). I will therefore turn to discussing the ways in which rituals, by regulating people's behavior, ensure the smooth running of society.[53]

Restraining Desires

Rituals, I just argued, help individuals restrain their short-term desires in favor of long-term ones. For Xunzi, restraining desires in this way prevents conflicts in society. Thus Xunzi starts his chapter "On Rituals" with the premise that humans are "born with desires," adding that the problem with these desires is that they are many, and resources are few, so that any attempt to satisfy them will lead to wrangling with others in society. The origin of rituals thus lies in the attempt on the part of the sage kings of antiquity to find a solution to this specific problem. Rituals were meant to ensure "that desires did not overextend the means for their satisfaction, and material goods did not fall short of what was desired."[54]

Xunzi positions himself against ideas prevalent in his time which sought to solve the problem of conflicting desires by eliminating or reducing these. For Xunzi, this solution is anathema to the basic nature of human beings: "Beings that possess desires and those that do not belong to two different categories—the categories of the living and the dead." For him, the question of possession and nonpossession of desires has nothing to do with the question of good and bad government, because the idea of the absence of desires is a nonstarter: it is relevant only for the dead. Instead, the idea should be to regulate de-

---

[53] My argument about rituals follows Eirik Harris's in suggesting that rituals are better at fostering a society that is "long lasting and effective" than laws are (hence Xunzi's advantage over Han Fei). See Harris, "Role of Virtue," 101. My disagreement with Harris lies in my understanding of the relationship between rituals and virtue: on my reading, the qualities acquired by the common people through ritual practice (for example, self-restraint) are not necessarily stepping stones toward virtue, and rituals' success does not hinge on the continual presence of virtuous men on top.

[54] *Xunzi* 19.1a, quoted from Watson, 93.

sires through rituals. By regulating eating and drinking habits, for example, rituals prevent excessive consumption on the part of any one person, and thus help avoid fights over food resources. Rituals do so in two ways: first, they shift attention from material satisfaction to emotional, aesthetic, and/or intellectual satisfaction,[55] and second, as I will explain in what follows, they make standards of consumption and behavior relative to social position, and make social positions clear, thereby regulating interaction among members of society.

Social Distinctions

While rituals also promote social ties, they principally mark social distinctions (*fen* 分),[56] thus specifying what is owed to, and required of, each. One obvious example here is rituals of investiture involving gift exchange to symbolize allegiance and obligation. Gifts varied according to rank and involved decorated clothing, but also and less frequently, chariots, flags, bows, and arrows.[57] Whereas these exchanges were limited, during Zhou times, to the Zhou king and princes, they expanded to include lower rungs of society as social mobility increased with the fall of the Western Zhou. A more mundane example of the way in which rituals set social distinctions comes from one anecdote in the *Analects:* Confucius disapproves of the behavior of a young boy as he watches him sitting with adults, and walking with his elders, because the boy violates the standards of propriety reserved for the distinction between young and old.[58] Marriage, mourning, and ancestral rituals also all emphasize the proper roles to be played by young and old, men and women, near and far, eminent and humble.

To appreciate the nature and importance for Xunzi of the social distinctions highlighted by rituals, one should understand the extent to which Xunzi takes the drawing of such distinctions to be a basic human propensity:

> What is it that makes a man human? I say that it lies in his ability to draw boundaries. To desire food when hungry, to desire warmth

[55] Henry Rosemont, Jr., "State and Society in the *Xunzi*: A Philosophical Commentary," in *Virtue, Nature, and Moral Agency in the Xunzi*, ed. T. C. Kline III and Philip Ivanhoe (Indianapolis: Hackett, 2000), 12.

[56] *Xunzi* 5.4.

[57] See Hsu and Linduff, *Western Chou Civilization*, 178.

[58] *Analects* 14.44. In Book 10, we also learn of the proper demeanor (i.e., as exemplified by the Master himself) of responding when summoned by a ruler (*Analects* 10.3, 10.20), of bidding farewell to a guest (*Analects* 10.3), and of receiving a gift (*Analects* 10.23).

when cold, to desire rest when tired, and to be fond of what is beneficial and to hate what is shameful—these characteristics man is born possessing, and he does not have to wait to develop them. They are identical in the case of a [sage] Yu and in that of a [tyrant] Jie. But even so, what makes a man really human lies not primarily in his being a featherless biped, but rather in his ability to draw boundaries.[59]

The most important boundaries to be drawn, according to Xunzi, are boundaries between social classes. In turn, the most important way to draw such boundaries is through the use of ritual principles.[60] Since the propensity to draw boundaries is a faculty of the intellect, one can say that it is the human intellect (or at least that of the sages) that creates rituals.

Another thing to note is the importance of merit, for our three Confucians, in the assignment of social ranks, as I explained in the previous chapter. Though the Confucians recognize, as I have also argued, that the circumstances of the life one is born into greatly affect the possibility of meritorious achievement, yet when merit is achieved, it determines, along with seniority, a person's position in the social hierarchy. This is why, as Michael Nylan argues, "In the well-governed state . . . it is not just that each unit in society admirably fulfills its specific functions like cogs in a wheel. It is rather that the person experiences a zest for his profession, sensing that it is well suited to his capacities and predilections."[61]

Public Display

One obvious way to make distinctions clear, which is crucial if everyone is to know their position in society, is to make them literally visible for everyone to see, hence the importance of public display. The *Analects,* as mentioned earlier, recounts approvingly Yu's sparing no sumptuousness in his ceremonial clothing. The importance of ceremonial clothing is also echoed in Xunzi's detailed description of the attire befitting officials of different ranks: "Hence, the [emperor] wears the dragon robe of royal red with its ceremonial cap, the [regional rulers] wear the black dragon robe with its ceremonial cap, the grand officers wear a skirt with an ornamented border at the bottom and the appro-

[59] *Xunzi* 5.4.
[60] *Xunzi* 5.4.
[61] Michael Nylan, "The Politics of Pleasure," *Asia Major* 14, no. 1 (2001): 115.

priate cap, and [men of service] wear a hat of skin with their clothes."[62] In short, the higher one is positioned, the more lavish should one's attire and sponsored ceremonies be.[63] Sumptuousness not only clarifies one's position; it also legitimizes it: as Xunzi argues in the quotes cited earlier, the people are more likely to obey their ruler and have an incentive to be productive if they are "charmed" by the blowing pipes and the carved jade and the fattened animals and the various aromas displayed by the ruler.

Xunzi criticizes the argument, presumably Mozi's, that the reason robbery was less frequent in past times lies in the fact that the ancients gave humble burials, while presently people give lavish burials, causing much crime and disorder. For Xunzi, the cause of robbery has to be found not in its target but in its motive: people steal because they are not provided for. Public display has nothing to do with it. For Xunzi, the assignment of people to their proper social position, a practice he takes to have been followed by the sage kings of antiquity, ensures that no one takes more than he needs: "Thus, robbers did not steal and thieves did not break in; dogs and pigs would turn up their noses at beans and millet; and both farmers and traders were able to give away some of their products and goods."[64]

The attention to sumptuousness and display in early Confucian political thought is reminiscent of Clifford Geertz's seminal work on the Balinese states, in which, as he puts it, "the interplay of status, pomp, and governance not only remains visible, but is, in fact, blazoned."[65] In its emphasis on status and pomp, the ideal Confucian state is indeed similar to the Balinese ones. But one important, and revealing, difference between the two systems is the through-and-through spiritual dimension of Balinese political life. Status in the Balinese states was arranged according to distance from divinity and the king was the "incarnation . . . of the Holy as such."[66] Whether this spiritual dimension is to be taken at face value or not, the contrast with the Confucians remains stark: the explanation for ritual and splendor in the Confucian vision of government is not, as is clear from the preceding, primarily tied to the workings of Heaven (I will have more to say about Heaven

---

[62] *Xunzi* 10.3a.

[63] Different occasions also require different attires, as we learn from Confucius's example in *Analects* 10.6.

[64] *Xunzi* 18.7.

[65] Clifford Geertz, *Negara: The Theatre State in Nineteenth-Century Bali* (Princeton: Princeton University Press, 1980), 121.

[66] Geertz, *Negara*, 124.

in Chapter 6) or to a belief in rituals' religious "efficacy,"[67] but rather to the recognition of the secular challenge of collective life, given human passions and the vagaries of the material world.

Harmony

Rituals, by clarifying positions and social distinctions, contribute to the avoidance of conflict in society. Perhaps the best illustration Xunzi gives of rituals as constituting the basic frame that allows society to run properly is the idea of rituals as markers. In Xunzi's words,

> People who ford streams mark out the deep places to cause others not to sink into the waters. Those who govern (zhi 治) men mark out the sources of disorder to cause the people not to fall into error. It is ritual principles that are the markers. The Former Kings employed ritual principles to indicate the causes of anarchy in the world. Those who have cast ritual principles aside have pulled up the markers. Thus, the people are beguiled and deluded and so sink into misfortune and calamity. This is the reason that penal sanctions and punishments are so very numerous.[68]

This passage also reveals that Xunzi takes rituals to do much of the work, and to do it better, than penal sanctions. By dividing society into classes based on distinctions of eminence, age, and merit, rituals cause the people "to perform the duties of their station in life and each to receive his due." This prevents a situation where everyone feels entitled to the same things, or where uncertainty about the future drives people to focus on satisfying immediate needs. Xunzi concludes, "This indeed is the Way to make the whole populace live together in harmony (he 和) and unity."[69]

The idea of harmony is also used in the *Analects* to convey the importance of rituals. Thus Confucius's disciple Youzi says that "Of the things brought about by the rites, harmony is the most valuable."[70] Xunzi and Confucius often cite music alongside ritual, suggesting that the use of music, presumably in public ceremonies and rituals of worship, would imprint music's own harmony on the people in the tem-

---

[67] Robert F. Company, "Xunzi and Durkheim as Theorists of Ritual Practice," in *Structure and Function in Primitive Society*, ed. A. R. Radcliffe-Brown (New York: Free Press, 1965), 157–58.

[68] *Xunzi* 27.12. See also *Xunzi* 17.11.

[69] *Xunzi* 4.12.

[70] *Analects* 1.12. He continues by saying that it does not do to aim at harmony without "regulating it by the rites."

ple, the household and the community.[71] Indeed, harmony is described as the climax of music: "What can be known about music is this: when it first begins, it resounds with a confusing variety of notes, but as it unfolds, these notes are reconciled by means of harmony, brought into tension by means of counterpoint, and finally woven together into a seamless whole. It is in this way that music reaches its perfection."[72] On Xunzi's account, "Music unites that which is the same, and ritual distinguishes that which is different."[73] Another way to put this is to say that rituals draw boundaries between people, assigning them to different positions and tasks, while music entices them to feel part of a harmonious whole. Xunzi tellingly uses a concept that was to become central to Neo-Confucianism, namely *li* 理, which Willard Peterson and Stephen Angle translate as "Coherence."[74] Xunzi sometimes uses the concept simply to refer to patterns or lines, as in silk or jade,[75] but he also employs it to refer to order in general,[76] an orderly person,[77] and an ordered society,[78] particularly in relation to ritual.[79] Xunzi's use of the concept suggests the idea that a properly patterned and ordered society conforms to underlying patterns in the world,[80] arguably revealing the beginnings of a metaphysical conception of order that took shape in Neo-Confucianism.[81]

Enriching and Strengthening the State

To return to the theme with which this chapter started, rituals, by encouraging people to take the long view of things, hedge against wastefulness, and ensure increased productivity, thus contributing to the

[71] *Xunzi* 20.1.

[72] *Analects* 3.23, quoted from Slingerland.

[73] *Xunzi* 20.3.

[74] Willard Peterson, "Another Look at Li," *Bulletin of Sung-Yuan Studies* 18 (1986); Angle, *Sagehood*, 31. See also Angle, *Contemporary Confucian Political Philosophy*, 158–59n48.

[75] *Xunzi* 21.7b, 22.5, 22.6d, 26.1, 26.4, 26.5, 30.4.

[76] *Xunzi* 3.9a, 5.5, 5.9, 6.2, 6.3, 6.4, 6.11, 8.4, 9.15, 9.17, 10.14, 11.9a, 11.11, 11.12, 15.1c (in reference to the army), 15.2,18.5c, 18.9, 19.2b, 21.9, 23.3a, 23.5a, 27.21, 27.55.

[77] *Xunzi* 2.3, 7.2, 7.3, 8.7, 12.7, 15.1c (in reference to army conduct), 19.1d, 19.6, 19.9c, 21.5e, 21.7d, 22.5a, 25.51, 27.81.

[78] *Xunzi* 7.1 (hegemons do not attain it), 11.1c (hegemons do and do not use orderly principles), 12.7, 13.7.

[79] *Xunzi* 19.2d, 19.3, 20.3, 22.4b, 23.1e, 23.2a.

[80] In his translation of the *Xunzi*, Knoblock translates *li* as "natural order," "rational principle," "great ordering principle," and "reason."

[81] This topic is beyond the scope of this book, but for more on the Neo-Confucian conception of *li*, see Angle, *Sagehood*, 31–50.

economic well-being of the realm. In other words, whereas, as pointed out earlier, economic success is necessary for rituals, rituals are also necessary for economic success. Xunzi explains the importance of moderation in the use of resources, achieved by rituals, as follows:

> Such moderation in the use of goods will cause overflowing surpluses and allow the people to make a generous living. If the people are allowed to make a generous living, they will become rich. If the people are rich, their fields will be fat because they are well cultivated. If the fields are fat and well cultivated, they will bear a harvest a hundred times over. When the upper classes take from the harvest as provided by law and the lower classes moderate their use of goods according to ritual principles, the surplus will pile up to veritable mounds and hills so that it will seem on occasion that it must be burned to destroy what there is no more room to store. How could a gentleman face the calamity of having no surplus?[82]

The rhetorical question here is clearly meant as a rebuke to Mozi, whose teachings, according to Xunzi, "too narrowly worry about the problem of the world suffering from the hardship of inadequate supplies." For Xunzi, if rituals are implemented, so that each person's task is made clear and he becomes expert at it, and so that consumption is regulated and production increased, then the stage is set for a well-supplied society.[83]

By regulating the interaction among people and engendering increased productivity, rituals ensure that the state is strong.[84] Indeed, to quote one of the proverbial expressions Xunzi is fond of using, to desire peace but still relinquish rituals is like "desiring old age and slitting one's throat. No stupidity could be greater!"[85] In another analogy, Xunzi compares forming a state to molding copper. Just as, once the mold is broken, one needs to remove the outer debris and sharpen with a whetstone to obtain a strong sword, so in the case of a state, one needs to instruct and unify before "breaking the mold" can produce a strong state. The sharpening with a whetstone in the case of the state involves the use of rituals: "Thus, just as the fate of men lies with

---

[82] *Xunzi* 10.2.

[83] *Xunzi* 10.8.

[84] Xunzi says the same about music which, by bringing about unity and harmony, makes the people orderly and the troops strong (*Xunzi* 20.1 and 20.2).

[85] *Xunzi* 16.4.

Heaven, so too the fate of the state lies with its ritual."[86] The problem with the state of Qin (which was actually later to spearhead the unification of the Chinese empire) was precisely that it relied on military power and ignored ritual.[87] According to Xunzi, "strong armor and keen soldiers will not assure victory; high walls and deep moats will not assure defensive strength; stern commands and manifold punishments will not assure majestic authority. If they proceed in accordance with the Way of ritual principles, then they will succeed; if they do not, then they will fail."[88] As Schwartz says, rituals "might seem to many moderns to refer to trivial forms of ceremony rather than 'fundamental' institutional matters."[89] My aim, however, has been to show how the Confucians took them to contribute to the smooth running of society. In my discussion so far, however, I have mainly mentioned *Xunzi* and the *Analects*. The question thus arises as to how Mencius views rituals. As has been widely argued, though rituals are a part of Mencius's view of society, he emphasizes them less than Xunzi does because of their different views on human nature.

The Question of Human Nature

Mencius clearly assumes rituals to be an intrinsic part of social life. Indeed, of the four "hearts" Mencius identifies as being possessed by all humans and from which moral dispositions spring, one is the heart of courtesy from which the observance of rituals arises.[90] For Mencius, anyone who lacks these four hearts is a "lackey" of others.[91] Mencius, however, does not say much to explain the importance (political or otherwise) of rituals: he says that they regulate and adorn the other three moral tendencies (*ren*, rightness, and wisdom),[92] that they cannot be encouraged in the populace when people are hungry,[93] that they should

---

[86] *Xunzi* 16.1. The statement is repeated in 17.9.

[87] *Xunzi* 16.5.

[88] *Xunzi* 15.4.

[89] Schwartz, *World of Thought in Ancient China*, 66.

[90] The others are the heart of compassion from which *ren* arises, the heart of shame from which rightness arises, and the heart of right and wrong from which wisdom arises. See *Mencius* 2A.6. In 6A.6, the observance of rituals is associated with the heart of respect (*gongjing* 恭敬), rather than with the heart of courtesy and modesty (*cirang* 辭讓). Also in 6A.6, the four hearts are described not as the sprouts (*duan* 端) of the virtues, but as the virtues themselves.

[91] *Mencius* 2A.7, quoted from Van Norden.

[92] *Mencius* 4A.27.

[93] *Mencius* 1A.7.

determine behavior in official posts,[94] and that the source of rituals lies with worthy men.[95] In short, though Mencius clearly does not question the place of rituals in society, he does not devote much consideration to them either.[96] This is in stark contrast to Xunzi who, as should be clear from the above, discussed rituals at length. To understand this difference in focus between Mencius and Xunzi, one should turn to their conceptions of human nature.[97]

Mencius argues that "human nature" (xing 性) is good and only gets corrupted by society.[98] The idea of the "four hearts" is effectively meant as an illustration of the natural goodness of human beings. This idea is first developed through a hypothetical example in Mencius 2A.6: Mencius asks us to imagine a situation in which a child is about to fall in a well. Who would not feel compassion and alarm at seeing this? One feels alarm neither "because he wanted to get in the good graces of his parents, nor because he wished to win the praise of his fellow villagers or friends, nor yet because he disliked the cry of the child."[99] From this

[94] Mencius 3B.1 and 5B.7. Ritual propriety is also one of the standards based upon which one should determine whether to take or leave an official post (see Chapter 5).

[95] Mencius 1B.16.

[96] Sato contends that "contrary to other general impressions, Mencius contributed greatly to the semantic expansion and the conceptualization of li [rituals]. By combining li with gongjing (modesty and reverence) and cirang (yielding), Mencius facilitated its internalization as a moral value, and by combining it with yi [rightness], he broadened the range of discussion about li to include the operation of state institutions, not merely individual behaviours." But he also acknowledges that "Mencius had not proposed a complete system of political discourse in which the term li occupied its central place as he had with the term renyi (benevolence and righteousness)." See Sato, Confucian Quest for Order, 208.

[97] Robert Eno argues that another reason for the difference (which is not unrelated to the differing opinions on human nature) concerns Mencius's preoccupation with defending Confucianism against Mozi's charges (which diminished in force by Xunzi's time). He thus argues that "the defensive nature of the Mencius, its responsiveness to the Mohist challenge, and the frequent functional equivalence of yi and li adequately explain the diminished role of li in the text." See Eno, Confucian Creation of Heaven, 113.

[98] There is an important debate in the literature about whether "human nature," for the early Confucians, is a biological concept (an essence) or a cultural concept (a process), but my discussion in what follows does not hinge on taking a stance on it, since my purpose is primarily to explain the difference between Mencius's and Xunzi's views. For more on the debate, see A. C. Graham, "The Background of the Mencian Theory of Human Nature" and Irene Bloom, "Mengzian Arguments on Human Nature," in Liu and Ivanhoe, Essays on the Moral Philosophy of Mengzi, 1–63, 64–100; Roger T. Ames, "Mencius and a Process Notion of Human Nature" and Irene Bloom, "Biology and Culture in the Mencian View of Human Nature," in Mencius: Contexts and Interpretations, ed. Alan Chan (Honolulu: University of Hawaii Press, 2002), 79–90, 91–102.

[99] Mencius 2A.6.

example, Mencius deduces the existence of a heart of compassion. He then continues to list the three other hearts (without offering similar proof for their existence).

As commentators have pointed out, Mencius only claims that one is moved to pity by the sight of the child, rather than moved to action. D. C. Lau argues that this distinction between our feelings and our actions actually saves Mencius's argument from the charge of implausibility. Indeed, if humans, as Mencius himself seems to acknowledge, do bad things all the time, in what sense is it meaningful to say of them that they are naturally good? Lau argues that Mencius thinks that humans' "heart of right and wrong" allows them to recognize their fault when they do wrong, and their "heart of shame" induces in them a gut feeling of shame when that happens.[100] This reaction is what justifies the description of human nature as good. But it is also of course possible for humans to actually act upon these natural tendencies and thus do good, which requires only that they nurture their four sprouts. Once these sprouts develop "it will be like a fire starting up, a spring breaking through,"[101] and "they will be sufficient to care for all within the Four Seas." On the other hand, if left undeveloped, "they will be insufficient to serve one's parents."[102] The variation in whether human beings *become* virtuous or not thus arises out of the fact that some people have the opportunity to develop their natural tendencies while others do not.[103] In fact, most people fall short of nurturing their sprouts—a feat usually left for the sages.[104]

Xunzi finds Mencius's argument implausible: "One may sit down and propound such a theory, but he cannot stand up and put it into practice, nor can he extend it over a wide area with any success at all. How, then, could it be anything but erroneous?"[105] For Xunzi, human nature is actually bad (*e* 惡): humans are born with a desire for profit, feelings of envy and hatred, and fondness for the indulgence of the senses.[106] This said, Xunzi, like Mencius, also ultimately believes that

[100] Lau, "Theories of Human Nature in *Mencius* and *Xunzi*," in Kline and Ivanhoe, *Virtue, Nature, and Moral Agency in the Xunzi*, 196.

[101] Also see *Mencius* 6A.2 for the idea that the human nature develops into goodness just like water naturally gushes downward.

[102] *Mencius* 2A.6.

[103] *Mencius* 6A.6, 6A.8.

[104] *Mencius* 6A.7: sages are "first to apprehend what our minds have in common," namely the taste for "order and rightness"(quoted from Bloom).

[105] *Xunzi* 23.3b, quoted from Watson, 167.

[106] *Xunzi* 23.1a.

not only some extraordinary people, but everyone can become good; according to him, there is truth to the claim, cited earlier in this book, that "the man in the street can become a Yu."[107] How is this so?

Xu Fuguan argues that Xunzi makes a distinction between natural desires and faculties and describes only the former as bad.[108] Xunzi indeed admits that all humans have the faculties necessary to understand ethical principles such as rightness and benevolence; it is only that, since these faculties are related to the intellect and learning and not to desires and emotions, he does not count them as part of human nature.[109] But there remains another difficulty in Xunzi which Xu also points to, concerning whether humans' desires are themselves actually bad. Xu thus points to a passage in Xunzi's discussion of rituals where the latter argues that all living creatures love their kin and that humans love their parents until the day they die.[110] Human desires and emotions are thus good to some extent, that is, to the extent that they are "amenable to being shaped toward a love of virtue and a delight in ritual," as David Wong argues.[111] Wong clarifies that these natural feelings have no moral content; thus expressing love for one's parents and mourning for them at their death are done without awareness for Xunzi, while for Mencius these are done at least partly because of an awareness that they are the right things to do.[112]

The reason why, despite these "feelings congenial to morality,"[113] Xunzi describes human nature as bad is that, on his view, desires left uncontrolled do lead to badness, given the fact of the scarcity of resources.[114] What is important to underscore for my purposes here is thus that Xunzi's insistence on describing human nature as bad goes,

---

[107] *Xunzi* 23.5a.

[108] Xu Fuguan, *Zhongguo renxing lunshi: xian Qin pian* 中國人性論史：先秦篇 [The history of the Chinese philosophy of human nature: The pre-Qin period] (Taizhong: Sili Donghai daxue, 1963), 255.

[109] *Xunzi* 23.5a.

[110] *Xunzi* 19.9b. Watson tellingly translates the sentence 故人之於其親也至死無窮 as "man *ought* to love his parents until the day he dies" (emphasis added). See Watson, 110.

[111] Wong, "Xunzi on Moral Motivation," in Kline and Ivanhoe, *Virtue, Nature, and Moral Agency in the Xunzi*, 148.

[112] Wong, "Xunzi on Moral Motivation," 149. Both Bryan Van Norden and Eric Hutton disagree with Wong's assessment of the role of human feelings and desires in Xunzi in the forging of morality. See Bryan Van Norden, "Mengzi and Xunzi: Two Views of Human Nature," in Kline and Ivanhoe, *Virtue, Nature, and Moral Agency in the Xunzi*, 127–28 and Hutton, "Does Xunzi Have a Consistent Theory of Human Nature?," in Kline and Ivanhoe, *Virtue, Nature, and Moral Agency in the Xunzi*, 231.

[113] Wong, "Xunzi on Moral Motivation," 150.

[114] Xu, *Zhongguo renxing lunshi*, 255–56; Wong, "Xunzi on Moral Motivation," 150.

as Xu and Wong argue, hand in hand with his emphasis on honing human desires through rituals. In other words, what is at stake is the importance of human effort, or what Xunzi calls "conscious exertion" (*wei* 偽).[115] Xunzi indeed argues that though it is possible (*keyi* 可以) for everyone to become a sage, it is not necessarily the case that everyone can be made to do so (*keshi* 可使) or that everyone will be capable (*neng* 能) of doing so.[116] Presumably, the thought refers to the significant amount of training necessary to attain sagehood, given the need to modify the direction that human emotions would take if left to their own devices. Seen this way, the contrast with Mencius is made more apparent. As Graham puts it, "the issue seems to come down to different proportions of trust and distrust in human spontaneity, with practical consequences for education."[117] For Mencius, moral training is noninterventionist: one has to leave people to their natural tendencies by ensuring that their surrounding environment is not corrupting. For Xunzi, on the other hand, one works both on the environment and on the natural emotions.

Xunzi describes human nature as being like "a warped piece of wood [which] must wait until it has been laid against the straightening board, steamed, and forced into shape before it can become straight" or like a "piece of blunt metal [which] must wait until it has been whetted on the grindstone before it can become sharp."[118] There is no talk here of patiently watering natural sprouts so that they flower into good moral behavior. Another way to put the contrast between Mencius and Xunzi is in terms of the role of the sages and the nature of morality. Xunzi explains that the straightening and the sharpening of human nature are the work of teachers and rituals.[119] As Lau puts it, since it was sages of antiquity who invented rituals, we can thus say that they invented morality.[120] In contrast, the sages in Mencius's view do not so much "invent" morality, as "awaken" people to the morality latent in

---

[115] *Xunzi* 23.1a.

[116] *Xunzi* 23.5b. David Nivison takes *bu neng* here to mean the same thing as *bu keshi*, i.e., that Xunzi is not saying that some people lack the capacity to become moral but that some people will be "unwilling" or "could not be induced to" do so because they judge it to be a bad idea. In other words, it is a question of motivation, not ability. See Nivison, "Mengzi: Just Not Doing It," in Liu and Ivanhoe, *Essays on the Moral Philosophy of Mengzi*, 135.

[117] Graham, *Disputers of the Tao*, 250. See also Van Norden, "Mengzi and Xunzi," 123.

[118] *Xunzi* 23.1b, quoted from Watson, 162.

[119] *Xunzi* 23.1b, 23.3c.

[120] On the question of how the sages invented morality if it is not ingrained in human nature, see David Nivison, "Xunzi and Zhuangzi," in Kline and Ivanhoe, *Virtue, Nature,*

them.[121] This is, in conclusion, the reason why Xunzi lays much more emphasis on propounding ritual than Mencius does.

Filiality

That Mencius does not emphasize rituals' importance for the regulation of society does not mean that he leaves the ordering of society to the "subjective intentionality of noble men," as Schwartz puts it.[122] In fact, in addition to the schemes of economic regulation mentioned in the previous chapter, and to some—albeit limited—role for ritual generally, Mencius focuses on the development of a specific type of behavior in society, which can actually be considered a subset of ritual, namely filiality. To understand the role of filiality for Mencius, it might be helpful to see, first, its place in the *Analects*. Here, we get, by the second anecdote, a statement about the sociopolitical importance of filiality, spelled out by Youzi, a disciple of Confucius: "It is rare for a man whose character is such that he is good as a son and obedient as a young man to have the inclination to transgress against his superiors; it is unheard of for one who has no such inclination to be inclined to start a rebellion. The gentleman devotes his efforts to the roots, for once the roots are established, the Way will grow therefrom. Being good as a son and obedient as a young man is, perhaps, the root of man's character."[123] The thought here is clear: the best way to get disciplined subjects who are not likely to defy the rules of their community is to start first by encouraging the development of proper attitudes in the family. This argument clarifies the meaning of Confucius's statement that there is no need to "actively take part in government," citing a passage from the *Classic of Documents* to the effect that to be a good son and brother is to exercise influence upon government.[124] While this statement is alone in reducing all political engagement to family obligations,[125] it can be

---

and Moral Agency in the Xunzi, 176–87, and David Wong, "Reasons and Analogical Reasoning in *Mengzi*," in Liu and Ivanhoe, *Essays on the Moral Philosophy of Mengzi*, 216.

[121] Lau, "Theories of Human Nature in *Mencius* and *Xunzi*," 208–9. Lau concludes from this that the real difference between Xunzi and Mencius lies in the thorny question of morality as such (whether morality is innate or acquired). Edward Slingerland describes the difference as one between "externalist" and "internalist" metaphors for self-cultivation. See Slingerland, *Effortless Action: Wu Wei as Conceptual Metaphor and Spiritual Ideal in Early China* (Oxford: Oxford University Press, 2003).

[122] See Schwartz, *World of Thought in Ancient China*, 290.

[123] *Analects* 1.2.

[124] *Analects* 2.21.

[125] More on the topic of political participation in Chapter 5.

interpreted as another way of saying that all correct political comportment is an extension of dutifulness at home.

This argument about the sociopolitical importance of filiality is echoed by Mencius.[126] Mencius thus says, "There is a common expression, 'The Empire, the state, the family.' The Empire has its basis in the state, the state in the family, and the family in one's own self."[127] Making sense of the last of these connections, that is, the connection between self and family, would take us off track, but it is worth mentioning here that fulfilling one's family responsibilities, for both Confucius and Mencius, requires more than material and physical support for parents; it also requires having the correct dispositions, like respectfulness.[128] As for the idea that the state has its basis in the family, it is clearly another version of Youzi's principle of "working on the roots." Mencius clarifies the importance of filiality for society as a whole by arguing that if filiality is pursued, victory over contending states follows suit,[129] and peace ensues.[130] Indeed, for Mencius, filiality is so central that the disruption of family relationships is his favorite way of illustrating bad rulership.[131] Here is one instance: "If he who is father and mother to the people makes it necessary for them to borrow because they do not get enough to minister to the needs of their parents in spite of having toiled incessantly all the year round, and causes the old and young to be abandoned in the gutter, wherein is he father and mother to the people?"[132]

But why should filiality be so central in the Confucian thinking about politics? I said above that Mencius argued against Mozi's principle of impartiality, taking partiality to one's family members to be so central to what it means to be a human being—it sets humans apart from animals—that he found it incongruous that people would not love their parents. As he puts it, "Since man came into this world, no one has succeeded in inciting children against their parents."[133] The

---

[126] It is also echoed in the *Great Learning*, one of the "Four Books" of Neo-Confucianism (see prologue).

[127] *Mencius* 4A.5.

[128] See, for example, *Analects* 2.7. Similarly, in an answer to Zixia, Confucius says that "what is difficult to manage is the expression on one's face" and that filial piety consists in more than helping parents in their work or serving them food (*Analects* 2.8).

[129] *Mencius* 1A.5.

[130] *Mencius* 4A.11.

[131] *Mencius* 1B.1. See also 7B.27.

[132] *Mencius* 3A.3.

[133] *Mencius* 2A.5.

naturalness of people's filial sentiments is also suggested in Mencius's account of the emergence of burials for parents: "Presumably there must have been cases in ancient times of people not burying their parents. When the parents died, they were thrown in the gullies. Then one day the sons passed the place and there lay the bodies, eaten by foxes and sucked by flies. A sweat broke out on their brows, and they could not bear to look. The sweating was not put on for others to see. It was an outward expression of their innermost heart."[134]

This naturalness of humans' love for their parents is precisely what makes the child-parent relationship the basis of all other relations of care and respect in society.[135] To see how this works, consider another anecdote where Mencius draws again a distinction between human and beast: "Slight is the difference between man and the brutes. The common man loses this distinguishing feature, while the gentleman retains it. Shun understood the way of things and had a keen insight into human relationships. He followed the path of morality. He did not just put morality into practice."[136] Bryan Van Norden quotes Zhu Xi as interpreting this passage thusly: "Benevolence [ren] and righteousness were already based in Shun's heart, and all that he did came from them. It is not that he regarded benevolence and righteousness as fine things and only then forced himself to act."[137] Zhu Xi's gloss follows from Mencius's thought, cited above, that human action stems from one source (the heart), rather than two (a heart and a mind distinct from each other). This means that when one's heart-sprouts develop and one acts morally, one can say both that one does the right thing and that one does it naturally. To nurture one's moral sprouts so that one spontaneously exudes moral worthiness, what is a better way than to start with the spontaneous feelings of affection toward one's family? In Mencius's words, "What a man is able to do without having to learn it is what he can truly do; what he knows without having to reflect on it is what he truly knows. There are no young children who do not know loving their parents, and none of them when they grow up will not know respecting their elder brothers. Loving one's parents is ren;

---

[134] *Mencius* 3A.5.

[135] On the relationship between filiality (*xiao* 孝) and *ren*, see Alan Chan, "Does *Xiao* Come Before *Ren*?" and Sin Yee Chan, "Filial Piety, Commiseration, and the Virtue of *Ren*," in *Filial Piety in Chinese Thought and History*, ed. Alan Chan and Sor-hoon Tan (New York: Routledge, 2004), 154–75 and 176–88.

[136] *Mencius* 4B.19.

[137] Van Norden, trans., *Mengzi*, 107.

respecting one's elders is rightness. What is left to be done is simply the extension (*da* 達) of these to the whole Empire."[138]

Filiality thus seems to be the obvious springboard for developing a good character, and becoming, probably not, in most cases, a sage like Shun, but someone who exhibits loyalty and reciprocity in interacting with others in society. The process of "extension" is well illustrated in the story of Mencius's meeting with King Xuan of Qi. Mencius tries to show the king that he has a heart of compassion because he decided to save an ox that was to be sacrificed. The king, the story goes, could not bear to see the ox "shrinking in fear."[139] To Mencius, the king's reaction is the work of his heart of compassion.[140] Hence his task is to convince the king to extend his compassion from animals to the people he governs: "all you have to do is to take this very heart here and apply it to what is over there. Hence one who extends (*tui* 推) his bounty can tend those within the Four Seas; one who does not cannot tend even his own family. There is just one thing in which the ancients greatly surpassed others, and that is the way they extended (*tui* 推) what they did."[141] Thus, the idea is to start with things that one naturally loves, and to proceed to what one does not love naturally.[142]

How is filiality promoted in society? Though it is important for the ruler to provide a model of filial behavior himself, this is not the only way that Mencius conceives of this task. Indeed he proposes two other ways: one, implicit in the earlier quote about bad rulers, is to provide for the people, using the noninterventionist policies described in the preceding chapter, thus ensuring that young and old can support each other: "an enlightened ruler must regulate the people's livelihood to ensure that it is sufficient, on the one hand, to serve their fathers and mothers, and on the other hand, to nurture their wives and children."[143] The second is to teach the people about filial duties: in one passage

---

[138] *Mencius* 7A.15.

[139] *Mencius* 1A.7. It should be noted here that the king ordered the ox to be saved by using a sheep instead.

[140] *Mencius* 6A.6.

[141] *Mencius* 1A.7.

[142] *Mencius* 7B.1. For discussions of how the process of extension is supposed to work, see, among others, Nivison, "Motivation and Moral Action in Mencius," in Van Norden, *Ways of Confucianism*, 91–119; Kwong-loi Shun, "Moral Reasons in Confucian Ethics," *Journal of Chinese Philosophy* 18 (1991): 353–70; Wong, "Is There a Distinction between Reason and Emotion in Mencius?," *Philosophy East and West* 41, no. 1 (1991): 31–44; and Philip Ivanhoe, "Confucian Self Cultivation and Mengzi's Notion of Extension," in Liu and Ivanhoe, *Essays on the Moral Philosophy of Mengzi*, 221–41.

[143] *Mencius* 1A.7, quoted from Van Norden.

Mencius mentions village schools in which some sort of education is given, and this is presumably where the inculcation of filial duties starts, so that "those whose heads have turned hoary will not be carrying loads on the roads."[144] In another, Mencius speaks of the appointment of a minister of education "in order to teach people about human relations: that between parents and children there is affection; between ruler and minister, rightness; between husband and wife, separate functions; between older and younger, proper order; and between friends, faithfulness."[145]

Before closing this section, it is worth discussing a central difficulty with the idea that loving one's parents is a good training ground for political obligations, namely the potential for conflicts of interest that frequently pit obligations to family against obligations to others in society. The *Analects* and the *Mencius* offer a few anecdotes that deal with such conflicts, though mostly as they arise for the ruler rather than subjects. One concerns Shun's treatment of his brother Xiang, who was cruel to him and plotted to kill him several times. Instead of simply banishing his bad brother, Emperor Shun enfeoffed Xiang. Wan Zhang complains,

> Shun dismissed the Supervisor of Works to You Zhou and imprisoned Huan Dou on Mount Chong. He killed the rulers of the Three Miao in San Wei and executed Kun on Mount Yu. He punished these four and so all the world submitted. This was because he was executing those who were not *ren*. Xiang was consummately lacking in *ren*, yet he gave him the territory of Youbi to administer. What crime did the people of Youbi commit??! Is a *ren* person inherently like this? In the case of other people, he punishes them. In the case of his younger brother, he gives him a territory to administer.[146]

Mencius's answer is twofold. On the one hand, he maintains the importance of family ties and the kindness one owes to one's brother: "*Ren* people do not store up anger nor do they dwell in bitterness against younger brothers." On the other hand, he qualifies the privileges given to Xiang in order to show that Shun actually recognized how bad his brother was and consequently tried to restrict his powers in the new fief, even to such an extent that his enfeoffment was akin to banish-

[144] *Mencius* 1A.3, repeated in 1A.7.
[145] *Mencius* 3A.4, quoted from Bloom.
[146] *Mencius* 5A.3, quoted from Van Norden.

ment: "Xiang did not have effective power in his state. The [emperor] instructed officials to administer the state and collect tributes and taxes. Hence it was referred to as 'banishment.' "[147] In short, Mencius tries to show that Shun was not partial toward Xiang to the extent that he reneged on his duties as a ruler. As Stephen Angle argues, this anecdote exemplifies the attempt to harmonize between conflicting values—in this case, three: brotherly affection, duty toward the people, and the fair treatment of criminals.[148]

Another interesting story about Emperor Shun concerns his relationship to his father, the Blind Man:

> Tao Ying asked, "When Shun was Emperor and Gao Yao was the judge, if the Blind Man killed a man, what was to be done?"
>
> "The only thing to do was to apprehend him."
>
> "In that case, would Shun not try to stop it?"
>
> "How could Shun stop it? Gao Yao had his authority from which he received the law."
>
> "Then what would Shun have done?"
>
> "Shun looked upon casting aside the Empire as no more than discarding a worn shoe. He would have secretly carried the old man on his back and fled to the edge of the Sea and lived there happily, never giving a thought to the Empire."[149]

As Shun is faced with the dilemma of fulfilling obligations both toward his father and toward the empire, he decides to fulfill the former, though, importantly, by giving up on his role as emperor. The thought presumably is that once he is no longer emperor, he cannot be said to violate his official duties toward the empire by being partial to his father. Yet resigning his position can be considered an abnegation of duty. Moreover, emperor or not, Shun is still violating the law. Interestingly, however, Shun takes his father away to the "edge of the Sea." In other words, Shun removes his father from all extant political community, precisely perhaps because he violated its norms. This is akin to a form of self-banishing for both.[150]

---

[147] *Mencius* 5A.3, quoted from van Norden.

[148] Angle, *Sagehood*, 96.

[149] *Mencius* 7A.35.

[150] Sor-hoon Tan is not sure that Mencius resolves this dilemma in a convincing way. She writes that Shun's father could be accused of "cowardice" for escaping, and that the escape would "deprive the empire of a sage-king—a potentially greater crime than killing one person." She also adds that Shun could have fulfilled his filial obligations by of-

Finally, consider Confucius's infamous response to the governor of She, who boasts of a man who testifies against his father for stealing a sheep. Confucius insists that the moral thing to do is to cover up for one's father.[151] In this case, one is to protect one's parents but, differently from the anecdote above, one is not asked to withdraw from society. Two differences, however, distinguish this case from that of Shun above: first, the person concerned is not a ruler, so he is not the representative of the "law" as such. Second, the man's father did not kill anyone; he just stole a sheep.[152] These differences explain why filiality is upheld here without any qualifiers.

In conclusion, though the move from family obligations to political obligations is fraught with tension, the Confucian stance is that the proper course of action when obligations conflict can be decided given the context of the situation and the choices available to the one facing it.[153] While priority is given to the value of filiality,[154] the Confucians also attempt to remain as faithful as possible to political obligations.[155] Wong describes this feature of the *Analects* and the *Mencius* as "value pluralism."[156]

---

fering to be punished instead of his father. See Tan, "Between Family and State: Relational Tensions in Confucian Ethics," in Chan, *Mencius*, 179.

[151] *Analects* 13.18.

[152] Erin Cline points out that the character translated as "stealing," namely *rang* 攘, is not the one used otherwise in the *Analects* to connote robbery (namely *dao* 盗) and, drawing on Zhu Xi's commentary, suggests that the word choice reveals that the stealing was done for a reason, potentially involving "extenuating circumstances" (158). Combining this idea with the argument that, for Confucius, "a sense of justice is inextricably bound up with filial piety" (162), she argues that "this passage does not imply a lack of concern for justice in the *Analects*" (162). See Cline, *Confucius, Rawls, and the Sense of Justice*.

[153] Wong, "Reasons and Analogical Reasoning in *Mengzi*," 208–9.

[154] Tan points to a few anecdotes where she argues that it is not necessarily obvious that filiality always takes precedence: *Mencius* 4B.29 (where Yu and Hou Ji [who also served under Shun] are said to have passed the doors of their family houses three times without going in, presumably because they were too busy fulfilling their official responsibilities toward the people), and *Analects* 16.13 (where Confucius is said not have shown partiality in teaching toward his own son) and 11.10 (where Confucius weeps for Yan Hui—see above). See Tan "Between Family and State," 176.

[155] On the tension between filiality and political obligation in practice (i.e., as experienced by the emperor during Chinese history), see Patricia Ebrey, "Imperial Filial Piety as a Political Problem," in Chan and Tan, *Filial Piety in Chinese Thought and History*, 122–40.

[156] Wong identifies two "forms of pluralism" in Mencius: "a plurality of appropriate specifications for any single value . . . and a plurality of basic values that are balanced against each other in multiple ways depending on the particular context." See Wong, "Reasons and Analogical Reasoning in *Mengzi*," 210.

Conclusion

This chapter has presented the institutional mechanisms favored by the early Confucians for the establishment and maintenance of an ideal orderly society. While there exists a vast and rich literature on the importance of Confucian filiality for making a person moral,[157] and the importance of ritual for self-mastery,[158] I have discussed them in this chapter as necessary for making society stable and orderly.[159]

In her article on "The Politics of Pleasure," Michael Nylan argues that the emphasis on "delayed pleasure-taking," which she takes to be the basis for Xunzi's ritual system, arose "when the vast scale and unprecedented scope of sociopolitical and economic changes occurring at the time drew attention to two issues: what form of equitable distribution would best serve as foundation for a stable state? and what methods of rule would allow the expanding states to integrate new populations?"[160] I disagree with Nylan on the centrality she gives to the idea of "pleasure" as such,[161] but agree with her emphasis on the political importance of ritual. As Nylan explains, the Zhou political system was based on a system of distribution which its members considered as consistent and fair: "With each member of that elite sharing in the life-force contained within the sacrificial meats, each sacrifice serves as an outward visible sign of the inner commitments binding the partakers to the same clan or body politic, despite their potentially disparate interests."[162] With the decline of the Zhou clan, the weakening of he-

[157] See, for example, the articles cited earlier from Chan and Tan, *Filial Piety in Chinese Thought and History*.

[158] See, for example, Paul Goldin, *Rituals of the Way: The Philosophy of Xunzi* (Chicago: Open Court, 1999); Schwartz, *World of Thought in Ancient China*, 290–320. Various articles in Kline and Ivanhoe's edited volume *Virtue, Nature, and Moral Agency in the Xunzi* touch on the issue of the relationship between virtue and rituals. Antonio Cua argues, in *Human Nature, Ritual, and History* (Washington, DC: Catholic University of America Press, 2005), that the political function of rituals (in preventing conflict) and their ethical function (as moral education) cannot be separated from one another in Xunzi's thought (49). I agree with this claim only to the extent that the limited training in rituals required of commoners can be described as moral (I used the adjective "civic" in Chapter 1).

[159] Chris Fraser also emphasizes order as Xunzi's "fundamental value," but he considers order to be "partly or even predominantly an aesthetic notion for him," while I read order as, at least as importantly, a political concept. See Fraser, "Happiness in Classical Confucianism: Xunzi," *Philosophical Topics* 41, no. 1 (2013): 68–69.

[160] Nylan, "Politics of Pleasure," 78.

[161] I find the concept of "pleasure" to be too loaded a term, suggesting a hedonistic tendency that is not necessarily applicable to the Confucian discussion of, and emphasis on, human needs and desires.

[162] Nylan, "Politics of Pleasure," 78.

reditary prerogatives, and the rising importance of a whole new segment of society, new methods of government had to be devised to hold together the rising, warring states. Part of the concern was to ensure that the people were fed, consequently the Confucians discussed mechanisms for the regulation of the economy, such as the well-field system, discussed in the previous chapter. But political order requires more than economic regulation, for competition over ranks and over material resources, however plentiful, was inevitable in a period of rising social mobility and the weakening of long-established privileges. The concern was thus to ensure that people's quests did not necessarily conflict. This is a familiar problem, perhaps best epitomized in Hobbes's thought.[163] What makes their solution special, however, was that, rejecting what they took to be artificial solutions propounded by the Mohists (they would have likely found Hobbes's solution, based as it is on the sanction of penal force, to be artificial too), the Confucians' starting point was to take advantage of humans' better features: their propensity to be social, their ability to delay gratification of the senses (according to Xunzi), or their tendency to feel compassion toward others (according to Mencius). The Confucians' solution was not artificial in another sense as well: it took advantage of a long-existing institution. As Henry Rosemont writes in discussing Xunzi's rituals, they "were not . . . to be cut out of whole cloth, nor were they to be grounded in any 'grand lie,' supernatural or otherwise; they were the ancient religious and other rituals and customs that already served as the cultural cement of the Chinese peoples."[164]

In some sense, then, the pessimism described in Chapter 1 about the potential of the masses to become virtuous is counterbalanced here by optimism about the possibility of turning human tendencies into qualities worthy of an orderly and diligent populace.[165] While rituals cannot

[163] Sungmoon Kim points out that the differences between Xunzi and Hobbes are not simply restricted to their proposed visions of government, but also involve their conceptions of human nature. More specifically, he contends that Hobbes attributes the conflict in the state of nature to "unsocial passions" whereas Xunzi attributes it to humans' "appetitive desires." See Kim, "From Desire to Civility: Is Xunzi a Hobbesian?," *Dao* 10 (2011): 291–309. But Kim downplays the extent to which Hobbes's "unsocial passions" are triggered by self-interest, or the quest for self-preservation, and exaggerates the extent to which Xunzi's humans are motivated by material self-interest (for not all human desires are strictly appetitive or material—for example the desire to serve one's parents—and in any case it is not the desires as such that are the problem for Xunzi but the combination of desires with the fact of scarcity of resources).

[164] Rosemont, "State and Society in the *Xunzi*," 10.

[165] I should note here one passage in the *Xunzi* that could be taken to contradict my

by themselves achieve moral perfection (they have to be linked with *ren*, rightness, trustworthiness, and wisdom),[166] they are to the common people what Confucian training in virtues is for the Confucian disciples. As Philip Ivanhoe puts it in relation to Xunzi's rituals, "The lowest members of society are protected from the ravages of unrestricted competition, insured a comfortable life, and encouraged to pursue simple virtues."[167] And, as to these "simple virtues" for the people, Benjamin Schwartz (discussing Confucius's thought) glosses these as "no more than the rudiments of proper family relationships."[168]

The reliance on rituals as institutional mechanisms for the regulations of society, at least in the case of Xunzi, also suggests optimism of another sort: that society can actually be regulated without the constant presence of a sage king on top. Rituals are, in Schwartz's words, the "cement of the entire normative sociopolitical order."[169] Thus, in principle, once the frame is set, as when the sage kings of antiquity instituted the rites, the emergence of an imperfect ruler should not necessarily disrupt the running of the system. I will turn to this question of the ruler's role in the Confucian vision of government in the next chapter.

---

emphasis on rituals: it is *Xunzi* 10.3a where Xunzi says that "the ordinary masses, the Hundred Clans, must be controlled by laws (*fa*) and norms of behavior (*shuzhi* 數制)" (in contradistinction to the class of men of service and above, who are regulated through ritual and music). I take this passage to suggest two ideas discussed in this and the previous chapter: first, that regulations, including punitive ones, are accepted by Xunzi when it comes to controlling the people below; and second, that the common people do not internalize rituals and music in the way that those above do. Harris also takes it as suggesting that the masses "cannot be regulated simply through rituals," not that they are regulated exclusively through laws. See Harris, "Role of Virtue," 98.

[166] See *Analects* 3.3, 15.18, 15.33.

[167] Philip Ivanhoe, "A Happy Symmetry: Xunzi's Ethical Thought," *Journal of the American Academy of Religion* 59, no. 2 (Summer 1991): 311–12.

[168] Schwartz, "Some Polarities in Confucian Thought," 52.

[169] Schwartz, *World of Thought in Ancient China*, 67.

CHAPTER 4

Rulers and Ministers

⤳

The ruler looms large in Classical Confucian political thought. He is after all the son of Heaven (*tianzi* 天子), the magnet toward which all the actors and events of the realm are pointed.[1] As I suggested at the end of the previous chapter, this portrait is misleading. It misconstrues the influence the ruler has on the workings of the realm. As I argued, the Confucian reliance on rituals as an institutional mechanism for political regulation raises the question of the role of the ruler in regulating society, especially as rituals are not of his creation but are inherited through the generations. In this chapter, I ask what exactly is the "job description" of the ruler in the Confucian vision of government, especially vis-à-vis his ministers, which raises the concomitant question of the qualities required for political rulership.

The first part of the chapter focuses on Xunzi, since he offers the most sustained view of the role of ministers in government. I will show here that in Xunzi's vision of a ritual-centered, patterned order, the ruler plays an essential but limited role; it is ministers who are assigned the responsibility of running day-to-day government. I also show that a similar distinction between virtuous kings and hegemons applies in the case of ministers: while sage ministers are favored, meritorious ministers are also accepted. As with the discussion of hegemons in Chapter 2, I argue that this appreciation of less-than-virtuous ministers

[1] For example, Yuri Pines argues that for the Confucians, as well as for all other early Chinese thinkers, the "political system was intrinsically ruler-centered and . . . all institutional power was supposed to be in the monarch's hands." See Pines, *Envisioning Eternal Empire*, 204.

reveals Xunzi's concern with political order and his recognition that a basic level of order is all that can be achieved at times.

In the section that follows, I broaden the inquiry to the three Confucians and show that, even though the *Analects* and the *Mencius* do not share the same ideal vision of government offered by the *Xunzi*, all three texts share the thought that it is permissible, even obligatory, for ministers to remonstrate against rulers. This highlights the importance of ministers in the former two texts as well.

In the last part of the chapter, I broaden the inquiry from the question of the division of labor between ruler and ministers to revisiting the question of the relationship between virtue and government in the Confucian conception of politics.

Xunzi's Vision

Xunzi's view is summed up in the following statement: "these rulers of men who have no worthies are like the blind without their assistant. How aimlessly they [wander] about!"[2] Indeed, in Xunzi's vision, much of the business of government can be undertaken only with the help of competent ministers chosen through the rigorous method of selection described in Chapter 2. To see this, note their role in the division of labor envisioned by Xunzi: the farmers and common people are responsible for the cultivation of the soil, the "leaders of men" are responsible for ensuring that people labor according to the seasons and that they fulfill their duties appropriately, Heaven is responsible for preventing floods and droughts: "As to universally (*jian* 兼) protecting the people, universally loving them, and universally regulating them, the responsibility for ensuring that the Hundred Clans do not suffer the misfortunes of cold and hunger, even though the year has been marked by calamities, natural disasters, floods and droughts, belongs to the sage [ruler] (*shengjun* 聖君) and the worthy . . . minister (*xianxiang* 賢相)."[3]

We thus get a recounting of the duties of government described in Chapter 2, here specified as the responsibility not of the ruler alone, but also of his worthy minister. But how is this shared responsibility negotiated between ruler and minister? Consider first the official duty of the ruler alone: he is not to worry about daily "minutiae," which would require him to sacrifice "the pleasures derived from excursions, amuse-

---

[2] *Xunzi* 25.1.
[3] *Xunzi* 10.7.

ments, ease and repose." Instead, he should be concerned with "selecting a single man as his assistant" and "depute to him universal authority to lead the government."[4] The ability to appoint officers to handle their affairs for them is indeed, in Xunzi's view, what characterizes rulers: "Ability as the ruler of men consists in appointing other men to office. Ability in a commoner consists in his capacity to do things himself."[5] For the ruler to take on additional tasks himself is to exceed his capacities, exhausting himself so much that even a servant would not wish to exchange positions with him.[6] On the other hand, the delegation of tasks allows the ruler to be concerned with the near, the clear, and the essential, rather than the far, the obscure, and the detailed. Hence the reason why the ruler's main task is the appointment of an appropriate minister, and it is the minister's task to handle government affairs. Xunzi sums this division of labor up as follows: "The Way of a ruler lies in knowing men; that of a minister in knowing affairs of state."[7] Xunzi goes so far as to argue that the ability "to appropriately employ one individual" (neng dang yiren 能當一人) would lead to "gaining the empire," but to lack this ability is to endanger the state.[8] "Forsake this principle and nothing else is worth trying," he adds.[9]

Xunzi specifies the duties of the prime minister to include to a large extent the administration of the affairs of the lower officials: these duties include "establishing the foundation of government and instruction, rectifying the legal code (faze 法則), receiving all reports and proposals and reviewing them at fixed times, measuring accomplishments and merits and considering appropriate rewards and commendations, and cautiously following the appropriate season in his preparations so as to cause the Hundred Officials to exert their best efforts and the mass of commoners not to be careless."[10] In the same passage, Xunzi describes the duties of the ruler in a way that suggests that they are more abstract and exalted than those of the prime minister: he is "to bring to perfect completion the Way and its virtue (de 德), to attain what

---

[4] *Xunzi* 11.5a.

[5] *Xunzi* 11.5b.

[6] Indeed, Xunzi says of ruling alone that it is "the way of the menial laborer that Mozi advocates" (*Xunzi* 11.5b) though Mozi actually agrees with Xunzi on the need for delegating tasks to ministers. Indeed, Mozi offers a sustained account of the division of labor (involving the emperor, ministers, regional rulers, and local officials) needed to govern the empire. See the chapter on "Identifying with One's Superior" in Watson.

[7] *Xunzi* 27.69.

[8] *Xunzi* 11.9b.

[9] *Xunzi* 11.9c. For the importance of ministers, see also *Xunzi* 24.5.

[10] *Xunzi* 9.17, quoted from Watson, 51. Also see 11.11.

is best and most noble, to found himself on culture (*wen* 文) and reason (*li* 理), and to unify the world down to the tip of the smallest hair so as to cause the whole world, without exception, to join with him obediently and to follow him with allegiance." He sets the duties of the other high officials (*bigong* 辟公)[11] to involve the reform of the rites and music. He finally concludes by saying, "If governmental affairs are in a state of disorder (*luan* 亂), it is the fault of the [prime minister] (*zhongzai* 冢宰). If the customs of the nation are defective, it is the error of the [high officials]. And if the world is not unified and the [regional rulers] desire to rebel, then the man who holds the title is not a king appointed by Heaven."[12]

It should be clear from this account that the business of day-to-day government, which includes the administration of the government bureaucracy with its many officials, is the prerogative of the prime minister. On the other hand, the ruler upholds public morals and the ritual order. As Edward Machle says of the importance of the ruler in Xunzi's vision, "In Xunzi's view of administration, the sage-king attracts the people into orderliness by his DE [virtue], the winsome power of his moral perfection, but the administration of the state is in the hands of his ministers."[13] Machle's formulation underscores that the ruler's virtue does not make the people virtuous, but rather induces them into orderliness. On my account, the ruler does so not merely by providing a model of good behavior, but more specifically by conferring legitimacy on the hierarchical system and thus encouraging the people to abide by it: people will find the hierarchical system legitimate if it is indeed organized according to merit and if it is indeed the case that the highest position is filled by one who is worthy of it. When the ruler is virtuous, his ceremonial standing at the apex of the political hierarchy ensures its successful functioning.

The only exertion the ruler needs to make is in finding the suitable individual to employ, after which he can be at rest: Thus the ruler labors only when it comes to choosing him, but is at ease when employing him (*gu junren lao yu suo zhi, er xiu yu shi zhi* 故君人勞於索之，而休

---

[11] Watson explains that he takes these to be the grand tutor, the grand protector, and the director of music who are responsible for everything related to manners and moral education, though he says that others take *bigong* to refer to the "feudal lords" (regional rulers). See Watson, trans. *Xunzi*, 52n.25.

[12] *Xunzi* 9.17.

[13] Edward Machle, *Nature and Heaven in the Xunzi: A Study of the Tian Lun* (New York: State University of New York Press, 1993), 176.

於使之).[14] Once this minister is found, the ruler "unifies the world and makes for himself a reputation comparable to that of Yao and Yu. Such a ruler restricts himself to the essentials of policy, yet tasks are carried out in precise detail. His undertakings involve the extreme of ease, yet they result in achievement. He can let the lower and upper garments hang down and not get up from his seat on the mat, yet none of the people within the seas does not long to have him as their Di ancestor or [king]. Truly, this may be called being 'restricted to the essentials.' No pleasure is greater than this."[15] The image of the ruler comfortably seated on his mat, calmly surveying his well-ordered realm, "reigning" as opposed to "ruling,"[16] is evoked numerous times in the *Xunzi*.[17] Fond as he is of contrasts, Xunzi compares it to the portrait of the ruler obsessed with power and influence, who fails to employ the appropriate minister and then, toil as he might, his realm remains disorderly and his reputation shameful.[18] Xunzi cites a supposed saying of old: "Undertaken with ease, yet well-ordered (*zhi* 治); restricted to essentials, yet carried out in full detail; not involving trouble, yet resulting in real achievement—this is the perfection of government."[19] As for the inevitable historical illustration, Xunzi provides the example of Emperor Shun who did not get involved in government affairs and proclamations, yet they were brought to completion.[20] It must be recalled that Shun was assisted by no other than the sage, soon-to-be-emperor, Yu.

This said, the ease with which the ruler rules when assisted by a worthy minister should not be confused with a lack of substance of his role. Xunzi continues the anecdote about Shun with the statement that, though a farmer be skilled in working the land, it would be inappropriate to make him director of the fields.[21] Although Xunzi extends the argument to artisans and merchants only, it is clear that he means to apply it to ministers as well: though a minister handles the affairs of state, he need not also be suitable for the position of ruler.

[14] *Xunzi* 11.11 and 12.1.
[15] *Xunzi* 11.5a.
[16] Rosemont, "State and Society in the *Xunzi*," 22.
[17] *Xunzi* 11.9b.
[18] *Xunzi* 12.1.
[19] *Xunzi* 16.6. Note that Xunzi argues that a minister's actions are not necessarily toilsome either, although he knows things in detail. He manages affairs with ease and reaches the ultimate of what is enjoyable. This is why the ruler treats him as a treasure (*Xunzi* 11.7a). He also admonishes the minister, "When given heavy responsibilities, do not presume to keep them all for yourself" (*Xunzi* 7.2).
[20] *Xunzi* 27.69.
[21] *Xunzi* 27.70.

The ruler has to be able to assume the removed aura of an overseer, which does not necessarily follow from the ability to handle the business of government.

Xunzi indeed says that the talents of the prime minister and those of the ruler's assistants, which include exalting rituals, welcoming scholars, loving the people, maintaining constant principles so as to unify customs, honoring the worthy, encouraging the primary occupations, knowing not to quarrel with inferiors over minor profits, understanding standards and regulations, and evaluating things and appraising their functions, do not rise up to the Way of the ruler. And what is this Way of the ruler that cannot be matched? Xunzi declares this to be the ability "to identify these three grades of talent [i.e., of lower officials; men of service and grand officers; and the prime minister and the ruler's assistants] and not to miss the proper rank in assigning them office." When this is so, "the ruler may be personally at ease yet the country will be well ordered (*zhi* 治), his accomplishments great, and his reputation enhanced. At the highest he could become a true king, at the lowest [a hegemon]."[22]

Besides specifying the Way of the ruler, this last quote is also important for the last sentence. Indeed, this is not the only instance when, in speaking of the inevitable success accruing to the ruler from the appointment of a worthy minister, Xunzi says that this would enable him to be a true king at best, and a hegemon at the least (*shang keyi wang, xia keyi ba* 上可以王，下可以霸).[23] Following upon arguments I made in Chapter 1 about hegemons, I argue in what follows that, though it is preferable for the ruler and the ministers to be virtuous, there is also a level at which their performance is acceptable although it falls short of virtue.

---

[22] *Xunzi* 12.11.

[23] See, for example, *Xunzi* 11.9b and 12.1. The statement is illustrated by the usual historical examples: at the level of sage kings, Tang made use of Yi Yin, King Wen made use of Lü Shang (though not otherwise cited in the Confucian texts, he is known in the Chinese tradition for his patient fishing during eighty years with a hookless rod, believing that the fish would come to him of their own volition when ready; a former minister of Zhou Xin's against whom he turned, he was appointed by Duke Wen as prime minister), King Wu employed Duke Shi of Shao (the half-brother of the Duke of Zhou encountered above), and King Cheng made use of the Duke of Zhou. At the level of hegemons, Xunzi cites Duke Huan of Qi who "spent his time in the inner palace in suspending musical instruments and in excursions and amusements," and yet was able to unite and order the world, and assemble the regional rulers in allegiance to him. The secret to his success is of course none other than his employment of Guan Zhong (see Chapter 1). See *Xunzi* 11.9c.

The idea that a ruler who employs a worthy minister will become a true king at best, and a hegemon at the least, can be understood to suggest a distinction between a ruler who, with the assistance of a good minister, is able to raise himself to the position of a true king, and another, less capable one, who can raise himself only to the position of a hegemon even while relying on similar assistance.[24] On the other hand, the ministers themselves can be of different calibers: on the one hand, there are ministers who follow rituals and rightness; on the other hand, Xunzi mentions ministers who are merely "correct" (*duan* 端), "sincere" (*cheng* 誠), "trustworthy" (*xin* 信), and "complete" (*quan* 全).[25] Xunzi calls the former sage (*sheng* 聖) ministers and the latter meritorious (*gong* 功) ministers. He explains that meritorious ministers are able to unify the people within and overcome difficulties outside. The people love them and the scholars trust them. They are, in turn, loyal to the ruler and love the common people. The examples of meritorious ministers include Guan Zhong, but also a certain Uncle Fan of Jin and Sunshu Ao of Chu (encountered in Chapter 2 in Mencius's list of able statesmen).[26] One could also cite Boli Xi, mentioned in Chapter 2, who made Duke Mu one of the five hegemons.[27] As for the sage ministers, they too honor their ruler and love the people. In addition, however, they instruct the people, adapt to changing circumstances, and draw inferences from similar cases to respond to cases for which a standard of response is unavailable. In short, sage ministers exhibit wisdom and virtue that is not attained by the meritorious ministers and that enables them to understand the rationale behind rituals and other regulative principles, and thus choose when and how to apply them.

Assisted by a sage minister, a ruler can become either a true king, or a hegemon, depending on his own qualities. On the other hand, if the minister employed is less than a sage, though good enough, then the ruler can either value (*gui* 貴) him and become a hegemon, respect (*jing* 敬) him and merely survive, or neglect (*man* 慢) him and perish. To be-

[24] This is the view suggested in the *Mencius* where Mencius is encouraged to take up an official post with the argument that he can turn the ruler either into a king or at least into a hegemon, indicating that what matters is the character of the ruler, not that of the minister. See *Mencius* 2A.2 and 3B.1.

[25] Answering a question about what makes a person a minister, Xunzi lists the following qualities: "to wait on the [ruler] according to ritual principles, to be loyal, obedient and not lazy" (*Xunzi* 12.3). Though rituals are listed here, rightness and *ren* are not. Moreover, the qualities listed are more akin to orderly conduct than to virtuousness.

[26] *Xunzi* 13.1.

[27] *Xunzi* 25.10.

come a sage king he would need to honor (*zun* 尊) a sage, not merely value a worthy.[28]

To conclude, there are two ways to understand the significance of ministers for Xunzi: On the one hand, whether sage assistants to sage kings or meritorious assistants to powerful rulers, ministers are always responsible for the business of daily government and of running the state bureaucracy. Though he recognizes the crucial role ministers play in Xunzi's vision of government, Yuri Pines argues that the delegation of powers to ministers is a "practical" solution to the problem of having bad monarchs.[29] This allows him to maintain that Xunzi believes that "the power of the monarch should be theoretically limitless."[30] This claim is true to the extent that the Confucians do not propose legal and institutional mechanisms for checking the ruler's power. But the preceding (and following) account of the importance of ministers does not rest on the likelihood of having a bad ruler; rather, the division of labor between ruler and ministers holds universally. On the other hand, when in fact an average ruler arises, ministers' responsibility simply increases, as they work to ensure his becoming a hegemon, that is, someone who can enforce order and unite the country. In other words, at the level of "suboptimality," ministers are themselves the guarantors of political order. This is made evident by the references to Duke Huan of Qi, Duke Mu of Qin, and the ruler of Chu in the three Confucian texts in that they are all references to the effect that they were assisted by Guan Zhong, Boli Xi, and Sunshu Ao, respectively. Indeed, in order to show the Confucian support for hegemons in Chapter 1, I had to resort to a discussion of Guan Zhong, not Duke Huan, precisely because more was said about the former than about the latter.

Insubordinate Ministers

I have elaborated in the preceding part of the chapter on Xunzi's vision of government, arguing that ministers are assigned the task of government administration. The importance of ministers, however, goes further than this: not only are they the government's enforcers, but they

---

[28] *Xunzi* 24.5.

[29] See Pines, *Envisioning Eternal Empire*, 90, 93, 96, 106.

[30] See Pines, *Envisioning Eternal Empire*, 106. Similarly, Sa Mengwu argues that Xunzi favors a "unitary autocratic ruler" and that he is similar to Hobbes in this regard. See Sa, *Zhongguo zhengzhi sixiang shi*, 50. I find the charge of "autocracy" misleading in both Xunzi's and Hobbes's cases (the latter case is beyond the scope of this book).

also check the ruler's potential mistakes and abuses. They do so by remonstrating against the ruler when he fails to fulfill his duties or makes decisions harmful to the country. In other words, they rule not only in an administrative sense, but also in a more ambitious political sense, with an eye to ensuring that political order is maintained in their societies. This further explains the importance of their being virtuous, or at least meritorious. This feature of Xunzi's thought, namely the political independence of ministers from rulers, is also shared by Confucius and Mencius. I start with Xunzi:

> Desiring to reply with inward good feelings
> even when his words of advice are not heeded,
> he fears he will endure the difficulties of [Wu] Zixu[31]
> who went forward in remonstrance, but was not heeded
> so his throat was cut and he was put in a sack
> to be cast away, thrown into the Yangzi.[32]

The fear of a fate similar to Zixu's notwithstanding, Xunzi admonishes ministers to remonstrate. But the call to remonstrate is not merely a blank call on the part of Xunzi. It is a layered, conditional, and qualified call. First, obedience and disobedience are both dependent on benefiting the ruler (not personally, but rather in his pursuit of political order). So when a minister follows the commands of the ruler for the ruler's benefit, this is "obedience," but contravening the ruler's commands, when this is also done for the benefit of the ruler, also counts as "loyalty." On the flip side, following a ruler's commands even though they do not benefit him is called "flattery," and contravening his commands for the minister's personal benefit is "usurpation." Finally, not to care about the ruler's honor and disgrace or about the state's fate, and to be concerned only with one's own revenue and relations, is tantamount to being "a threat to the state."[33]

---

[31] A famous protagonist of Chinese lore, he became a minister in the state of Wu during the Spring and Autumn period. Upon the ascendancy of a new king, he lost favor and the king offered him a sword to cut his own throat with.

[32] *Xunzi* 25.43.

[33] *Xunzi* 13.2. Furthermore, contravening the ruler's wishes, even when undertaken for the benefit of the ruler and the state, is not of a single genus, and is subject to Xunzi's fondness for categorization. Xunzi offers a four-fold classification: "remonstrating," "contesting," "assisting," and "opposing." See *Xunzi* 13.2. It is not easy to see what classification principle is at use to distinguish these four praiseworthy categories of ministers. Remonstrating and contesting seem to be related to giving advice, while opposing and assisting seem to be related to taking action. Though historical examples follow the four categories to illustrate them, it actually seems as if the categories are based on the

On the other hand, Xunzi also offers a three-tier ranking of loyalty in which remonstration is actually given an inferior position.[34] According to him, loyalty at the highest degree is to use the Way to protect and transform the ruler. Loyalty at a second degree is to use one's virtue to conciliate the ruler and assist him. Loyalty at a third degree is to use right to remonstrate against wrong and, in so doing, anger the ruler. There is finally the category of one who is a threat to the state, concerned with one's personal, rather than public, welfare.[35] The example Xunzi gives for the second degree of loyalty is that of Guan Zhong in relation to Duke Huan (which is somewhat baffling, because Guan Zhong is never otherwise mentioned as relying on "virtue" in assisting Duke Huan). The example given for the third degree of loyalty is Wu Zixu, who was killed for remonstrating against the new king of Wu. On one level, Guan Zhong ranks higher than Wu Zixu simply because he happened to serve a ruler more open to advice than the ruler served by Wu Zixu. On the other hand, another reading of the ranking of these two is possible, which revolves around asking about the results of the actions of both ministers. What is the consequence of Wu Zixu's action, however virtuous it might have been? To get him killed without having effected any change in the ruler. What is the consequence of Guan Zhong's assistance to Duke Huan, however lacking in morality his motives might have been? To help Duke Huan become one of the leading hegemons of his time, thus ensuring security and order in his state. A comparison of both results explains why Guan Zhong is more praiseworthy, and thus higher on the scale of loyalty, than Wu Zixu. This reasoning also makes sense of Xunzi's statement that though one should remonstrate against and contest an average ruler, one should not seek to oppose or correct a cruel one, for futile morally motivated

---

historical examples themselves, rather than the other way round—which would explain the absence of an evident classification principle.

[34] This leads Sa Mengwu to argue that Xunzi supports obedience (in comparison to Mencius who advocates remonstration). See Sa, *Zhongguo zhengzhi sixiang shi*, 44–45. A few remarks can be made in response to this interpretation: first, it is clear from the preceding passage that Xunzi does not consider obedience as such to be good (obeying bad commands is actually bad). On the other hand, it is clear from the passage under study that Xunzi prefers there to be no need to resort to remonstration in the first place, arguably because of his emphasis on hierarchy, while Mencius's tone, as will be clear below, is more combative than his. Yet Mencius is more combative about the respect owed to worthy ministers (rather than about remonstration as such). I am thus inclined to the view that Xunzi's and Mencius's positions are ultimately similar, both advocating remonstration, but only when strictly necessary.

[35] *Xunzi* 13.6.

actions are less politically good than efficacious actions that are lacking in moral motivations.[36]

That the obligation to remonstrate should be sensitive to the consequences of such remonstration is also made clear in Xunzi's account of a supposed encounter between Duke Ai of Lu and Confucius. The anecdote is meant to illustrate the meaning and importance of filial piety and ministerial integrity: the Duke asks the Master whether a son is filial who follows the commands of his father, and whether a minister acts with integrity who follows the commands of his ruler. Confucius does not respond but later on puts the question to Zigong who answers in the affirmative. Confucius disagrees with Zigong's answer on both counts. What is interesting in this disagreement for my purposes here is the way in which Confucius lays out the importance of remonstrating ministers. According to him, the presence of "contesting ministers" (*zhengchen* 爭臣) ensures that the state is preserved, when it comes to its territory, its "altars of soil and grain," and its "ancestral shrine."[37] Xunzi's Confucius does not say that the ministers' contestation leads the ruler to undertake a virtuous act or refrain from committing an immoral one (whereas, in what follows, he says that a father who has a remonstrating son will conduct himself according to ritual principle, while a man of service [*shi*] who has remonstrating friends will not act against rightness). The importance of ministers' integrity is glossed rather as engendering the security of the state. In other words, the standard of good political conduct, as I argued in Chapter 1, is intimately tied to the preservation of political order. This is not an ideal of virtuous ministers opposing the demands of realpolitik. It is an ideal of ministers who understand what it takes to maintain a state and protect its people. This, again, explains why Guan Zhong ranks higher than Wu Zixu.

Turning now to the *Analects*, the principle it proposes for organizing the relationship between ruler and minister is the unsurprising idea that "the ruler should employ the services of his subjects in accordance with the rites. A subject should serve his ruler [with loyalty]."[38] Extant

---

[36] *Xunzi* 13.3. On serving a cruel ruler, Xunzi says, "With him, one proceeds 'as though one were driving unbroken horses,' 'as though one were caring for an infant,' or 'as though one were feeding a starving man.' Thus, one should avail oneself of his fears to modify his excesses, use his distress to acquaint him with its causation, depend on his pleasures to get entrance for the Way, and avail oneself of his wrath to eliminate those who bear him animosity—these are the indirect ways to obtain the goal" (*Xunzi* 13.4).

[37] *Xunzi* 29.3.

[38] *Analects* 3.19.

ministers are judged according to this principle. Thus, Zichan, a minister in the state of Zheng, is said to be a gentleman because of his respectful deportment and his caring for the people, but also for being "reverent in the service of his [superiors]."[39] That said, not all superiors deserve the same reverence. For example, Zilu and Ran Qiu are called "place-holders" (*juchen* 具臣)[40] or in Lau's translation, "ministers appointed to make up the full quota." Their failure does not stem from a lack of loyalty, but rather from a misplacement of loyalty, since they faithfully obey the commands of the Ji family (the usurpers of Zhou prerogative). Because of their perseverance in serving rulers who will not follow advice that accords with the Way, Confucius refuses to give them the title of "great ministers," which he defines as ministers "who serve their [ruler] according to the Way and who, when this is no longer possible, relinquish office."[41]

We can already see, in this definition of great ministers as ones who should not serve when it is no longer possible to advise on the right path, that the ministers of the *Analects* are not supposed to always follow the commands of their rulers—notwithstanding the language of "loyalty" and "reverence."[42] Indeed, even Zilu and Ran Qiu are said not to be willing to obey the ruler if asked to do something as outrageous as killing their own father.[43] But moving away from such an extreme example, consider the importance of remonstration. Asked about a saying that can lead a state to ruin, Confucius answers, "There is a saying amongst men: 'I do not at all enjoy being a ruler, except for the fact that no one goes against what I say.' If what he says is good and no one goes against him, good. But if what he says is not good and no one goes against him, then is this not almost a case of a saying leading the state to ruin?"[44] On the flip side of this advice to rulers, Confucius advises Zilu on the way to serve a ruler: "Make sure that you are not being dishonest with him when you stand up to him."[45] Clearly, then, the necessity of remonstration is enshrined both in the duty of the ruler

---

[39] *Analects* 5.16.

[40] See *The Analects of Confucius: A Philosophical Translation*, trans. Roger T. Ames and Henry Rosemont (New York: Ballantine Books, 1998).

[41] *Analects* 11.24.

[42] *Analects* 13.23: "The gentleman harmonizes (*he* 和) with others without agreeing (*tong* 同) with them" (quoted from Slingerland) is taken by Slingerland to represent the attitude ministers should have toward the ruler.

[43] See also *Analects* 11.24 where it is said that they would also not kill their ruler (i.e., the ruler of Lu), presumably if asked to do so by the Ji family.

[44] *Analects* 13.15.

[45] *Analects* 14.22.

to maintain the state and in the responsibility of the minister to do his best to help the ruler achieve this duty.

Two anecdotes from the *Analects* illustrate the duty of the minister. One anecdote revolves around Confucius himself: Upon hearing the news that Chen Chengzi assassinated Duke Jian of Qi, he bathes himself ceremonially (as is required before a minister meets the ruler) then reports the news to Duke Ai of Lu, asking him to punish the perpetrator. The king asks him to report it instead to the heads of the three important families in the state of Lu. Confucius says, "Having rank below the [counselors], I did not dare to not report this. Now you tell me: 'Report it to the Three.'" When the Three refuse his request, Confucius repeats the same statement: "Having rank below the [counselors], I did not dare to not report."[46] As it stands, this anecdote suggests a rather subdued form of remonstration, where Confucius seems to merely go through the motions, so to speak, reminding his ruler of his duty to avenge a wrongful crime, without the insistence characteristic of Xunzi's remonstrating minister. Remonstration takes a more pronounced form, however, in the second anecdote: Ran Qiu and Zilu complain to Confucius that the Ji family whom they serve (and who de facto rules the state of Lu) is preparing to attack Zhuanyu, a small dependent state located inside the state of Lu. Confucius asks about the reasons for the attack, and Ran Qiu answers, "It is what our master wishes. Neither of us is in favor of it."[47] Confucius scolds Ran Qiu—the most senior of the two, saying,

> "Qiu! There is a saying of Zhou Ren's which goes: let men who have strength to display join the ranks, let those who lack the strength give up their places. What use to a blind man is the assistant who does not steady him when he totters or support him when he falls. Moreover, what you said is quite wrong. Whose fault is it when the tiger and the rhinoceros escape from their cages or when the tortoise shell and the jade are destroyed in their caskets?"
>
> Ran Qiu said, "But Zhuanyu is strongly fortified and close to Bi [a Ji family stronghold]. If it is not taken now, it is sure to be a source of trouble for the descendants of our master in the future."

[46] *Analects* 14.21, quoted from Slingerland.
[47] Slingerland explains that the ruler of Zhuanyu was appointed by the Zhou King to serve the altars of the state of Lu, a fact that the Ji family resented.

Confucius said, "Qiu, the gentleman detests those who, rather than saying outright that they want something, can be counted on to gloss over their remarks . . . you and Zilu have not been able either to help your master to attract the distant subjects when they are unsubmissive or to preserve the state when it is disintegrating. Instead, you propose to resort to the use of arms within the state itself. I am afraid that Ji Sun's worries lie not in Zhuanyu but within the walls of his palace."[48]

In an exemplary move, Confucius shifts the locus of responsibility from the Ji family to the ministers themselves. When the rhinoceros escapes from his cage, one cannot blame the rhinoceros himself. The guardian is to be blamed. In language reminiscent of Xunzi's, Confucius admonishes the two ministers to take on their duty as brave assistants and remonstrate against the ruler's bad decision, fulfilling what Schwartz describes as "ministerial initiative" in the *Analects*.[49]

This said, it is not obvious that ministers will necessarily be successful in their attempts at persuading a bad ruler, especially if the latter is cruel like Zhou Xin. In this case, means other than persuasion are in order: indeed, Weizi had to leave Zhou Xin, Jizi became a slave because of him, and Bigan was killed.[50] As Slingerland explains, the responses of the three "*ren* men of Yin," as Confucius calls them,[51] differ because their situations differ: Weizi, as the eldest son of the previous Shang ruler, felt that he had a duty to maintain the sacrifices in the family's ancestral temple, and thus fled in order to do so. Jizi, on the other hand, was the eldest uncle of Zhou Xin's and, seeing that his remonstration came to naught, feigned madness to get enslaved. He wanted to preserve his life because he felt that, as the senior uncle, he might have important official roles to fulfill in the future. Finally, Bigan was a younger uncle of Zhou Xin's and a minor official, and thus felt less bound to family and official obligations, and freer to engage in forthright remonstration (and to get himself killed for it).[52] The fact that Confucius approves of these three ministers shows that candid remonstration against all odds is not the Confucian ideal of ministerial conduct. Instead, remonstration is to be thought of in relation to family and political obligations.

[48] *Analects* 16.1.
[49] Schwartz, *World of Thought in Ancient China*, 114.
[50] *Analects* 18.1.
[51] *Analects* 18.1.
[52] Slingerland, trans., *Confucius: Analects*, 213.

Finally, Confucius also offers, besides his advocacy of remonstration, a conception of ministerial responsibility in the absence of a worthy ruler similar to Xunzi's. For example, in one relevant anecdote,
Confucius speaks about the licentiousness of Duke Ling of Wei. Ji
Kangzi asks how he never lost his state. Confucius answers, "Zhongshu
Yu was responsible for foreign visitors, Priest Tuo for the ancestral temple and Wangsun Jia for military affairs. That being the case, what
question could there be of his losing his state?"[53] The ministers mentioned by Confucius are all lacking in virtue: though Zhongshu Yu
(also known as Kong Wenzi) is said to be fond of learning and to be
accepting of inferiors' advice, Slingerland explains that Confucius de-
fends him thusly precisely because he is otherwise known to be a dis-
solute person.[54] Priest Tuo, on the other hand, is known for his
"glibness,"[55] and Wangsun Jia for going against the demands of ritual.[56]
Morally deficient as they are, these three ministers appropriately fulfilled their ministerial duties. They might not have propagated virtue,
but they certainly maintained order and security for their state. Here,
like in the *Xunzi*, we find ministers stepping in, in the absence of sage
rulers, to uphold political order themselves. Moreover, this is combined with an account of lofty rulers also similar to Xunzi's. Here are,
for example, pieces of a portrait of sage Emperors Yao and Shun:

> How lofty Yao and Shun were in holding aloof (*buyu* 不與) from
> the Empire while they were in possession of it.[57]
>
> Great indeed was Yao as a ruler! How lofty! It is Heaven that is
> great and it was Yao who modeled himself upon it. He was so
> boundless that the common people were not able to put a name to
> his virtues. Lofty was he in his successes and brilliant was he in
> his accomplishments.[58]
>
> If there was a ruler who achieved order without taking any ac-
> tion (*wuwei* 無為), it was, perhaps, Shun. There was nothing for

[53] *Analects* 14.19.

[54] *Analects* 5.15. See Slingerland, trans., *Confucius: Analects*, 45.

[55] *Analects* 6.16, quoted from Slingerland.

[56] *Analects* 3.13. The passage is complicated and can be read to suggest either Wangsun Jia's prioritization of food over ritual, or his belief that he should be consulted as the
real wielder of power in Wei, not the ruler of Wei himself. On this, see Slingerland, trans.,
Confucius: Analects, 22.

[57] *Analects* 8.18. On Heaven as a model of effortless rule, since it does not spell out its
orders ("Heaven does not speak"), see *Analects* 17.19 and Slingerland's commentary on
it.

[58] *Analects* 8.19.

him to do but to hold himself in a respectful posture and to face due south.[59]

Slingerland writes that two interpretations have been proposed for the notion of *wu wei*. Either it refers to the ruler's disposition after filling all the ministerial posts or, alternatively, it symbolizes his rule by virtue through which he effortlessly transforms those around him.[60] The evidence adduced in the previous chapters concerning the regulations and institutional mechanisms through which Confucian government works weighs against the latter interpretation. The first one is therefore more plausible on my account.

Like Xunzi and Confucius, Mencius offers a conception of independent-minded ministers, but he focuses more on the rulers' need to heed their ministers' advice than on the duty of the latter to remonstrate. He offers an analogy to the master carpenter and the jade cutter: if the king wants to build a big house, he expects the master carpenter to find timber for it. Similarly, if the king has a piece of uncut jade, he entrusts it to a jade-cutter, however expensive it is. Now, "when it comes to the government of your state, you say, 'Just put aside what you have learned and do as I tell you.' In what way is this different from teaching the jade-cutter his job?"[61] The thought here seems to be that the aptitude required to advise on matters of government is a skill like carpentry and jade-cutting. However, this does not necessarily mean, when Mencius says of the person entrusted with a ministerial position that "since his childhood, [he] has been acquiring knowledge, naturally wishes to put his knowledge to use when he grows up,"[62] that this refers to a specialized kind of knowledge and training. A more generalist education is more probably what Mencius means here, as explained in Chapter 2. In any case, the point is that the ruler should listen to those who understand affairs of state. Special courtesies are even due to the ones whose advice benefits the people.[63]

This is at the level of how the ruler should respond to a worthy minister. As to how ministers should treat their ruler, this strongly depends on how they are treated by him: if he treats them as his "hands and

[59] *Analects* 15.5.
[60] Slingerland, trans., *Confucius: Analects*, 175.
[61] *Mencius* 1B.9.
[62] *Mencius* 1B.9.
[63] Such as escorting him out of the country when he decides to leave and not confiscating his land before three years of absence (*Mencius* 4B.3).

feet, they will treat him as their belly and heart. If he treats them as his horses and hounds, they will treat him as a mere fellow country-man. If he treats them as mud and weeds, they will treat him as an enemy."[64] To see how this works, consider an example of a minister being treated like a horse and a hound. The example involves Zisi who kept receiving gifts in the name of Duke Mu of Qin and, according to protocol, had to bow every time he did. Zisi became indignant. As Mencius explains, "to make him bob up and down rendering thanks for the gift of meat for the tripod was hardly the right way to take care of a gentleman (*junzi* 君子)."[65] To see how Zisi preferred to be treated, we can refer to Mencius's recounting of a conversation between Duke Mu and Zisi, where Duke Mu asks, "How did kings of states with a thousand chariots in antiquity make friends with [men of service] (*shi* 士)?" Zisi does not like the question. Mencius explains Zisi's reasoning: "In point of position, you are the prince and I am your [minister]. How dare I be friends with you? In point of virtue, it is you who ought to serve me. How can you presume to be friends with me?" Mencius continues that if a ruler cannot presume to be friends with a scholar, then he surely cannot feel free to summon him.[66]

We thus get to the key idea in Mencius, mentioned in Chapter 1, on the relationship between rulers and ministers, namely that of "ministers who cannot be summoned" (*suo buzhao zhi chen* 所不召之臣). This idea is expounded in an anecdote involving Mencius himself: One day, while Mencius was getting prepared to go to court, he receives a message from the king saying that he wanted to go see him, but feeling sick, prefers that Mencius comes to him the next day instead. Mencius, feigning illness, replies that he will not be able to make it. Avoiding a doctor sent to him by the king, Mencius spends the night at Jing Chou's. Jing confronts Mencius with the stipulations of the rites: "When summoned by one's father, one should not answer, I am coming [but go immediately]. When summoned by one's prince, one should not wait for the horses to be harnessed." Mencius answers with a supposed saying by Zengzi: "They may have their wealth, but I have my *ren*; they may have their exalted rank but I have my rightness. In what way do I suffer by comparison?" He adds that, among the three things that people value (rank, age, and virtue), having only one (i.e., rank) is no excuse to treat others with condescension, especially that,

---

[64] *Mencius* 4B.3.
[65] *Mencius* 5B.6.
[66] *Mencius* 5B.7.

though rank is important at court, and age in the village, virtue (*de* 德) is the most valuable of the three for government. Mencius concludes with the idea that "a prince who is to achieve great things must have [officials] he does not summon."[67]

Mencius's vision is, as I will discuss more fully below, more virtue-laden than Xunzi's: it involves, as the foregoing reveals, virtuous men refusing to submit to the mere prerogative of rank when devoid of virtue. This said, what is noteworthy about the historical examples Mencius uses to illustrate the idea of ministers who cannot be summoned is that he cites Guan Zhong. I have already discussed, in Chapter 1, Mencius's clear ambivalence about Guan Zhong, which is evident in his statement that if "even Guan Zhong could not be summoned, much less someone who would not be a Guan Zhong." Ambivalent as he might be, the fact is that Mencius cites Guan Zhong as an example of a minister who cannot be summoned, and a minister from whom Duke Huan learned, helping him to "become a leader of the [regional rulers] without much effort."[68] In a sense, then, we find in Mencius echoes, albeit faint, of Xunzi's view that what makes the position of a minister who stands up to the ruler important is not necessarily (or, more accurately in Mencius's case, not only) that he stands up for morality against vice, but also that he stands up for successful government against weakness and disorder.[69] This would be particularly important in the absence of a sage king.

---

[67] *Mencius* 2B.2. This said, Mencius seems to qualify his idea of ministers who cannot be summoned in his answer to Wan Zhang's claim that Confucius (contrary to Mencius himself) answered the summoning of his prince without waiting for his horse to be harnessed. This is how Mencius justifies Confucius's behavior: "Confucius was in office and had specific duties, and he was summoned in his official capacity" (*Mencius* 5B.7). This answer thus suggests that only scholars who do not hold official positions can resist the ruler's summoning (in which case, one could translate, with Lau, 所不召之臣 as "subjects who cannot be summoned" rather than as "officials who cannot be summoned"). But this goes counter to the historical examples Mencius provides, which involve two ministers, Yi Yin and Guan Zhong, who were not to be summoned by their respective rulers, Prince Tang and Duke Huan. It is therefore likely that Mencius's statement about Confucius being warranted in rushing to meet his prince is an attempt on Mencius's part to find exceptions for Confucius's behavior, as he does for the sage kings of antiquity (as I mentioned in Chapter 1).

[68] *Mencius* 2B.2.

[69] Pines argues that it is only Xunzi among our three Confucians who equates, like his student Han Feizi, the ministerial role with the preservation of the political realm (rather than of the moral Way). My contention is that Confucius and, to some extent, Mencius also understand ministers as stepping in to defend the state (rather than only virtue as such). See Pines, *Envisioning Eternal Empire*, 177–79.

On the other hand, Mencius neither portrays an aloof and lofty ruler nor talks about ministers as frequently as Xunzi and Confucius do. He argues, as mentioned above, that rulers should honor ministers and listen to them, and that ministers should refuse to obey improper commands, but he does not say that ministers should be left to run the daily business of government. Yet to the extent that Mencius argues for the hereditary succession of rulers, as I discussed in Chapter 1, it is the ministers who are left with the reins of government, and this is precisely why these ministers should be such that they "cannot be summoned."

Revisiting the Question of Virtuous Rulership

In the preceding section, I argued that Mencius and Confucius agree with Xunzi that kings should heed their ministers' advice and that, when they do not, ministers not only can, but should, remonstrate against them, or at least refuse to obey their commands (as applies more accurately to Mencius). I also showed that ministers are often left with the reins of government, not only for Xunzi, but also for Confucius and even for Mencius.

Highlighting the role of ministers is not only important, however, for explaining the way government functions. It also leads us back to the question of the relationship between virtue and government since, while rulers can be chosen through hereditary succession, ministers are chosen on the basis of merit. I also argued above that for Mencius the basis for ministers' and advisors' defiance of rulers is their virtue. And Xunzi, although he accepts meritorious ministers, also offers a category of sagely ones. In fact, even though rulers are preferably to be chosen through hereditary succession, this does not stop the Confucians from expressing preference for the rise of sage kings. Thus, Xunzi's ruler is described as embodying rightness,[70] and ritual propriety,[71] in addition to being fair,[72] and promoting the worthy.[73] Similarly, in the *Analects*, despite the large role left for ministerial initiative, the qualities that distinguish rulers are ritual propriety (*li* 禮),[74] trustworthiness (*xin* 信),[75]

---

[70] *Xunzi* 9.3, 9.9, 9.18, 11.1a, 11.2b 15.1c, 15.5.
[71] *Xunzi* 11.1a, 11.2b, 15.1c, 15.5.
[72] *Xunzi* 9.4.
[73] *Xunzi* 9.4, 15.5. For a more complete discussion, see Chapter 2.
[74] *Analects* 1.9, 2.3, 3.19, 4.13, 7.31, 13.4, 14.41, 15.33, 16.2.
[75] *Analects* 1.5, 12.7, 13.4, 19.10, 20.1.

reverence (*jing* 敬),[76] the promotion of the worthy,[77] and impartiality.[78] Mencius's ruler is said to embody rightness (*yi* 義),[79] wisdom (*zhi* 智),[80] and virtue (*de* 德) more generally.[81] We also find in the *Mencius* and the *Xunzi*, the idea of a *ren* ruler,[82] and specifically in the former, the idea of a "*ren* government" (*renzheng* 仁政).[83] The question then that the preceding raises concerns the relationship between the ruler and/or the minister's virtue and the promotion of political order, which I have been emphasizing in this and previous chapters.

Let me start with the idea of a "*ren* government" (*renzheng* 仁政). *Ren* is a complicated concept meant to capture an ideal of Confucian virtuousness, characterized by the aptitude to respond well to others, near and far. As Stephen Angle defines the concept, it is "not just caring, not just sympathy, but warm and compassionate concern that extends, in an organic fashion, to all related and relevant aspects of one's context."[84] The interesting aspect of *ren* that I want to point to here is that it is not clear that it means exactly the same thing as an attribute of government as when it connotes a more general virtue (which is as it should be, to the extent that virtues are differently instantiated in different contexts). While on the personal level it is not defined in relationship to the idea of giving to others,[85] *ren* government is defined precisely as one that

[76] *Analects* 1.5, 6.2. See also related ideas such as deference (*rang* 讓) in 4.13, respectfulness (*gong* 恭) in 15.5, and dignity (*zhuang* 莊) in 2.20 and 15.33.

[77] *Analects* 2.19, 2.20, 12.22, 13.2. For a discussion of the promotion of the worthy, see Chapter 2.

[78] See Chapter 1. It is interesting to note that *ren*, rightness, and wisdom are not mentioned in relation to the ruler in the *Analects* (except if one takes *Analects* 12.22 as indicating that the ruler should be wise and *ren*).

[79] See *Mencius* 1A.1, 4A.20, 4B.5, 7B.12.

[80] *Mencius* 1B.3, 2B.9, 4A.1, 4A.4.

[81] *Mencius* 2B.2.

[82] *Mencius* 4A.3; *Xunzi* 9.9, 9.18.

[83] See *Mencius* 1A.5, 1B.11, 1B.12, 2A.1, 3A.3, 3A.4, 4A.1, 4A.14. Variations on this idea can also be found in *Mencius* 1A.7, 4A.7, 4A.9, 7B.4.

[84] Angle, *Sagehood*, 78. Even though Angle's definition is related to the concept of *ren* in Neo-Confucian, rather than Classical Confucian, thought, it applies to the latter as well.

[85] Part of the problem with capturing the meaning of *ren* concerns whether the concept is universally connected to a notion of generosity, or providing for others. For *ren* is associated with material generosity only when it comes to the depiction of the ruler in the *Mencius*. In the *Analects*, all we find is the idea that the exemplary person should provide for his parents, making sure they are well nourished and well clothed (see, for example, 2.8). Otherwise, in his dealings with others, he should mainly be trustworthy (*xin* 信), be dutiful (*zhong* 忠), and treat others with reciprocity (*shu* 恕), i.e., according to Confucius's version of the Golden Rule, "Do not impose on others what you yourself do not desire" (see *Analects* 15.24; also see, for the other qualities, *Analects* 1.6, 1.7, 2.22, 4.15).

provides for the people in the way described in Chapter 2. Indeed, Mencius himself says that one could have a *ren* heart but still fail in benefiting the people,[86] suggesting that what is *ren* about *ren* government is not so much that the ruler has a *ren* heart but that he provides for the people.[87] This is much more likely to happen when a ruler (or his minister) is himself *ren*, but one wonders whether this is actually strictly speaking necessary.

Immediately after the previous statement, Mencius quotes approvingly the following saying:

> Goodness (*shan* 善) alone is not sufficient for government;
> The law (*fa* 法) unaided cannot make itself effective.[88]

Xu Fuguan, citing this passage, as well as another telling passage from the *Mencius* (The gentleman should not be in the business of helping each individual cross the river, but should rather rely on the bridges to be built),[89] in addition to Mencius's statements on providing for the people, including the economic principles he advocates and which I discussed in Chapter 2, argues that whenever Mencius speaks about government (*zheng* 政) in these passages, he is speaking about methods of governing (*zhifa* 治法).[90] The point then is to highlight the importance of government regulations for Mencius, and thus to suggest that his emphasis on virtuous rulers to a large part stems from the latter's ability to initiate such regulations, like opening schools, limiting tariffs, setting up a merit-based promotion system, and so on in order to achieve political order. Virtue is not, in other words, effortless. And if it holds transformative power, the transformation happens through the mechanisms virtuous rulers (and/or ministers) set into place, not through the power of example. This is not to deny all role for the power of example: virtuous rulers can be said to provide a public model of

---

Nowhere is there any reference, in any of the three Confucian texts, to a general requirement to provide for the poor and help the needy, or even to be simply generous. The requirement to provide for others is thus distinctive of the ruler (mainly of Mencius's ruler), not part of the general definition of virtue or *ren*.

[86] *Mencius* 4A.1. See also *Mencius* 4B.16, where Mencius argues that one can never subdue the people through goodness (*shan* 善), but that one can use goodness to provide for them.

[87] This reasoning would explain why, in *Analects* 14.16, Guan Zhong's actions could appear to be *ren* even if he is not. See chapter 1, note 106 of this volume.

[88] I thank Aaron Stalnaker for alerting me to this passage and to the importance of *fa* for Mencius and the early Confucians more generally.

[89] *Mencius* 4B.2.

[90] Xu, *Zhongguo sixiang shi lunji*, 138.

filial conduct for the people to follow, as I argued in the previous chapter.

It is the link between *ren* and regulations (*fa*) that Xunzi opens up in his account of hegemons. Like Mencius, Xunzi appreciates the importance of a virtuous ruler as well as good regulations/laws, but he is much more explicit about the idea that one is not necessary for the other. It is indeed by delinking them that he opens up in a systematic manner the space for hegemons as a category of decent rulers and meritorious ministers as a category of good ministers. As I mentioned in Chapter 1, the difference between a true king and a hegemon is glossed more than once in the *Xunzi* as consisting in the fact that a ruler who extols rituals and honors the worthy becomes a king, while one who stresses *fa* and loves the people becomes a hegemon (*renjunzhe, longli zunxian er wang, zhongfa aimin er ba* 人君者，隆禮尊賢而王，重法愛民而霸).[91]

On the other hand, the idea that one can pursue *fa* without being *ren*, or virtuous more generally, is in tension with a discussion by Xunzi to the effect that it is the gentleman (*junzi*), that is, the noble or virtuous man, who is the wellspring of *fa* (which also leads Xunzi to maintain that the order brought about by *fa* is really the work of men, thus one can speak of orderly men, but not of orderly *fa*: *you zhiren, wu zhifa* 有治人，無治法).[92] One way to solve this tension, which is compatible with the multiple uses of *fa* in the *Xunzi*, is to posit two senses of it: in one sense, *fa* is simply an abstract model, a template so to speak, and both the idea that we need a template to organize society, together with the actual template, can be attributed to gentlemen (just like the initial "discovery" of rituals can be attributed to sage kings).[93] In the second sense, *fa* is closer to meaning what we would call "laws" and involves regulations of the sort discussed in Chapter 2, meaning taxation schemes, economic regulations, standards for rewards and punishments, and so on.[94] As Harris argues, the latter can be taken to be a "subset of [the] broader sense of *fa*."[95] It is the second type of *fa* only

[91] *Xunzi* 16.1, 17.9, and 27.1.

[92] *Xunzi* 12.1.

[93] Sa Mengwu points to the relationship between *fa* (in the abstract sense) and rituals by citing *Xunzi* 2.11, in which Xunzi says that "to oppose ritual is the same as lacking a model" (非禮是無法也). See Sa, *Zhongguo zhengzhi sixiang shi*, 40. For *fa* as a model, see *Xunzi* 2.11, 9.2, 13.7, and 21.9.

[94] This is indeed how the *fa* are specified in *Xunzi* 9.13. For *fa* as laws, see *Xunzi* 4.3, 10.2, 11.8, 15.6a, 16.3, 22.2a. See also 21.4 where the "Legalist" Shen Dao is criticized for a narrow focus on *fa* that blinded him to worth.

[95] Harris, "Constraining the Ruler," 50.

that can be attributed to hegemons. Hegemons (and their ministers) can be described as mere enforcers of *fa*, whereas gentlemen and sage kings are both enforcers and creators. Since enforcers are necessary, it is not surprising that Xunzi would say that order requires men, rather than simply *fa* as such. Yet creators of *fa* can also tune them to different situations, and thus produce order that is more durable than that produced by the former.[96] This explains why Xunzi says, "although there have been cases in which good *fa* nonetheless produced disorder, I have never heard of a case, from the most distant past to the present day, where there was a gentleman in charge of the government and chaos ensued."[97]

Moreover, it is not only that gentlemen are important as the sources of *fa*, but sage kings are also actually important at the apex of the sociopolitical system. Xunzi's case in this regard is both more difficult and easier than Mencius's. It is more difficult because Xunzi is the one who assigns the highest virtues to the ruler, as can be seen from the summary above, while also offering a complex ritual order that seems even less in need of a virtuous ruler than Mencius's educational vision does. On the other hand, it is easier to see the importance of a virtuous ruler for Xunzi precisely because of this fully worked-out ritual system. As I argued above, in Xunzi's system, in addition to his role in appointing officials, the ruler plays a symbolic role at the apex of a hierarchical, merit-based, sociopolitical order; it is thus important that it be seen that he, the person who occupies the highest political position, is worthy of it. Since he symbolizes the system as a whole, he has to be a symbol worthy of the name. This is what Xunzi means when he says that "when a sage king occupies the highest position and responsibility and duties proper to each social class are observed by his subjects . . . the majesty of his conduct will overawe the people like flooding waters," removing the need for penal sanctions to maintain the system.[98] He does not, however, primarily govern through the power of his example, but through the ritual system that he sets into place.[99] This is

[96] Justin Tiwald argues in relation to Xunzi that "the stage of history in which the models themselves needed to be revised is long past," but he suggests that it would be plausible to assume that Xunzi would give present-day rulers the authority to revise them to the extent that they can prove that the changes they make to these models derive from failures in the latter. In other words, they are "accountable" to these models. See Tiwald, "Xunzi on Moral Expertise," 289. See also Harris, "Constraining the Ruler," 54–58.

[97] *Xunzi* 14.2.

[98] *Xunzi* 24.2.

[99] As well as the establishment of schools to instruct the common people. See *Xunzi* 27.52.

why, while there is more certainty that order will be maintained if sage kings rule, it should not collapse the moment they are replaced by less virtuous rulers. As Rosemont argues,

> If the primary function of the ruler is to appoint his officials, and he is even to be guided in this task by the present office-holders, an unending procession of philosopher-kings will not have to be guaranteed in order to insure the continued harmony and prosperity of the state. As long as the appointments are made and the ceremonial duties fulfilled the ruler may otherwise deport himself in accordance with his desires. It might well require a man of exceptional ability to establish the state, but once founded, Xunzi believed the officials would be able to manage affairs well even during the reigns of less than ordinary monarchs.[100]

To conclude, I have been emphasizing in this book the idea that Confucian political thought is motivated by a concern with political order, not virtue, and have evidenced this idea in Chapter 1 by showing that virtue is not expected from the people and that the Confucians accept a category of rulers, namely hegemons, who are not virtuous. Yet no one can deny that the Confucians also express a preference, even longing, for a sage ruler like Yao and Shun. I have attempted in this section to show why this longing is not incompatible with my insistence on the centrality of order in their political vision: while political order is an end in itself, and not a means toward virtue, a more durable order, as described in the previous chapter, is more likely to obtain with the rule of virtuous men. For Mencius, moreover, even the more basic level of order, described in Chapter 2, requires virtuous men because Mencius links good regulations with virtuous rulers (though, strictly speaking, to the extent that hegemons do pursue at least some good regulations, they also promote order).

Conclusion

In Chapters 1 to 3, I argued that the early Confucians are concerned with the promotion and maintenance of political order. In this chapter, I zoomed in on the government agents responsible for the production of this order: in Xunzi's vision, it is government ministers who administer the realm, while ceremonial kings have the task of appointing

---

[100] Rosemont, "State and Society in the *Xunzi*," 23.

these ministers and, more broadly, of providing legitimacy for society's ritual order.

What I wish to stress in this conclusion is the way in which the arguments I make in this chapter concerning the responsibilities of ministers fit with my overall thesis about the sensitivity of the early Confucians to political realities (in contradistinction to the view that sees them as primarily morally idealistic and distant from politics). There are three ways to see this: first, I argued, in Chapter 1, that the Confucians favored hereditary appointment for the rulers. The reasoning was that hereditary succession provided the most orderly and secure avenue for succession, given the rising competition over the highest political offices and the dangerous conflicts that ensued from it. But hereditary succession means that it is difficult to guarantee the virtuousness of the ruler. This is why it is important to insist on merit as the standard for appointment to all ministerial positions. As Herrlee Creel argues in relation to Confucius, "Confucius did not ... demand that the hereditary rulers vacate their thrones ... Instead, he tried to persuade the hereditary rulers that they should 'reign but not rule,' handing over all administrative authority to ministers chosen for their qualifications."[101]

Second, as I have shown above, even when the ministers are not fully virtuous, they can be, at least for Confucius and Xunzi, effective, brave, and resolute like Guan Zhong, or more generally, correct, loyal, and caring for the common people. This allows them to guarantee political order, propping up their rulers as hegemons.

Finally, I have argued that the explanation for why the early Confucians emphasize the importance of virtuous rulers lies for Xunzi in the thought that the order produced by virtuous men, who are not only holders, but also creators, of rituals and regulations, is longer-lasting (because adapted to the passage of time). Mencius envisions less of a possibility of anyone other than virtuous rulers (or ministers) capable of instituting the sorts of policies and setups that would bring about political order. This said, my interpretation does not rule out the possibility, for both Mencius and Xunzi, that virtuous rulers could also serve as moral exemplars for the people to follow, if it is understood that to take someone as an example is not necessarily to imitate them in their essential traits (but merely in their secondary traits, like honesty, or

[101] Creel, *Chinese Thought*, 417.

dutifulness).[102] In fact, for Mencius, the promotion of filiality, as I showed in Chapter 3, and thus the durable political order which it encourages, does rely on the ruler offering himself as a model of good filial behavior.

The question of ministers' role vis-à-vis rulers was not simply a theoretical one for the early Confucians. They faced the actual dilemma of seeking ministerial positions themselves and of recommending such pursuit to their disciples. But does this mean that the Confucians recommend that their disciples take up positions in the courts of corrupt or incompetent rulers, with the hope of making some improvement on government? In other words, how do their assessments of historical cases of minister-ruler relationships translate into a view of personal obligation? Is there an obligation to take part in politics? Under what conditions does the obligation hold? Should we describe this obligation as moral, political, or both? These are the questions that I will turn to in the chapter which follows.

---

[102] As Eric Hutton argues in "Han Feizi's Criticism of Confucianism and Its Implications for Virtue Ethics," *Journal of Moral Philosophy* 5 (2008): 423–53, there are many ways in which one can understand the Confucian idea of imitating the sages. Hutton favors a middle position where the model to be imitated is not specific such as to encourage emulation *à la lettre* by the wrong people or in the wrong context, and not so general such as to be vacuous.

CHAPTER 5

Political Involvement

ン☉

In the previous chapter, I delineated the responsibilities of ministers vis-à-vis rulers. This chapter deals with the ministerial question again, but from a different, more personal, angle. It asks whether the Confucians saw the pursuit of ministerial positions as a corollary to their teachings, and what limits, if any, they imposed upon such a pursuit. Is involvement in government a duty? If it is a duty, is it a moral one, flowing from the Confucian conception of personal virtue, or a political one, following upon what I have presented as the Confucian concern with political order? Is it permissible, let alone advisable, to seek an official position in the court of a debased ruler?

The question of when it is proper to take up an official post is greatly discussed in the early Confucian texts, especially in the *Analects* and the *Mencius*. Robert Eno has offered the only systematic account of the Confucian view on this question. He argues that Confucian "purism" and idealism isolated "the ritual community of early Confucians from the political hazards of a chaotic era and endowed a style of social withdrawal with the ethical status of conscientious objection."[1] On Eno's view, the early Confucians linked political involvement to the availability of "moral government" and, given the unavailability of such government at the time, "the functional message which these doctrines conveyed to disciples was to enter and persist in Ruist [Confucian] training for ideal political opportunities, while avoiding involvement in actual government."[2]

---

[1] Eno, *Confucian Creation of Heaven*, 1.

[2] Eno, *Confucian Creation of Heaven*, 44–45. For arguments in the same vein, see Roetz, *Confucian Ethics of the Axial Age*, 83–92, and Sim, *Remastering Morals with Aristotle and Confucius*, 185.

I will question Eno's reading in this chapter, showing ways in which the Confucians reveal themselves to be in favor of political engagement, even in troubled times. The chapter will proceed as follows: I start out with some historical preliminaries about the Confucians' own political activities. I then turn to the question of political involvement on the ideal level, that is, to showing that political involvement follows from the Confucian conception of virtue. In the third and central section, I show that the duty of political involvement holds even in troubled times, and that it is justified through a concern with promoting political order.

Biographical Preliminaries

Recall from the prologue that the early Confucians went from one state to another hoping to obtain a ministerial position that would allow them to counsel rulers. Confucius managed to obtain a junior position in his native state of Lu, but one that he eventually lost, causing him to travel to the states of Wei, Song, Chen, and Cai hoping to obtain another. Mencius also traveled around, and the text of the *Mencius* reports encounters between him and the rulers of the states of Liang and Qi, suggesting he might have taken on some advisory role in these. Finally, Xunzi seems to have made a stop in the state of Qi, which was endeavoring to attract scholars, and eventually held a position as a magistrate of the region of Lanling in the state of Chu.

While these biographical data suggest that the early Confucians personally sought to take part in government, it is also true that it is difficult to ascertain the exact motivation behind, and significance of, this quest and the positions they obtained. Eno thus argues that while Confucius's quest is "generally taken to demonstrate that Confucius's commitment to political activism remained undiminished," another way to interpret it is as revealing Confucius's "unwillingness to be flexible about the conditions under which he would seek office," thus suggesting that it was not that the opportunities for holding office were lacking but that Confucius's ethical standards were "too high to seize them."[3] Also in line with his argument that the early Confucians shunned political activism, Eno points out that Mencius sought political experience only as an old man, and that he was not so much a "frustrated politician" as much as an "aging philosopher hoping to use the leverage of his reputation as a wise man to break into politics at the

---

[3] Eno, *Confucian Creation of Heaven*, 45.

highest levels." He also describes Mencius's position in Qi as an "advisory position without administrative duties."[4] He suggests that the post that Xunzi took up in the state of Qi might have been taken under pressure, or at least reluctantly, and that it was an office that did not present the possibility of much political influence anyway, warning that this post "should not lead us to portray the man as an office seeker, or to view the philosophy of the *Xunzi* as springing from the motivations of political ambition."[5]

The historical evidence alone is not sufficient to determine the exact nature of Mencius's and Xunzi's official positions,[6] and the opportunities that were in fact available to Confucius. Given that much of what we know about Confucius, Mencius, and Xunzi comes from the respective texts associated with their names, it is ultimately the interpretation of their philosophical project as presented in these texts that affects the interpretation of the biographical history, rather than the other way round. Indeed, Eno says that his interpretation of Confucius's quest relies on "the evidence of the *Analects*."[7] If one disagrees with him on his reading of the *Analects*, then one will also likely disagree with Eno's view of Confucius's involvement. Similarly, if one reads the *Mencius* as emphasizing the necessity of political participation, then one will likely take Mencius to have appreciated its importance not merely when he was aging, and thus to interpret his actual political pursuits as more than a desperate attempt in old age to leave a mark on the world. While I will offer a view of "political activism" below, it will not thus rely on any evidence of Confucianism's historical role, as is the strategy of Frederick Mote (who contends that Confucian students and their descendants historically dominated the market for government positions),[8] but rather on the Confucians texts' content, to which I now turn.

The Virtue of Political Involvement

When interpreters speak about the relationship between ethics and politics in early Confucianism, they often speak of the notion of "inner sageliness outer kingliness" (*neisheng waiwang* 內聖外王), that is, the

---

[4] Eno, *Confucian Creation of Heaven*, 52.

[5] Eno, *Confucian Creation of Heaven*, 135–36.

[6] Edward Machle, for example, argues that one would be hard pressed to describe Xunzi's position in Chu as a mere "sinecure." See Machle, *Nature and Heaven in the Xunzi*, 192–93n9.

[7] Eno, *Confucian Creation of Heaven*, 45.

[8] Frederick Mote, *Intellectual Foundations of China* (New York: Knopf, 1971), 41.

notion that the inward development of virtue makes one properly suited for the position of king. This notion is in fact not of Confucian provenance. As Stephen Angle explains, some scholars have traced it to the shamanic Chinese kings of antiquity, while the actual slogan comes from the Daoist text, the *Zhuangzi*. Angle points out, however, that it was "widely used by the Neo-Confucians to express the intimate relation, or even identity, that they saw between inner moral cultivation and external, political action."[9] As I argued in the prologue, Neo-Confucian developments, starting with Zhu Xi (1130–1200), are often read back into early Confucianism, and I have questioned, throughout this book, the argument about the "identity" between ethics and politics in Confucianism by questioning the dependency of politics on ethics. I will continue doing so in this chapter as I show that many of the political actions recommended by the early Confucians do not strictly conform to the ethics of self-cultivation. This said, there is truth to the flip side of the equation: as I argue in this section, the domain of ethics is itself dependent on the domain of politics insofar as one cannot become fully virtuous in isolation from all political involvement.

I presented in Chapter 3 the Confucian view, especially expounded by Mencius, that qualities important for the ruler and the people alike, such as loyalty, reciprocity, and compassion, are first learned at home; in other words, how civic dispositions develop from personal and family ethics. What I wish to emphasize here is the fact that the Confucians view this extension of virtue, from the realm of the family, to the wider realm of society, to be necessary for the full-fledged development of virtue itself. As Angle puts it, "sagehood is not just a matter of personal ethics: on any traditional Confucian's view, it is intimately involved in shaping one's broader community both unofficially and through participation in government. In other words, to aim at sagehood is to aim at some sort of political involvement and impact."[10]

[9] Angle, *Sagehood*, 182.

[10] Angle, *Sagehood*, 179. Eno argues that the Confucian texts link ethical cultivation (he specifically focuses on "ritual mastery") and political activism in three ways: sequentially ("self-cultivation precedes political action"), predictively ("the man whose virtue has been cultivated through ritual education is supremely competent to oversee the restoration of political order, either as a ruler, or as the administrator of enlightened policy"), and proscriptively ("being moral, the Ruist sage or [*junzi*] will not participate in corrupt government, lest he set a bad example, needlessly expose himself to danger, become himself corrupted, or legitimize corruption by his presence. Instead, he will bide his time, perfecting himself, until the proper opportunity for political action presents itself. This is the doctrine of 'timeliness' (*shi*)"). I agree with Eno on the first two links (though, in what concerns the second, my argument, as laid out at the end of the previ-

The political aspect of sagehood is exemplified through the model kings the early Confucians constantly cite. These are Yao, Shun, and Yu from the largely mythical Tang, Yu, and Xia dynasties, respectively (twenty-fourth to sixteenth centuries BCE), Tang and Yi Yin from the Shang dynasty (sixteenth to eleventh centuries BCE), and then Kings Wen and Wu and the Duke of Zhou from the Zhou dynasty (1045–770 BCE). While all these are good rulers, when they are given as models, the suggestion is not simply that they are good at ruling, but that they are good persons as well, that is, their political performance is a direct manifestation of their virtue.[11] This is clearest in the case of Shun. As I mentioned in the prologue, Shun is cited both for his unwavering filial piety (which he maintained even as his parents and brother conspired to kill him), and for his accomplishments as a ruler.[12] Indeed, Yao gave his daughters in marriage to Shun even while the latter was still a commoner,[13] presumably on account of his filial reputation, and then raised him to the position of regent to the throne before he died. In this position, and in line with the idea that the ruler is primarily responsible for choosing good ministers—see Chapter 4—Shun is said to have appointed Yi in charge of fire, Yu in charge of rivers, and Hou Ji in charge of education, exhibiting an acute concern with "the affairs of the people" and bringing order to the realm.[14] Both his filial piety and his political acumen are thus interrelated manifestations of Shun's core virtuous disposition.

Personal and political qualities are also bundled up in passages in the early Confucian texts that offer descriptions of what a Confucian gentleman (*junzi* 君子) is like, suggesting, as Sor-hoon Tan argues, that "many aspects of the exemplary person's way . . . are sociopolitical."[15] For example, when asked by Zilu about being a gentleman, Confucius replies,

"He cultivates himself and thereby achieves reverence."
  "Is that all?"

---

ous chapter, is that sagehood is not strictly necessary for political order), but disagree with his account of the third (as will become clear below). See Eno, *Confucian Creation of Heaven*, 44.

[11] See *Mencius* 7A.46, 7B.33, 7B.38; *Analects* 8.21; *Xunzi* 18.2, 23.5a.

[12] In *Mencius* 6B.2, Yao is mentioned alongside Shun as exhibiting filiality: "The way of Yao and Shun is simply to be a good son and a good younger brother."

[13] *Mencius* 5A.1, 5B.6.

[14] *Mencius* 3A.4.

[15] Tan, *Confucian Democracy*, 129. Tan cites *Analects* 1.7, 5.16, 19.10, and 20.2, in addition to 14.42. All these passages describe the *junzi* as undertaking political tasks.

"He cultivates himself and thereby brings peace and security to his fellow men."

"Is that all?"

"He cultivates himself and thereby brings peace and security to the people. Even Yao and Shun would have found the task of bringing peace and security to the people taxing."[16]

The question remains whether the political tasks attributed to the gentleman in the early Confucian texts are simply supererogatory, rather than a necessary part of virtue. This possibility is in fact suggested in a passage from the *Analects* mentioned in Chapter 3:

Someone said to Confucius, "Why do you not take part in government?"

The Master said, "The [*Classic of Documents*] says, 'Oh! Simply by being a good son and friendly to his brothers a man can exert an influence upon government.' In so doing a man is, in fact, taking part in government. How can there be any question of his having actively to 'take part in government?' "[17]

This passage suggests that the fulfillment of family duties produces a positive influence on government, presumably through its indirect effects on society, and that therefore there is no need to actually participate. The view presented in this passage is, however, as I also mentioned earlier, a lonely one, and the idea that political duties are supererogatory is hard to sustain given the many discussions in the early Confucian texts dealing with whether, when, and how it is appropriate for the Confucians and their disciples to take part in politics.[18] It seems therefore more plausible to see these latter discussions as acting as a bridge between the purely ethical and intellectual discussions of virtue (what being *ren* consists in, how to treat one's parents, whether rightness is externally imposed or an internal quality, what learning requires, etc.), and the political discussions. They act as a bridge insofar as they define a duty for Confucian disciples, as individuals, to participate in politics. This duty is emphasized in Mencius's saying, "A [man of service] takes office as a farmer cultivates his land." Mencius also cites the historical records as saying that "when Confucius was not in the service

---

[16] *Analects* 14.42.

[17] *Analects* 2.21.

[18] See, for example, *Analects* 2.18, 4.14, 5.6, 6.1, 6.8, 6.14, 11.17, 11.24, 11.25, 11.26, 13.20, 19.13, *Mencius* 2B.5, 2B.12, 3B.1, 7B.23, 7B.29, *Xunzi* 27.90.

of a ruler for three months, he became agitated" and Gongming Yi comments that "in ancient times when a man was not in the service of a [ruler] for three months he was offered condolences."[19]

This duty can, moreover, be understood to have two dimensions: it is a duty that stems from the Confucian understanding of virtue itself, and it is a duty that stems from their concern with politics. These two ideas can be culled from Benjamin Schwartz's statement of the importance of political cultivation for the early Confucians: "The superior man can achieve complete self-realization only in his public vocation. It might indeed be stated that a commitment to public service—even when such service is unattainable—forms one of the basic criteria distinguishing the Confucian ideal of self-cultivation from some competing ideals in the Chinese world. Conversely, society can be harmonized and set in order only when men who have approached the ideal of self-realization are in public office."[20] Self-realization and the harmonization of society are thus two goals that political involvement helps achieve.

Concerning self-realization, Confucius says that virtue "never stands alone. It is bound to have neighbors."[21] There are many ways to understand this claim: it could be that virtuous persons entice others around them to become virtuous, or that virtuous people are naturally attracted to one another. But another interpretation is that it is necessary to be around others to become virtuous, that, except perhaps for wisdom (*zhi* 智), the Confucian virtues *ren* (仁), rightness (*yi* 義), trustworthiness (*xin* 信), ritual propriety (*li* 禮), dutifulness (*zhong* 忠), and reverence (*jing* 敬), are all qualities that we can have only in relation to others.

One theme that clearly reveals the importance of social relations for the early Confucians is their rejection of recluses. These were men who had shunned the world and had gone on to live isolated, self-sustaining lives with their families (they plowed their own lands, wore unwoven clothes, etc., prompting Mencius to condemn their lack of appreciation for the principle of division of labor).[22] Confucius, defending himself against two recluses' charge that it would have been better for him to shun the world altogether than to simply shun bad men, replies, "A person cannot flock together with the birds and the

[19] *Mencius* 3B.3.
[20] Schwartz, "Some Polarities in Confucian Thought," 52.
[21] *Analects* 4.25.
[22] *Mencius* 3A.4.

beasts. If I do not associate with the followers of men, then with whom would I associate?"[23] Confucius thus suggests that it is part and parcel of being a human being to want to associate with other human beings; as Brooks and Brooks point out, in a language somewhat foreign to the Confucians but clarifying nonetheless: "Humankind, such as it is, is all that human beings can validly labor for."[24] It is presumably this natural tendency to associate with, and care for, other humans that also creates the motivation for wanting to improve society.

We can of course limit our relations to family and friends, but to limit ourselves in this way is in fact to limit the range of possible relations we could have, and thus the range of proper dispositions we could develop. It is to fail, as Mencius argues, to "extend" our moral dispositions to apply them to less personal relationships, including political ones.[25] One should keep in mind here the unavailability for the early Confucians of the range of political careers one can envision in the modern world: to engage in politics for the early Confucians is to take up an advisory or official position at a ruler's court. Confucius's disciple Zilu makes the point about the importance of such a position starkly: "Not to enter public life is to ignore one's duty. Even the proper regulation of old and young cannot be set aside. How, then, can the duty between ruler and subject be set aside? This is to cause confusion in the most important of human relationships simply because one desires to keep unsullied one's character. The gentleman takes office in order to do his duty. As for putting the Way into practice, he knows all along that it is hopeless."[26] The passage almost overstates the case for the duty of political participation. It presents the duty as absolute, regardless of the prevailing political situation, including the character of the ruler. As we will see below, the Confucians are actually concerned with both the potential for sullying one's character or, more accurately, derailing one's ethical pursuits, and for putting the Way, or at least some lower-level version of it, into effect. What this passage underscores, however, is the extent to which the duty to participate is central to the Confucian vision of the good life.

[23] *Analects* 18.6, quoted from Slingerland.

[24] Brooks and Brooks, *Original Analects*, 174.

[25] It might be worth noting here that though virtue involves a necessary political manifestation, the relationship does not hold the other way round. In other words, a person's ability to take on a political position is not necessarily a sign of all-round virtue. The obvious case here is Guan Zhong. See also *Analects* 5.8.

[26] *Analects* 18.7.

If the concern with self-cultivation creates the motivation to participate in politics, another part of the motivation stems, as mentioned
above, from the concern with the good of society. Recall from Chapter 3
that the Confucian ideal society is hierarchically organized, where hierarchy ideally tracks merit, and from Chapter 2 that merit, especially in
ministerial positions, is defined as all-around worthiness. This system
is reflected in a revealing passage where Xunzi associates gradations of
virtue with gradations of rank, arguing thus that the most virtuous
Confucians can become emperors or one of the three highest officials
while the lesser Confucians can become regional rulers, grand officers,
or men of service (shi 士).[27] This means not only that the virtuous Confucian disciples are most suited to ministerial positions in society, but
also that the regulation of society depends on their willingness to assume their positions in the hierarchical system.

Dilemmas of Political Life

I have argued so far that the Confucians identify a duty to participate
in politics that derives, on the ethical level, from the Confucian conception of self-cultivation and, on the political level, from the Confucian
conception of a harmonious society. But the Confucians are aware, perhaps all too aware, that ideal conditions do not exist in the actual
world: precisely because their conception of virtue is relational, other
parties to social relationships might not exhibit the same concern with
self-cultivation that the Confucian gentleman shows. Moreover, the argument that one contributes to the ordering and harmonization of society by assuming one's proper role is rendered moot by a deeply disordered society where positions are not typically filled by the worthy. On
an even more basic level, financial strains might force one to take up an
official post even against one's principles. Robert Eno argues, as I mentioned above, that the Confucians' response to a disordered world is an
"idealistic" one, since they recommend, according to him, withdrawal
as a way to fend off corruption and to maintain ethical purity.[28] My aim
in what follows is to raise questions about this interpretation by discussing numerous anecdotes which suggest that the Confucians actually tilt more toward political engagement rather than withdrawal. I
first briefly discuss the issue of the propriety of seeking office for the

[27] *Xunzi* 8.12.
[28] Eno, *Confucian Creation of Heaven*, 31.

sake of financial remuneration, then turn to the issue of whether and when the Confucians allow for the compromise of ethical principles for the sake of political effectiveness.

Financial Need and Reward

Mencius lays out three conditions for taking, and relinquishing, office. The first condition stipulates that the gentleman should be "sent for with the greatest respect, in accordance with the proper rites," and that he should be "told that his advice would be put into practice." This is reminiscent of the idea expressed in *Mencius* 5B.7, and discussed in Chapter 4, of ministers who "cannot be summoned" but should rather be sought after because of their virtue. On this first condition, Mencius argues that, even while the courtesies are still observed, leaving office is justified when the gentleman's advice is "not put into practice." The second condition is a diluted version of the first: Mencius removes the requirement of having one's advice put into practice, arguing that one should take up office as long as it is offered according to the proper rituals, and leave when the rituals are no longer observed.[29] The third condition stipulates that even the lack of observance of proper ritual form can be overlooked in case of dire economic need. He thus argues that though "poverty does not constitute grounds for taking office . . . there are times when a man takes office because of poverty."[30]

I will discuss the concern with having one's advice heeded in the following section. In this section, I simply elaborate on the requirement of ritual propriety, which is part of the more general issue of the propriety of accepting remuneration and gifts in the *Mencius*. The question of whether the Confucians allowed for profit, broadly conceived, as a reason to pursue office is not merely theoretical but also historical. Mark Edward Lewis argues that the scholars of the Warring States period were not dependent on the different states for revenue. He contends that they ensured their living through teaching, technical jobs (medicine, astronomy, divination), the provision of ritual expertise, such as for ceremonies of noble households, and patronage.[31] As I mentioned

---

[29] *Mencius* 6B.14.

[30] *Mencius* 5B.5.

[31] Patronage, according to Lewis, is no sign of alliance between states and scholarly traditions, because it was not exclusive to rulers, as regional rulers and high-ranking officials also acted as patrons, and because patronage was not based on necessity, but merely on prestige. Lewis, *Writing and Authority in Early China*, 75–78.

in the prologue, Lewis argues that "the *ru* [Confucians] and the technical experts, in contrast to other wielders of texts [such as court scribes], enjoyed a bipolar character—able to move between the courts and local society, between public service and private retirement."[32] Yuri Pines disagrees with Lewis. He argues that teaching did not ensure sufficient revenue, and that official posts were more economically lucrative than any other,[33] concluding that "many, probably most" Warring States scholars "sought careers primarily for economic and social reasons."[34] Edward Slingerland points out that because Confucian training consisted in large part of the "mastery of the Zhou classics and traditional ritual etiquette," it was particularly valued for state officials, and thus led many to seek it in order to acquire posts.[35]

Putting the historical debate aside, what do the Confucian texts have to say on the issue of remuneration? In one entry in the *Analects*, Confucius is said to remark that "it is not easy to find a man who can study for three years without thinking about earning a salary,"[36] suggesting the ubiquity of this trend but also, more important, his opposition to it. When Yuan Si asks him about what is "shameful," the Master responds that "it is shameful to make salary your sole object, irrespective of whether the Way prevails in the state or not."[37] In many other passages, Confucius's emphasis is on showing that the pursuit of virtue should never be sacrificed for the pursuit of riches.[38] Mencius similarly argues that one should not accept any position, however attractive the salary associated with it, when it is not properly offered:

> Here is a basketful of rice and a bowlful of soup. Getting them will mean life; not getting them will mean death. When these are given with abuse, even a wayfarer would not accept them; when these are given after being trampled upon, even a beggar would not accept them. Yet when it comes to ten thousand bushels of grain one is supposed to accept without asking if it is in accordance with the rites or if it is right to do so. What benefit are ten thousand bushels of grain to me? [Do I accept them] for the sake of beautiful houses,

[32] Lewis, *Writing and Authority in Early China*, 83.
[33] Pines, *Envisioning Eternal Empire*, 138–39.
[34] Pines, *Envisioning Eternal Empire*, 141.
[35] Slingerland, trans., *Confucius: Analects*, xxi.
[36] *Analects* 8.12.
[37] *Analects* 14.1.
[38] See *Analects* 1.14, 4.5, 6.11, 7.12, 7.16, 15.32, and 15.38.

the enjoyment of wives and concubines, or for the sake of the gratitude my needy acquaintances will show me?[39]

As for his inescapable metaphor on the topic of preferring profit over morality, Xunzi, defending Zilu's preference to wear clothes that looked like "hanging quails" over serving a ruler that treats him arrogantly, says that to prefer the opposite "is like obtaining something no bigger than a flea's suit of armor at the cost of losing your hand."[40]

What I want to emphasize here, however, in line with my argument about the Confucians' sensitivity to the vagaries of life and of the political world, is that they reject profit only when profit competes with virtue. They otherwise have no compunction as such about receiving salary in exchange for their counsel. As Pines writes, "The quest for riches and honor, which is associated with holding the office, is entirely legitimate and acceptable, but it should be subordinate to the moral imperatives of the Way."[41] The clearest instance of the Confucian acceptance of riches and honor is *Mencius* 3B.4, where Mencius answers Peng Geng, who asks whether "it is not excessive to travel with a retinue of hundreds of followers in scores of chariots, and to live off one [regional ruler] after another." Mencius first repeats that the pursuit of office should be in accordance with the Way, but then he argues that there is nothing wrong with the Confucians accepting remuneration for the advice they give to rulers. The argument rests on the notion of division of labor, wherein the Confucian gentleman, like the carpenter and the carriage-maker, has something special to offer to society: "he can make the prince secure, rich and honoured, and, if the young men come under his influence, he can make them dutiful to their parents and elders, conscientious in their work and faithful to their word."[42] This contribution should earn him a living, just like the carpenter and carriage-maker garner a living off of their work. Indeed, the Confucians do not simply argue that gentlemen are allowed to take remuneration, but that they should do so. Xunzi thus criticizes Prince Fa for refusing to take a reward for his success during a military expedition. While the latter finds it inappropriate to use the achievements of his soldiers for the sake of a personal reward, Xunzi says that the proper

[39] *Mencius* 6A.10. On the topic of when it is appropriate to accept a gift or food (when given according to ritual, and when there is a justification for it), see *Mencius* 2B.3, 5B.4, 5B.6, 6B.5.

[40] *Xunzi* 27.97.

[41] Pines, *Envisioning Eternal Empire*, 145.

[42] *Mencius* 7A.32.

regulation of society requires that the worthy be rewarded, since this is a central way in which ranks and distinctions are maintained.[43] Similarly, Confucius criticizes Yuan Si for declining a salary of nine hundred measures of millet in return for his services as a steward. "Could you not use it to aid the households in your neighborhood?" Confucius asks.[44]

Finally, to return to his third condition for taking office, it is clear that Mencius is not even absolutist about virtue trumping need, recognizing the constraints of dire poverty and the necessity to compromise when one has no other option. Part of Mencius's recognition stems from his rejection of asceticism as a viable way of life, even when it is a sign of protest against a corrupt world, for to live on grass and fruit is to live like an "earthworm" and not like a human being.[45] The other part stems from the Confucian idea that what is right to do might be different in different circumstances. Thus, in a response to Gaozi about whether it would be right to break the rules of propriety to get food when one is starving, Mencius responds that this would generally be right, but that it would not be right, for example, to twist one's brother's arm and snatch food from his hand for this purpose.[46] It should also be mentioned that Mencius advises that the person who accepts a position because of extreme hunger should opt for a low-ranking office, with a small salary. The thought seems to be that such an office, if it is problematic in some way (see discussion below), is at least far away from the position of power, and thus associated with a lesser responsibility for "putting the Way into effect." He gives as examples the positions of a gatekeeper and that of a watchman. He also mentions Confucius's attitude when he was a minor official in charge of stores ("All I have to do is to keep correct records") and in charge of cattle ("All I have to do is to see to it that the sheep and cattle grow up to be strong and healthy"), suggesting that Confucius considered these positions to provide limits on what he was supposed to do, and therefore on what he could be held accountable (or hold himself accountable) for, as a virtuous gentleman in office.[47]

---

[43] *Xunzi* 16.3.

[44] *Analects* 6.5, quoted from Slingerland. Yuan Si was famous for being extremely fastidious (*juan* 狷) or, in Lau's translation "over-scrupulous," a character aberration that Confucius tellingly equates with being "undisciplined" (*kuang* 狂) as second best (he prefers moderation). See *Analects* 13.21.

[45] *Mencius* 3B.10.

[46] *Mencius* 6B.1.

[47] *Mencius* 5B.5.

Ethical versus Political Pursuits

Confucius says that the gentleman is not "invariably for or against anything," but instead follows what is right.[48] Hsiao Kung-chuan concludes from this that "Confucius did not hold unalterably either to the view that one must serve in office or to the view that one must be a recluse."[49] But the question remains as to what sorts of considerations led the Confucians to sometimes advise seeking official positions under a corrupt ruler, and to sometimes condemn doing so. What I will elicit below are two central considerations: first, the extent to which one is likely to have to compromise on one's ethical duties, but second, and less obviously, the extent to which one is likely to actually influence the ruler. As Sor-hoon Tan puts it, "Withdrawal from the public life is not just to preserve one's life and limb. The point is to serve only where one could make a difference."[50] To make a difference need not mean to turn a corrupt ruler into a virtuous ruler. Rather, the Confucians recognize that it is sometimes possible, and sufficient, to influence the ruler to undertake policies favorable to the common people, and thus to peace and political order. I start with Mencius since he offers the most extended discussion of political involvement, then turn to the *Analects*, and finally to Xunzi.

MENCIUS

First, it should be noted that, in the case of serving a virtuous ruler, the two considerations of integrity and effectiveness are at play, but there is no tension between them. The two, in addition to the consideration about propriety mentioned above, are revealed in the story of how virtuous Yi Yin came to serve virtuous King Tang, which is worth quoting in its entirety:

> Yi Yin worked in the fields [of the ruler of Xin], and delighted in the Way of Yao and Shun. If it was contrary to what was right or to the Way, were he given the Empire he would have ignored it, and were he given a thousand teams of horses he would not have looked at them. . . . When Tang sent a messenger with presents to invite him to court, he calmly said, "What do I want Tang's presents for? I much prefer working in the fields, delighting in the

[48] *Analects* 4.10.
[49] Hsiao, *History of Chinese Political Thought*, 122.
[50] Tan, *Confucian Democracy*, 129.

way of Yao and Shun." Only after Tang sent a messenger for the third time did he change his mind and say, "Is it not better for me to make this prince a Yao or a Shun than to remain in the fields, delighting in the way of Yao and Shun? Is it not better for me to make the people subjects of a Yao or a Shun? Is it not better for me to see this with my own eyes? Heaven, in producing the people, has given to those who first attain understanding the duty of awakening those who are slow to understand; and to those who are the first to awaken the duty of awakening those who are slow to awaken. I am among the first of Heaven's people to awaken. I shall awaken this people by means of this Way. If I do not awaken them, who will?" When he saw a man or woman who did not enjoy the benefit of the rule of Yao and Shun, Yi Yin felt as if he had pushed them into the gutter. This is the extent to which he considered the Empire his responsibility. So he went to Tang and persuaded him to embark upon a punitive expedition against the Xia to succor the people. I have never heard of anyone who can right others by bending himself, let alone someone who can right the Empire by bringing disgrace upon himself. The conduct of sages is not always the same. Some live in retirement, others enter the world; some withdraw, others stay on; but it all comes to keeping their integrity (*jie* 潔) intact.[51]

This anecdote shows how Yi Yin was concerned with self-cultivation and the pursuit of the Confucian Way, how he was summoned to court in a respectful manner (he was invited three times, with presents), and how he recognized a duty to heed the invitation that was based both on his ability to keep his integrity intact (as Mencius says in the concluding sentence) and on his ability to bring about effective political results (he would be able to "awaken" the people to the rule of Yao and Shun by ensuring their welfare; I return to Heaven's role in Yi Yin's awakening in the next chapter).

Mencius's view becomes less straightforward when he approves of serving corrupt rulers, since the values of propriety, integrity, and effectiveness are not bundled up in the same way in these cases as they are in the case of serving a virtuous ruler. In fact, even Yi Yin appears in a different light when Mencius quotes him as saying, "I serve any prince; I rule over any people. I take office whether order (*zhi* 治) pre-

[51] *Mencius* 5A.7.

vails or not."[52] This statement follows from the account of Yi Yin going "five times to Tang and five times to [tyrant] Jie" before becoming minister to Tang when the latter finally overthrew Jie and founded the Shang dynasty.[53] Yi Yin's behavior is not too dissimilar from that of Liuxia Hui, an official in the state of Lu, who "was not ashamed of a prince with a tarnished reputation, neither did he disdain a modest post. When in office, he did not conceal his own talent, and always acted in accordance with the Way. When he was passed over he harboured no grudge, nor was he distressed even in straitened circumstances. When he was with a fellow-villager he simply could not tear himself away. 'You are you and I am I. Even if you were to be stark naked by my side, how could you defile me?' "[54]

On the other hand, the opposite behavior is exemplified by Bo Yi, who "was such that he would only serve the right prince and rule over the right people, would take office when order (zhi 治) prevailed and relinquish it when there was disorder."[55] Bo Yi "would not take his place at the court of an evil man, nor would he converse with him," for this would be like "sitting in mud or pitch wearing a court cap and gown."[56] He "could not bear to remain in a place where the government took outrageous measures and unruly people were to be found,"[57] and even when the regional rulers "made advances in the politest language, he would repel them" because he felt it was beneath him to serve them.[58] As Van Norden explains in relation to Mencius 5B.1, Bo Yi was the son of a ruler during the last period of the Shang dynasty who abdicated in favor of his brother when his father died, following what he believed to be his father's wish. Bo Yi admired King Wen but refused loyalty to King Wu, Wen's son, because the latter attacked tyrant Zhou, the last ruler of the Shang dynasty, of whom Bo Yi was a subject. Bo Yi died from starvation as a recluse.

Mencius approves of the behavior of all of these differently disposed individuals. He actually even describes them as "sages" (shengren 聖人) (though it is important to note here that Mencius uses the term much more freely than it is used in the Analects, which should

[52] Mencius 5B.1.

[53] See Mencius 6B.6.

[54] Mencius 5B.1. See also Mencius 2A.9, where Mencius adds that Liuxia Hui "stayed when pressed, simply because it was beneath him to insist on leaving."

[55] Mencius 2A.2.

[56] Mencius 2A.9.

[57] Mencius 5B.1.

[58] Mencius 2A.9. See Van Norden, trans., Mengzi, 131,

become clear below given that these individuals suffer from important character failings): Yi Yin is the sage who accepted responsibility
(*ren* 任), Liuxia Hui is the sage who was accommodating (*he* 和),[59] and
Bo Yi is the sage who was pure (*qing* 清).[60] Also, in a different passage,
Mencius argues that the different behaviors of Bo Yi, Liuxia Hui, and
Yi Yin all partake of *ren* 仁.[61] On the other hand, Mencius criticizes Bo
Yi for being too "constrained" (*ai* 隘) and Liuxia Hui for not being
dignified enough (*bugong* 不恭), adding that the gentleman will not
follow either.[62] The model Mencius ultimately recommends is none of
these, but rather that of Confucius who "would take office, or would
remain in a state, would delay his departure or hasten it, all according
to circumstances."[63] Mencius describes Confucius's actions as timely
(*shi* 時).[64]

The question that the preceding raises is why Mencius approves of
these different types of behavior, and what makes Confucius's model
better than the other three.[65] Concerning the first question, Mencius
says that Bo Yi, Yi Yin, and Confucius have an important thing in common: "Were they to become ruler over a hundred [leagues] square,
they would have been capable of winning the homage of the [regional
rulers] and taking possession of the Empire; but had it been necessary
to perpetrate one wrongful deed or to kill one innocent man in order to
gain the Empire, none of them would have consented to it. In this they
were all alike."[66] What this quote suggests is that even when Yi Yin
and, by implication, Liuxia Hui, accept to serve corrupt rulers, they do
so without ever agreeing to commit wrongful acts themselves.[67] This
perhaps explains why these two served many (different types of) rulers
in their lifetime (i.e., because they had to abandon a ruler whenever he
asked them to do anything wrongful). Moreover, as the quote above
about Liuxia Hui suggests, it must be the case that they did not believe

[59] Lau translates the adjective as "easy-going" and Van Norden as "harmonious."

[60] *Mencius* 5B.1. See also 7B.15.

[61] *Mencius* 6B.6.

[62] *Mencius* 2A.9.

[63] *Mencius* 2A.2.

[64] *Mencius* 5B.1.

[65] For a discussion of why the idea of sagehood applies to all of the figures above, see
Angle, *Sagehood*, 16.

[66] *Mencius* 2A.2. In 7A.28, Mencius says that Liuxia Hui "would not have compromised on his integrity for the sake of the three [highest offices in the state]."

[67] See also *Mencius* 4B.4: "When an innocent [man of service] is put to death, a [counselor] is justified in leaving, when innocent people are killed, a [man of service] is justified in going to live abroad."

that the mere association with corrupt rulers necessarily affects their character. On the other hand, there must also be some harm accrued from such association (otherwise, it would be unclear why they fall short of the model exemplified by Confucius). One potential interpretation is that, even though association with corrupt rulers does not corrupt (Yi Yin and Liuxia Hui would not have been described as "sages" if they were corrupt), perhaps it distracts ministers from other worthy pursuits of a more purely ethical nature, like learning, caring for parents and friends, and so on. Applying the same logic, there must be something that Bo Yi loses and Yi Yin and Liuxia Hui gain; in other words, it must be that some good follows from serving corrupt rulers. The only plausible candidate for such a good is the possibility of influencing the ruler to implement policies that, as I will show more fully below, promote the welfare of the common people or, to put it in terms of the argument of my book, bring about political order. This was indeed one of the motivations that led Yi Yin to serve King Tang, but it was also presumably the—principal—motivation for him serving Tyrant Jie. If all this is true, then Confucius's flexibility amounts to weighing the good of ethical relationships versus the good of political order based on the context of particular rulers and the opportunities they offer: speaking of Confucius in a different passage, Mencius explains how he "took office sometimes because he thought there was a possibility of practising the Way, sometimes because he was treated with decency, and sometimes because the prince wished to keep good people at his court."[68]

This kind of weighing is evident in Mencius's account of Boli Xi. Mencius's aim in the account is to refute the claim that Boli Xi gained the attention of Duke Mu of Qin by selling himself into slavery as a cattle keeper in the state of Qin. As mentioned above, Mencius believes that the taking of office should not be done through improper ways. He argues that selling oneself into slavery is one such improper way, and that this was not the route that Boli Xi actually followed. The more relevant aspect of Mencius's account for my discussion here is Mencius's explanation for why Boli Xi agreed to advise the ruler of Qin, but not the ruler of Yu. Mencius reports that the ruler of Yu had accepted gifts in exchange for letting the state of Jin use Yu's territory to attack the state of Guo. Boli Xi refused to give advice (it is not clear from the story whether he enjoyed any official post in Yu at the time) and left for

[68] *Mencius* 5B.4.

Qin. Mencius says that Boli Xi's refusal stemmed from his belief that "the ruler of Yu was beyond advice." When he left for the state of Qin, on the other hand, he did agree to help Duke Mu. Boli Xi believed that, unlike the ruler of Yu, Duke Mu could be influenced for the better. As Mencius concludes about Boli Xi,

> Can he be called unwise when he remained silent, knowing that advice would be futile? He certainly was not unwise when he left in advance, knowing the ruler of Yu to be heading for disaster. Again, can he be said to be unwise when, after being raised to office in Qin, he decided to help Duke Mu, seeing in him a man capable of great achievement? When prime minister of Qin, he was responsible for the distinction his prince attained in the Empire, and posterity has found him worthy of being remembered. Was this the achievement of a man with no ability?[69]

Boli Xi's example shows how it is permissible to advise less-than-virtuous rulers in some cases but not in others. Boli Xi did not make Duke Mu into a virtuous ruler, but he turned him, as mentioned in Chapter 2, into a hegemon. When it came to the ruler of Yu, however, he did not see any possibility of influencing him, and so preferred to divert his attention toward a more worthy pursuit (in this case, advising a different, more promising, ruler). Mencius actually uses Boli Xi's example to show the political utility of wise men for the state. Chunyu Kun asks,

> "In the time of Duke Mu of Lu, Gongyizi was in charge of affairs of state, and Ziliu and Zisi were in office, yet Lu dwindled in size even more rapidly than before. Are good and wise men of so little benefit to a state?"
> Mencius answers:
> "Yu was annexed for failing to employ Boli Xi, while Duke Mu of Qin, by employing him, became [a hegemon]. A state which fails to employ good and wise men will end by suffering annexation. How can it hope to suffer no more than a reduction in size?"[70]

What is revealing in this exchange is that it glosses the benefit of wise men not as promoting virtue, but as ameliorating the state's defenses, presumably by improving its internal workings. Like Guan Zhong,

---

[69] *Mencius* 5A.9.
[70] *Mencius* 6B.6.

who helped Duke Huan of Qi (see Chapter 1), Boli Xi allowed Duke Mu of Qin to become a hegemon. Recall that hegemons' acceptability to the Confucians stems from their ability to produce political order through security- and welfare-oriented policies. In other words, this passage reveals that political order is the benefit that gentlemen can bring to the state, even when they are employed by men less wise than them, and which therefore justifies their willingness to be so employed.

Similar considerations can be elicited in Mencius's willingness to advise all sorts of rulers.[71] Excepting for the anecdote relayed in Chapter 4, in which Mencius feigns illness to avoid seeing the king because he summoned him,[72] Mencius is more than willing to advise the ruler of Qi, leading a certain Yin Shi to comment that if Mencius "did not realize that the King could not become a Tang or a King Wu, he was blind, but if he came realizing it, he was simply after advancement." Yin Shi also criticizes Mencius for taking too long to leave when his advice was not needed, which is contrary to his stated principle of taking leave when one's counsel is not put into practice. Mencius responds that he was hoping that the king would change his mind, specifically that he would offer Mencius a proper position. Two sentences in his response are worth noting. First, he says that if the king had employed him, "it would not simply be a matter of bringing peace to the people of Qi, but of bringing peace to the people of the whole Empire as well." Then he also says, "I am not like those petty men who, when their advice is rejected by the prince, take offence and show resentment all over their faces, and, when they leave, travel all day before they would put up for the night."[73] In other words, the emphasis here is on attempting to improve the political situation in the Chinese world by pressuring its less-than-worthy rulers, but also on persevering in such an attempt, without being derailed by every rejection. This goal, however, is in tension with Mencius's attempt to justify his unwillingness to help solve the famine in Qi by claiming that he had no official post.

[71] There are numerous anecdotes in the *Mencius* that involve Mencius giving advice to a ruler: 1A.1, 1A.2, 1A.3, 1A.4, 1A.5, 1A.6, 1A.7, 1B.1, 1B.2, 1B.3, 1B.4, 1B.5, 1B.6, 1B.7, 1B.8, 1B.9, 1B.10, 1B.11, 1B.12, 1B.13, 1B.14, 1B.15, 2B.8 (Mencius gives advice to a high minister in Qi), 3A.1, 3A.2, 3A.3, 3B.6 (he gives advice to a minister of Song).

[72] *Mencius* 2B.2. As Eno argues, this passage suggests "rationalization of Mencius's most arrogant behavior." See Eno, *Confucian Creation of Heaven*, 257n39. Indeed, in 5B.7, as also mentioned earlier, Mencius faces the challenge of explaining the fact that Confucius himself did respond when summoned, which he does by pointing out that the latter was "in office and had specific duties" and was thus "summoned in his official capacity."

[73] *Mencius* 2B.12.

A more convincing reason would be that he simply had no power to influence the ruler on the issue of the famine. In other words, while he felt able, or at least hoped to be able, to be employed by the ruler to promote peace and unity, he could not, as merely an office-seeker, influence the ruler on matters of policy making, and did not want to be held accountable for these.[74]

To summarize, Mencius encourages political involvement even when one has to associate with a corrupt ruler, if there is a reasonable hope that one can influence the ruler to promote welfare-inducing, and thus order-inducing, policies.[75] One perseveres in such involvement, or the quest thereof, so long as there is reason for such hope.

THE *ANALECTS*

Startled, the bird rose up and circled round before alighting. He said, "The female pheasant on the mountain bridge, how timely (*shi* 時) her action is, how timely her action is!" Zilu cupped one hand in the other in a gesture of respect towards the bird which, flapping its wings three times, flew away.[76]

This passage comes at the end of book X of the *Analects*, which is devoted to showcasing Confucius's ritual propriety, and thus suggests, as Edward Slingerland argues, that it is a metaphor for Confucius's be-

---

[74] *Mencius* 7B.23: Mencius, using the analogy of a government official chasing tigers, argues that since he holds no official position, it is not his job to bring about an end to the famine. The analogy is not very plausible: there are clear reasons, relating to the proper fulfillment of one's role and to the need for a division of labor, for public officials not to chase tigers, but it is not obvious that the mere fact of not holding a position should prevent, let alone prohibit, Mencius from trying to exert influence on the ruler to open the state's granaries. A similar, unconvincing, excuse is given in *Mencius* 2B.5. It is worth quoting Eno's comment on 7B.23: "While this passage suggests Mencius' skill at literary repartee and sophisticated understanding of the role of the courtier, which naturally entails 'timeliness' in perceiving the limits of what one may achieve in the context of the court, against the background of starving people looking for a moral hero, Mencius' cool wit seems to emanate from a moral universe remote from that of the sage responding to the imperatives of the moral senses." See Eno, "Casuistry and Character in the *Mencius*," in Chan, *Mencius: Contexts and Interpretations*, 198.

[75] In commenting on *Mencius* 3B.1, Van Norden explains that Mencius uses three kinds of justification to explain his unwillingness to advise the ruler: deontological (it is intrinsically wrong to do so), virtue ethical (it corrupts one's character), and consequentialist (it will not do any good). That there is a deontological strain in Mencius is a large question beyond the scope of this book, but I agree with Van Norden that Mencius appeals both to an argument from effectiveness and to an argument from virtue. See Van Norden, trans., *Mengzi*, 77.

[76] *Analects* 10.27. See Slingerland, trans., *Confucius: Analects*, 110.

havior (admired by his disciple Zilu). This idea of "timeliness" (*shi* 時), also used by Mencius to describe Confucius as reported above, implies that there are times when it is appropriate, and others when it is inappropriate, to go forward in politics. To say that one acts according to context, or according to "the times," however, does not explain what factors one considers in a given context or period. To elicit these, I proceed by analyzing different passages from the *Analects*. I show that the two central considerations of integrity and effectiveness are at work in the former as they are in the *Mencius*.

Consider, first, the following passage from the *Analects*:

> The Master said, "Be sincerely trustworthy and love learning, and hold fast to the good Way until death. Do not enter a state that is endangered (*wei* 危), and do not reside in a state that is disordered (*luan* 亂). If the Way is being realized in the world then show yourself; if it is not, then go into reclusion. In a state that has the Way, to be poor and of low status is a cause for shame; in a state that is without the Way, to be wealthy and honored is equally a cause for shame."[77]

This passage makes recommendations both about when one should enter a given state, and about when one should take up an official position (which would allow one to show oneself, to be honored, and to become wealthy). The advice about entering or residing in a state is arguably targeted toward outsiders, and the advice about holding a position toward insiders. On the second front, the duty to hold an official position is made relative to the realization of the "Way." The most straightforward way to read the Way (*dao* 道) is as the all-encompassing Confucian Way. Doing so will lead to the conclusion that Confucius makes the duty of political involvement dependent on the preexisting realization of Confucian precepts. In other words, political involvement would depend on the availability of a reciprocal relationship between ruler and minister and, more generally, of a harmonious society. Moreover, the passage not only annuls the duty of political involvement when the Way does not hold, but also seems to argue for the opposite duty of withdrawal. No justification is explicitly offered for withdrawal; Eno argues, as mentioned above, that the concern underlying withdrawal is ethical purity. Here are two examples that illustrate Confucius's preference for such withdrawal in disorderly times:

---

[77] *Analects* 8.13, quoted from Slingerland.

The Master said, "How straight (*zhi* 直) Shi Yu is! When the Way prevails in the state he is as straight as an arrow, yet when the Way falls into disuse in the state he is still as straight as an arrow.

"How gentlemanly (*junzi* 君子) Qu Boyu is! When the Way prevails in the state he takes office, but when the Way falls into disuse in the state he allows himself to be furled and put away safely."[78]

While it is clear that "gentlemanly" connotes praise, it is not as clear how positive or negative the description of Yu as "straight" is, but as the case might be, "gentlemanly" seems more laudatory than "straight."[79] D. C. Lau says that Shi Yu was a prime minister in the state of Wei, which suggests that his stubbornness was likely directed at refusing to leave office as opposed to refusing to take up office. Confucius thus finds this model less gentlemanly and praiseworthy than the model of withdrawing from office during turbulent times.

Confucius's preference for the first version of the timeliness principle, recommending withdrawal, might also be said to be borne out by the following two examples: Nan Rong, to whom he gave his elder brother's daughter in marriage, and of whom Confucius says that "when the Way prevailed in the state he was not cast aside and when the Way fell into disuse he stayed clear of the humiliation of punishment,"[80] and Ning Wuzi, who became stupid when the Way did not prevail.[81] Both of these statements, however, are subject to differing interpretations. In Nan Rong's case, it is not clear whether staying away from humiliation required him to stay out of public office. As for Ning Wuzi, the literal reading of the passage is that he acted unwisely when the Way did not prevail; Slingerland's explanation that he "feigned" stupidity and his suggestion that this was in order to avoid being offered a position are based on a specific interpretive move: to make consistent the example with Confucius's timeliness principle.

In fact, another version of the timeliness principle is offered in the *Analects* recommending not withdrawal, but caution: "The Master said, 'When the Way prevails in the state, speak and act with perilous high-mindedness; when the Way does not prevail, act with perilous high-

[78] *Analects* 15.7.

[79] Slingerland, and Brooks and Brooks, are in agreement about this. Interestingly, straight (*zhi* 直) is also the adjective used in *Analects* 13.18, discussed in Chapter 3, to describe appropriate behavior in response to one's father's stealing of a sheep.

[80] *Analects* 5.2.

[81] *Analects* 5.21. See Slingerland, trans., *Confucius: Analects*, 48.

mindedness but speak with self-effacing diffidence.' "[82] Slingerland cites Wang Fuzhi's comment on this passage, in which he explains that "one is conciliatory in speech not out of fear of disaster but because actively courting disaster does no good, and is therefore something from which the gentleman refrains."[83] In other words, the justification for being cautious, in speech at least, arises not out of an instinct for self-defense as such, but precisely out of the concern with political effectiveness since, while it is worthwhile to have one's advice heard and heeded, there are ways of going about this that are counterproductive.

Moreover, like Mencius, Confucius not only approves of different models of behavior, but also prefers flexibility. To start out with the examples he shares with Mencius, he describes Bo Yi as someone who does not lower his purpose (*zhi* 志) or allow himself to be humiliated (*ru* 辱). He says of Liuxia Hui that he did lower his purpose and allow himself to be humiliated, but that nonetheless his words were in line with his status and his actions with his thoughts.[84] This is presumably because he was not "prepared to bend the Way."[85] Confucius also mentions a third category of those who "give free rein to their words while living as recluses" but are "unsullied in character and showed sound judgment in accepting their dismissal." He concludes, as Mencius reports him to do, with an affirmation of his own favored attitude: "I have no preconceptions about the permissible and the impermissible."[86] This attitude is in tension with the "preconception" that serving in office during disordered times is necessarily wrong. For this is precisely Bo Yi's attitude, and Confucius distances himself from the former as much as he does from the other personages he mentions in the passage.

Indeed, in a response to two models, one of political involvement and one of political withdrawal, Confucius—unlike Mencius—refuses to describe either as *ren*. He describes Prime Minister Ziwen who "gave no appearance of pleasure when he was made prime minister three times" nor of "displeasure when he was removed from office three times" as dutiful (*zhong* 忠), but not *ren*. On the other hand, he says of Chen Wenzi, who left the state of Qi when Cuizi assassinated its ruler,

---

[82] *Analects* 14.3.
[83] Slingerland, trans., *Confucius: Analects*, 154–55.
[84] *Analects* 18.8.
[85] *Analects* 18.2.
[86] *Analects* 18.8.

and went from state to state, finding none of their rulers to be better than Cuizi, as "pure" but not *ren*.[87]

As with Mencius, though Confucius in principle favors an attitude of flexibility, the accounts of his own behavior show that he was more determined to serve in office, even during corrupt times, than not. The clearest instance of Confucius's willingness to take up an official post even when the Way is not realized is his willingness to serve Gongshan Furao who wanted to use the stronghold of Bi to stage a revolt against the Ji family, the de facto rulers of Lu. As the story goes,

> Zilu was displeased and said, "We may have nowhere to go, but why must we go to Gongshan?"
>
> The Master said, "The man who summons me must have a purpose. If his purpose is to employ me, can I not, perhaps, create another Zhou in the east?"[88]

This passage makes clear that, as with Mencius's attempts to obtain a position in Qi, Confucius thought it worthwhile to attempt to serve, even under a nonlegitimate ruler, if there was hope of bringing back the unity, peacefulness, and orderliness of the preceding Zhou dynasty. As Confucius puts it in a different passage, "If anyone were to employ me, in a year's time I would have brought things to a satisfactory state, and after three years I should have results to show for it."[89]

Another anecdote has Confucius expressing his willingness to help Bi Xi, who was conspiring against the ruler of his own state of Jin, again to the dismay of Zilu:

> Zilu said, "Some time ago I heard it from you, Master, that the gentleman does not enter the domain of one who in his own person does what is not good. Now Bi Xi is using Zhongmou as a stronghold to stage a revolt. How can you justify going there?"
>
> The Master said, "It is true, I did say that. But has it not been said, 'Hard indeed is that which can withstand grinding'? Has it not been said, 'White indeed is that which can withstand black dye'? Moreover, how can I allow myself to be treated like a gourd which, instead of being eaten, hangs from the end of a string?"[90]

---

[87] *Analects* 5.19.
[88] *Analects* 17.5.
[89] *Analects* 13.10.
[90] *Analects* 17.7.

As Slingerland comments, the reference to the hard and white is a metaphor for Confucius's "incorruptibility": "Zilu's misgivings are unjustified, because Confucius can be employed by a less-than-ideal ruler without being led astray."[91] But what Confucius's response also underscores, as illustrated in the comparison to the uneaten gourd, is the concern with putting one's talent to use, in this case for political effect, in the attempt to create "another Zhou." This concern is similarly illustrated in Confucius's answer to Zigong, who asks whether one should put a piece of beautiful jade away or one should sell it: "The Master said, 'Of course I would sell it. Of course I would sell it. All I am waiting for is the right offer.' "[92]

A third anecdote, where Confucius is summoned by Yang Huo, a steward of the Ji family, is more ambiguous. In the *Mencius*, Confucius is said to avoid the summoning, and Mencius glosses this as an issue of propriety: as Mencius reports, Yang Huo sent a gift of a steamed piglet to Confucius while the latter was not at home, thus forcing him, as the rituals prescribe, to return the visit in order to express his gratitude in person. Confucius, in turn, waits for Yang Huo to be away from home to return the visit.[93] In the *Analects*, however, the story offers an additional twist, as Confucius ends up meeting Yang Huo on the way to his house and the latter tells him:

"Can the man be said to be *ren* who, while hoarding his treasure, allows the state to go astray? I should say not. Can the man be said to be wise who, while eager to take part in public life, constantly misses the opportunity? I should say not. The days and months slip by. Time is not on our side."

Confucius said, "All right. I shall take office."[94]

[91] Slingerland, trans., *Confucius: Analects*, 203.
[92] *Analects* 9.13. Slingerland comments on this that "Confucius . . . refuses to actively peddle his wares on the market, waiting instead for his virtue to be recognized by a ritually correct and morally cultivated ruler." See Slingerland, trans., *Confucius: Analects*, 203. In the same vein, Paul Goldin writes that "Confucius means to say that he would relish the opportunity to serve in government, but he will not do so until the regime has become worthy of his support. As long as his services are undervalued, he will keep himself off the labour market." See Goldin, *Confucianism*, 29–30. Both of these interpretations, especially Slingerland's, suggest more of a reluctance on the part of Confucius to serve in office than the anecdotes about him warrant, or so I argue.
[93] *Mencius* 3B.7.
[94] *Analects* 17.1.

Slingerland, following Zhu Xi, reads Confucius's answer as dismissive, an attempt to put off Yang Huo.[95] The thought behind this reading is that Yang Huo was revolting against the Ji family out of a concern with "self-aggrandizement," and thus should not be assisted, whereas Gongshan's and Bi Xi's motives, in the preceding anecdotes, were to restore the usurped power of the legitimate rulers of the states of Lu and Jin, respectively.[96] As Slingerland puts it, the latter two "though less than perfectly dutiful or moral, were at least moving in the right direction."[97] The same could not be said about Yang Huo and thus Confucius would not have agreed to serve under him. Although this reading of Confucius's response to Yang Huo is made plausible by the circumstances of the encounter, especially if one believes Mencius that Confucius was trying to avoid Yang Huo, it is not the most straightforward way to read the passage, and even Eno implicitly disagrees with it, seeing in this anecdote the closest that Confucius gets to accepting a political position.[98]

Slingerland's interpretation of the above anecdote rests on the assumption that Confucius cannot possibly be willing to help any ruler, bad or good, legitimate or illegitimate, yet more anecdotes about Confucius suggest precisely that. In one, for example, he went to see Nanzi, an ill-reputed consort of the ruler of Wei. Zilu was, yet again, displeased: "The Master swore, 'If I have done anything improper, may Heaven's curse be on me, may Heaven's curse be on me!' "[99] Similarly, in an anecdote in the *Mencius*, Mencius refutes the theory that Confucius stayed with Yongju when he visited the state of Wei and with Ji Huan when he visited Qi, both being favorites of their respective rulers. He contends that "Confucius went forward in accordance with the rites and withdrew in accordance with what was right."[100] Yet this an-

[95] Slingerland, trans., *Confucius: Analects*, 199.
[96] In 6.9, Min Ziqian declines the Ji family's offer to employ him as a steward for Bi. Slingerland comments that "Confucius' disciples, and even Confucius himself, were not averse to serving the Ji Family in public offices, where they would be formally serving the state of Lu as a whole and—at least in theory—serving as ministers to the legitimate lords of Lu." On the other hand, "Bi was the Family's private fortress-city, and . . . serving it as its steward would contribute nothing to the public good." Slingerland, trans., *Confucius: Analects*, 55.
[97] Slingerland, trans., *Confucius: Analects*, 203.
[98] Eno, *Confucian Creation of Heaven*, 51.
[99] *Analects* 6.28. Slingerland argues that some requirement of ritual propriety must have led Confucius to meet with Nanzi. Slingerland, trans., *Confucius: Analects*, 62.
[100] *Mencius* 5A.8.

ecdote is actually further evidence that Confucius might have been less scrupulous in his political involvement than he otherwise suggests, thus prompting Mencius to come to his defense. Finally, in one anecdote, the recluse Weisheng Mou asks Confucius why he is restless and whether he is trying to practice flattery, a question that can plausibly be taken to be aimed at criticizing Confucius's attempts at seeking office. Confucius answers that he does not practice flattery, but that he detests inflexibility (*jigu* 疾固), emphasizing the importance of keeping at what he does, that is, trying to obtain office.[101]

To recapitulate, I have tried to show that though Confucius, like Mencius, approves of different types of political behavior, and though he prefers an attitude of flexibility that is responsive to circumstances, he leans, especially in his own personal behavior, toward political engagement.[102] In other words, based on the preceding, it is hard to describe Confucius as an ethical purist or idealist, or as being against political involvement.[103] In fact, it is not even clear that the first version of the timeliness principle, frequently cited by interpreters, captures the essence of Confucius's position on political involvement. Recall that the timeliness principle advocated advancing in politics when the Way prevailed, and not advancing when the Way did not. In all of the situations faced by Confucius and relayed above, the Way, if taken to mean a situation where all the precepts of Confucian teaching are put into

---

[101] *Analects* 14.32. See also the anecdote in *Analects* 18.5, which also suggests Confucius to have been an advocate of political involvement, and to be criticized on precisely these grounds in the passage. *Analects* 14.39 is more ambiguous and open to differing interpretations.

[102] I thus agree with Schwartz that Confucius has no "fixed view" on the question of whether it is the duty of a Confucian scholar to try to influence rulers whose "life histories" do not "suggest an openness to virtue," but my interpretation above pushes toward seeing Confucius's default position to be favorable to the attempt. See Schwartz, *World of Thought in Ancient China*, 112.

[103] Eno's case for political idealism largely rests on a different set of passages from the ones discussed above, dealing with Confucius's decision to leave various states. Thus, in one passage, Confucius decides to leave the state of Wei because its ruler asked him about military formations, and this was not a topic he wanted to advise on (*Analects* 15.1). In another, he leaves Lu, where he held an official position, because its ruler was distracted by a gift of female entertainers and did not hold court for a few days (*Analects* 18.4). Finally, he leaves Qi because the ruler says that he is not able to treat him as he would the head of the Ji family (but somewhere between the rank of the Ji family and that of the Meng family), later conceding that he cannot employ him at all (*Analects* 18.3). What these passages could be taken to reveal, however, is not so much Confucius's political idealism but rather, as the commentator Jiang Xi, quoted by Slingerland, says, "that the sage is not inflexible," since he is willing to be employed, but leaves when he deems it proper to do so. See Slingerland, trans., *Confucius: Analects*, 214.

practice, is not realized. A better way to understand this principle is therefore to lower the standards for political involvement such as to allow for Confucian gentlemen's involvement precisely in order to bring the Way into being. If the standards are too low, then it is not worth trying, not only because one risks forgoing more worthy ethical pursuits, but also because trying is futile.[104] Commenting on the first version of the timeliness principle, Bao Xian (ca. 6 BCE–65 CE) interprets the need to leave a state to arise only "once a state has degenerated into immoral disorder" which he defines as "a situation where ministers are assassinating lords and sons killing fathers."[105] It is plausible to read the idea of the absence of the Way in a given state along these lines, suggesting that the condition for involvement in politics is not the full-blown realization of Confucian precepts, but the presence of a basic modicum of propriety in the key human relationships.

Xunzi

It is Xunzi who comes closest to the notion of political idealism and withdrawal suggested by Eno, leading one to wonder whether the passage of time, with its increasing warmongering and the fast-disappearing specter of a Zhou comeback, bred Xunzi's disillusionment.[106] Xunzi does not actually say much about the topic of political

---

[104] It is true that there are a couple of references in the *Analects* that suggest that it is worth pursuing tasks that one knows to be hopeless. One is a statement by Zilu cited earlier in which he says that one attempts to put the Way into practice even if one knows this is never going to work (*buxing* 不行) (*Analects* 18.7). The other is a statement by a gatekeeper to Zilu describing Confucius as one who "keeps working towards a goal the realization of which he knows to be impossible" (*zhi qi bu ke er wei zhi* 知其不可而為之) (*Analects* 14.38). Sor-hoon Tan thus argues that Confucius shows "faith . . . a willingness to try without guarantee of success, a positive attitude to the unknown and uncertain." See Tan, *Confucian Democracy*, 153. As Angle argues, however, and as I have tried to show in the preceding, associating his disposition with "faith" should not suggest that Confucius did not have a realistic sense of what he can actually achieve. See Angle, *Sagehood*, 201. Moreover, given that neither of the two preceding statements is attributed to Confucius himself, and that the second appears to be a statement by someone critical of Confucius, one should not necessarily take them as accurate representations of Confucius's own take on his mission.

[105] Slingerland, trans., *Confucius: Analects*, 82.

[106] On Sato's view, the increasing warfare and the development of bureaucratic states encouraged a shift away from the "advocacy of moral values" from the early to the late Warring States period. He notes, "In the capital of Qi, thinkers of the generation after Mencius seemed to turn their attention from the assertion of morality to analysis of socio-political dynamism. They began to analyse the dynamism of the rise and fall of a state extensively." See Sato, *Confucian Quest for Order*, 161. It is certainly true of Xunzi that he offered such an analysis, and one can thus argue that his elaboration of abstract

involvement, except to emphasize the need to maintain one's virtue under any circumstances. He thus says that success in serving a "disruptive" (*luan* 亂) ruler is not as good as obedience in serving an "impoverished" (*qiong* 窮) one—though this does not go as far as saying that it is never permissible to serve the former.[107] Xunzi's account of superior valor also emphasizes the importance of maintaining one's moral integrity in disordered times:

> When proper standards prevail in the world, to dare to bring your own conduct into accord with them; when the Way of the former kings prevails, to dare to follow its dictates; to refuse to bow before the ruler of a disordered age, to refuse to follow the customs of the people of a disordered age; to accept poverty and hardship if they are in the cause of *ren*; to reject wealth and eminence if they are not consonant with *ren*; if the world recognizes you, to share in the world's joys; if the world does not recognize you, to stand alone and without fear: this is superior valor.[108]

Xunzi compares the tenacity of the gentleman during adverse times to the cypress and cedar trees in winter,[109] adding that "although a gentleman is in dire straits and bitter poverty, he does not lose his way. Although he is tired and exhausted, he does not behave indecorously. Although he faces calamity or great difficulties, he does not forget the smallest measure of the doctrine."[110] As examples, Xunzi mentions Emperor Shun who persisted in his filial duties although his parents did not love him, Bigan and Wu Zixu who were loyal though their rulers did not employ them, and Confucius and his disciple Yan Hui who

---

blueprints for the regulation of society replace the more immediate, actual, and practical question of how and when to advise what ruler.

[107] *Xunzi* 2.5.

[108] *Xunzi* 23.7, quoted from Watson, 173. See also *Xunzi* 7.2, 8.2, 8.9, 22.4a, 22.4b.

[109] See also *Analects* 9.28: "The Master said, 'Only when the cold season comes is the point brought home that the pine and the cypress are the last to lose their leaves.'"

[110] *Xunzi* 27.77. Mencius actually makes a similar argument in 7A.9, though he still emphasizes the need to perfect the whole empire when one is able to (while Xunzi's statement suggests that he lost hope on this front): "A [man of service] never abandons rightness in adversity, nor does he depart from the Way in success. By not abandoning rightness in adversity, he finds delight in himself, by not departing from the Way in success, he does not disappoint the people. Men of antiquity made the people feel the effect of their bounty when they realized their ambition, and, when they failed to realize their ambition, were at least able to show the world an exemplary character. In obscurity a man makes perfect his own person, but in prominence he makes perfect the whole Empire as well."

were wise though their generation left them in poverty.[111] It should be mentioned, with regard to these examples, that they overstate their case. Shun was very filial, but he did get married without telling his parents. Mencius justifies Shun's decision on filial grounds, by emphasizing the importance of grandchildren but the point remains that in the dire situation of lacking his parents' love, Shun had to resort to the otherwise unfilial means of not seeking their approval. As for Wu Zixu, although he was loyal, Xunzi does not otherwise rank his loyalty high, precisely because it led to nothing but his death (see Chapter 4). Finally, as I showed in the preceding section, Confucius was far from merely putting up with a lack of an official position: he actually went around from ruler to ruler trying to obtain one.

Notwithstanding the inconsistencies involved with these historical figures, Xunzi seems to envision a scenario where a gentleman's only political involvement in a disorderly situation is to wait should the ruler or high officials ask him about government, in which case he is to tell them "what is right and what is wrong."[112] This distant but still engaged attitude is perhaps what Xunzi means when he speaks of restoring order (zhi 治) by "leaving what is chaotic behind and reaching over to what is well ordered."[113] By doing so, as Confucius did, according to Xunzi, "he will establish alone a noble reputation. Heaven cannot kill it, earth cannot bury it, the age of a Jie or Robber Zhi cannot tarnish it."[114]

The last segment of the *Xunzi*, which was probably added later to the corpus of the text (see the prologue), does suggest a certain indignation at Xunzi's not having enjoyed an official position worthy of him. Interestingly, the purpose of the passage is to answer the charge that Xunzi was not equal to Confucius in stature. The defense emphasizes the fact that Xunzi lived in chaotic times when rituals and rightness were not observed, when benevolent men were constrained, and when the transformative effects of teaching were not brought to completion. It was a time when "the wise had no opportunity to reflect, the able had no opportunity to govern, and the worthy had no opportunity

[111] *Xunzi* 27.112.
[112] *Xunzi* 27.76. On the other hand, when "one is detained and harassed in a cruel and violent land with no means of escape," then one should primarily "heap praise on its good qualities, display its fine points, discuss its strengths, but . . . not mention its shortcomings." *Xunzi* 27.112. See also 13.3.
[113] *Xunzi* 3.7.
[114] *Xunzi* 8.9.

to serve." This apparently forced Xunzi to cover up his true worth, hence the reason why his fame was not plainly evident and his followers were not many:

> Alas! He was a true worthy, fit to be a Di Ancestor or King. But the world did not recognize him, taking pleasure instead in the Jies and Zhou Xins of the age and killing the good and worthy. Bigan had his heart cut out; Confucius was seized in Kuang, . . . the Viscount of Ji had to feign madness. . . .
>
> It was impossible for him to exercise control over the government so that his true merit might have been perfected. Yet, since his aspirations were truly cultivated and his moral worth was highly developed, who can say that he was not a worthy man![115]

The thought here is that Xunzi would have been politically accomplished if the circumstances had allowed for it, suggesting perhaps that Xunzi did not try to be politically engaged not simply because he was focused on self-cultivation, but also because he thought that trying to get involved politically was futile. As he puts it elsewhere, the Confucian gentleman requires enabling conditions and resources to make his worth manifest: "Zaofu was the best charioteer in the world, but if he had lacked a chariot and team of horses, he would have had no way to make his ability manifest. Yi was the best archer in the world, but if he had had no bow and arrows, he would have had no way to make his skills known. A great *ru* [Confucian] is the best at adjusting and uniting the world, but if he lacks even so much as a hundred square [leagues] of territory, he has no way to make his skill manifest."[116] The great Confucian that was Xunzi thus lacked the means, not the will or the interest, to adjust and unite the world.

Conclusion

This chapter furthers my discussion of the Confucian conception of the political through a turn into the personal aspect of politics, or individuals' responsibility in relation to their government and society. While individuals, in the Confucian vision, cannot become fully virtuous without participating in political relationships, and while the possibility of a harmonious society rests on such participation, the duty of po-

[115] *Xunzi*, "Eulogy."
[116] *Xunzi* 8.9.

litical involvement is not limited to circumstances that would allow for the practice of virtue in a straightforward fashion. To the extent that one is able to preserve moral integrity by refusing to commit immoral acts, and to the extent that one sees a potential for convincing the ruler to undertake order-promoting policies, like the welfare-oriented policies delineated in Chapter 2, then one should get involved, even to the detriment of devotion to the pursuit of purely intellectual and moral cultivation. That politics involves corrupt actors and unforeseen events should not derail one's attempts to try to bring about a more orderly society. Or, to put it differently, humans' inability to control the various aspects of life, and especially political life, should not be an obstacle to political action. This inability is in fact what the early Confucians call fate, or the mandate (*ming* 命); how fate and its source, Heaven (*tian* 天), are mobilized in the service of their political agenda will be discussed in the next and final chapter.

CHAPTER 6

Heaven in Politics

The preceding chapters have mapped out the Confucian political vision, including the appointment of the ruler and his responsibilities, the relationship between ruler and ruled, and the place of ministers and Confucian gentlemen in government and politics, without reference to any metaphysical arguments. This is, on one level, as it should be, to the extent that this approach is suggested by the Confucians themselves. Thus Confucius, asked by Zilu about serving the spirits (*guishen* 鬼神), retorts, "You are not able even to serve man. How can you serve the spirits?"[1] This passage suggests Confucius's concern with turning one's focus from otherworldly matters to issues within human reach.[2] It is also said, in the *Analects*, that Confucius does not speak much of "prodigies, force, disorder and gods,"[3] of "profit, the mandate (*ming* 命) [of Heaven], and *ren*,"[4] and of "human nature and the Way of Heaven (*tiandao* 天道)."[5] Based on the *Analects* and other writings of the Eastern Zhou, some scholars have in fact concluded

---

[1] *Analects* 11.12.

[2] Another relevant passage in the *Analects* is 3.12, which speaks of sacrificing to the gods "as if the gods were present," thus emphasizing the psychosocial (rather than religious) importance of rituals of sacrifice. For more on the turn toward worldly concerns in early Confucianism, see Michael J. Puett, *To Become a God: Cosmology, Sacrifice, and Self-Divinization in Early China* (Cambridge, MA: Harvard University Press, 2002), 97–99; Erin Cline, "Religious Thought and Practice in the *Analects*," in *Dao Companion to the Analects*, ed. Amy Olberding (Dordrecht: Springer, 2014), 273–74; Slingerland, trans., *Confucius: Analects*, 44, 76; Graham, *Disputers of the Tao*, 15; and Eno, *Confucian Creation of Heaven*, 85.

[3] *Analects* 7.21.

[4] *Analects* 9.1.

[5] *Analects* 5.13.

that the period witnessed a continual decline in myths, cosmological arguments, and allusions to gods.[6]

That said, the metaphysical question cannot easily be dismissed. For, on the one hand, recent scholarship sheds doubt on the religious decline thesis and emphasizes instead the changing nature of the meaning of "religion" and of the religious outlook in early China.[7] On the other hand, even if one focuses only on the early Confucian texts as I have done in this book, and even just on the *Analects*, the statements cited above appear to be puzzling, because the *Analects* does not only discuss disorder, profit, human nature, and *ren* (all of which I alluded to in previous chapters), but also ghosts, spirits, prayers, and the Way of Heaven.[8] The question thus arises as to whether the political vision I have laid out in the previous chapters is lacking without mention of these metaphysical categories, especially Heaven (*tian* 天) and its mandate (*ming* 命).

Simply put, the answer to this question is yes and no. I argue in this chapter that Heaven provides legitimacy for the political vision discussed in the previous chapters without operating as an independent source of value. My argument largely follows that of Robert Eno, who argues that the early Confucians use Heaven as a legitimating device to justify political ideas that are not about Heaven per se. Eno also contends that Heaven is not a "defining interest" for the Confucians, and that "early Confucian philosophy seems directed away from meta-

[6] See, for example, Graham, *Disputers of the Tao*, 16, and Chad Hansen, *A Daoist Theory of Chinese Thought: A Philosophical Interpretation* (Oxford: Oxford University Press, 1992), 30.

[7] The argument of David Pankenier's *Astrology and Cosmology in Early China: Conforming Earth to Heaven* (Cambridge: Cambridge University Press, 2013) suggests that astrology and cosmology were central in early China, including for the state, well into the Han dynasty. See also T. C. Kline III and Justin Tiwald, eds., *Ritual and Religion in the Xunzi* (New York: State University of New York Press, 2014); Kelly James Clark and Justin T. Winslett, "The Evolutionary Psychology of Chinese Religion: Pre-Qin High Gods as Punishers and Rewarders," *Journal of the American Academy of Religion* 79, no. 4 (2011): 928–60; Philip J. Ivanhoe, "Heaven as a Source of Ethical Warrant in Early Confucianism," *Dao* 6 (2007): 211–20; and Cline, "Religious Thought and Practice."

[8] See *Analects* 2.24, 3.13, 6.22, 7.35, and 11.12. This tension in the text raises questions, discussed in the prologue, about the nature of the *Analects* and whether it contains different layers of content, some added later than others. Sor-hoon Tan argues in relation to Mencius that his references to Heaven could be attributed to his wish to make "an allowance for existing religious practices in his desire to win over new adherents to Confucianism," while also "reinterpreting it to serve Confucian purpose." See Tan, *Confucian Democracy*, 137. Eno points out that communist Chinese writers interpreted Confucius's appeal to Heaven as an appeal to a Zhou institution to legitimize archaic social divisions. See Eno, *Confucian Creation of Heaven*, 95.

physics and religion."[9] My aim in this chapter is not to assess the latter claim about the religious pedigree of early Confucianism: I intentionally bracket the question of the ontological status of Heaven, that is, whether the early Confucians really believed in it or not,[10] and whether one finds a realm of the religious, the sacred, or the divine in early Confucianism.[11] This is a big question that is beyond the scope of this chapter or book; my concern is only to address the way in which references to Heaven impact (or not) the Confucian conception of the political. It is of course true that I am able to disentangle the political and ontological dimensions of the religious question only because my argument is that the political vision stands on its own feet, but this argument is still compatible with a few, though perhaps not all, possible interpretations of the ontological status of Heaven.

A few background words about Heaven are in order here before I elaborate on the argument. "Heaven" is the translation adopted by the Jesuits when they first came to China in the sixteenth century. As Sorhoon Tan writes, it is "overburdened with Judeo-Christian theological and philosophical baggage."[12] Since the use of "Heaven" is common, however, I will keep to it here, while also sometimes using *tian* untranslated, as a reminder that the jury is still out on the adequacy of the English translation. As for the Mandate of Heaven, I briefly discussed the concept in the prologue. The mandate provided legitimacy for Zhou rule by suggesting that the Zhou kings had been appointed by Heaven to their position. Eno writes that the mandate made the Zhou king *"tian's* executor on earth," allowing him alone to sacrifice to Heaven, while in the preceding Shang dynasty, the king "had been merely chief

---

[9] Eno, *Confucian Creation of Heaven*, 5.

[10] I will thus not be doing for the early Confucians what Paul Veyne did for the early Greeks in his famous *Les Grecs ont-ils cru à leurs mythes? Essai sur l'imagination constituante* (Paris: Editions du Seuil, 1983).

[11] Graham argues that "the awe and resignation with which thinkers as far apart as Confucius and Zhuangzi accept the decree of Heaven has much more of the sense of the holy than anything in Mozi." See Graham, *Disputers of the Tao*, 48. Machle similarly argues, speaking of Xunzi's conception of Heaven, that just because *tian* "does not arbitrarily reward and punish, cannot be manipulated by rituals or special virtues, does no 'special acts' other than follow its proper 'office,' or is not spoken of in clearly anthropomorphic terms," does not mean it cannot partake of qualities that we usually associate with the "divine." See Machle, *Nature and Heaven in the Xunzi*, 175. See also Roetz, *Confucian Ethics of the Axial Age*, 194–97; Ivanhoe, "Heaven as a Source," 217n11; Puett, *To Become a God*, 181–88; and Cline, "Religious Thought and Practice," 285–89.

[12] Tan, *Confucian Democracy*, 137. This does not necessarily mean, however, that the translation is inappropriate; its appropriateness depends on the answer to the question of what Heaven is, i.e., to the ontological question mentioned above.

priest to the high gods."[13] He argues that Heaven legitimized Zhou rule as much as Zhou rule legitimized Heaven,[14] and that a crisis of legitimacy emerged from the collapse of this duality: as Zhou rule weakened, and its former territory descended into war, questions arose as to the role of Heaven, what Eno calls the "problem of theodicy": "how can a deity prescriptively good allow a world descriptively evil?"[15]

The early Mohists, presented in Chapter 3, offered an early simple view on the relationship between Heaven and the world: Mozi insisted on Heaven's goodness, arguing that Heaven desires rightness (yi 議), the survival (sheng 生) of the world, its richness (fu 富), and its order (zhi 治),[16] and that obedience to Heaven's desires brings rewards, while to oppose Heaven, by being partial and not helping others, is to incur Heaven's punishments.[17] The problem with the Mohist approach was evident: in the chaotic world of the warring states, it was not clear at all that tian actually rewarded the good and punished the bad.

The Confucian solution to the crisis was to insist both on the goodness and on the inscrutability of Heaven. This might seem contradictory at first sight,[18] but the early Confucians offer an account that does delimit the line where Heaven's commands end and its unfathomable work begins. Edward Slingerland puts the distinction in terms of an inner and outer realm;[19] Ning Chen puts it in terms of "moral decree"

[13] Eno, Confucian Creation of Heaven, 23–24. David Pankenier traces the development from a particularistic view of religion, including of the "Supernatural Lord" (Di) and of Heaven, under the Shang dynasty, to a universalistic approach, epitomized in the idea of the Mandate of Heaven, in the Zhou dynasty. See Pankenier, Astrology and Cosmology in Early China, 226–41.

[14] Eno, Confucian Creation of Heaven, 24.

[15] Eno, Confucian Creation of Heaven, 27. He also says that an old image of Heaven, as an "unpredictable ruler of the sky, whose whims were as likely to be malevolent as otherwise," started to reemerge during this period.

[16] Mozi bk. VII, chap. XXVI, 136. See Puett, To Become a God, 104.

[17] Mozi bk. VII, chap. XXVI, 138. For the Mohists, it was through ghosts and spirits that tian punished and rewarded, according to the standard of utilitarian logic explained in Chapter 3. See Csikszentmihalyi, Material Virtue, 41.

[18] Puett contends that the Confucian view is contradictory, not simply at first sight. He argues that there is an "agonistic" relationship between Heaven and humans in early Confucianism: Heaven is "the source of the patterns that should guide humanity but also the source of seemingly arbitrary commands that can disrupt those very patterns." See Puett, "Following the Commands of Heaven: The Notion of Ming in Early China," in The Magnitude of Ming: Command, Allotment, and Fate in Chinese Culture, ed. Christopher Lupke (Honolulu: University of Hawaii Press, 2005), 68–69. As I show in what follows, these two accounts of Heaven are not actually irreconcilable.

[19] Edward Slingerland, "The Conception of Ming in Early Confucian Thought," Philosophy East and West 46, no. 4 (1996): 568.

and "fixed fate."[20] Both share the idea that Confucius and Mencius use Heaven to point to both what is within and what is outside human control. As I will show in what follows, the domain of the inscrutable, or at least what is beyond human control, is threefold: biological life, political events and the actions of others (sometimes), and the course of Nature. To this correspond two areas that are within human control: improving oneself and improving society. Heaven thus provides the justification for the Confucian political program by both exhorting its followers to focus on what is within their control (most importantly for my purpose here, political engagement) and shielding them from responsibility for actions, especially political actions, well conceived but gone wrong, by attributing some types of failures to its own inscrutable work.

Most of this chapter is devoted to the *Analects* and the *Mencius*, elaborating on the argument just enunciated and showing how it sheds light on a few controversial passages in these two texts. While I understand Heaven's role similarly to Eno, Slingerland, and Chen, my conclusions regarding these controversial passages are different since my interpretation of the Confucian political program as a whole (and which I laid out in the preceding chapters) is different. The last section is devoted to Xunzi, who offers a sustained, but less controversial for my purposes here, view of *tian*.

Heaven's Allotments

Discussions of human nature constitute the most basic level at which references to Heaven play the dichotomous role I mentioned above.[21] This is clearest in the *Mencius*: Mencius thus argues that both the five senses and moral dispositions (*ren*, rightness, ritual propriety, and wisdom) are mandated (*ming* 命) by Heaven; but he also says that it is proper to associate only the first with what is decreed because the senses, as opposed to moral dispositions, are beyond our ability to control:

> The way the mouth is disposed towards tastes, the eye towards colours, the ear towards sounds, the nose towards smells, and the four limbs towards ease is human nature (*xing* 性), yet therein also

[20] Ning Chen, "The Concept of Fate in Mencius," *Philosophy East and West* 47, no. 4 (1997): 503.

[21] For Mencius's view of human nature, and how it differs from Xunzi's, see Chapter 3.

lies [the mandate] (*ming* 命). That is why the gentleman does not ascribe it to nature. The way *ren* pertains to the relation between father and son, [rightness] to the relation between prince and subject, the rites to the relation between guest and host, wisdom to the good and wise man, the sage to the way of Heaven, is [mandated] (*ming* 命), but therein also lies human nature. That is why the gentleman does not ascribe it to [the mandate] (*ming* 命).[22]

The idea of the "mandate" has, on the one hand, two interrelated meanings: what is given and what is fated (inescapable). A familiar conception of what is fated emerges in statements in the *Analects* to the effect that to be stricken by a disease is *ming*,[23] and that life and death are *ming*.[24] Such statements explain why it is a mark of a good Confucian to be ready to put one's life on the line when faced with danger.[25] For the idea is that fate (for example, whether one will live long or die young) should not influence one's "steadfastness of purpose" in being good.[26]

On the other hand, the moral senses are not just simply given to us; the reason why they are not to be described as *ming* (like the natural senses) is that we can significantly develop them. In fact, to develop them would be to fulfill Heaven's wishes;[27] this idea explains why virtue is sometimes described as being Heaven-ordained (rather than human-made), for example that "*ren* is the high honor bestowed by Heaven,"[28] and in the *Analects* Confucius is described as being set on the path of sagehood by Heaven.[29]

The link in this latter account that is relevant for my purposes here is not the relationship between Heaven and self-cultivation per se,[30] but

[22] *Mencius* 7B.24.

[23] *Analects* 6.10. In 7A.38, Mencius says that "only a sage can give his body complete fulfillment," implying that there is some level of control one has over one's physical existence. Xunzi makes a statement in a similar vein, suggesting that to rectify one's bodily faculties and nourish one's emotions is to complete *tian*'s undertakings (*Xunzi* 17.4).

[24] *Analects* 12.5. See also 11.9, where, in response to Yan Hui's death, Confucius laments, "Heaven has bereft me! Heaven has bereft me!"

[25] In *Analects* 19.1, to lay down his life (*zhi ming* 致命) in the face of danger, is as much a mark of a Confucian gentleman as to "not forget what is right at the sight of gain . . . not forget reverence during a sacrifice nor sorrow while in mourning." See also *Analects* 14.12.

[26] *Mencius* 7A.1.

[27] The confusing element here is that Mencius actually calls fulfilling Heaven's wishes "the mandate" too. See, for example, 7B.24.

[28] *Mencius* 2A.7.

[29] *Analects* 9.6.

[30] As Tan argues, the ethical dimension of *tian* is evidenced in "the description of the ethical life as the way of *tian* (*tiandao* 天道), the distinction between the nobility of *tian*

the way in which the achievement of merit, and concomitantly rank, in government, is also glossed as being Heaven-ordained: thus there are such things as "positions," "duties," and "revenue" given by Heaven,[31] and Mencius speaks of "Heaven-appointed" officers (*wei tianli* 為天吏), by which he means men worthy of ruling their countries.[32] Heaven thus favors the promotion of worthy men. In other words, it backs up the hierarchy of merit espoused by the Confucians and discussed in the preceding chapters.

The idea that Heaven's will tracks worthiness explains a difficulty I set aside in Chapter 1, when I discussed Mencius's account of the succession to the throne in *Mencius* 5A.5 and 5A.6. The difficulty lies in the fact that Mencius, on the one hand, attributes the choice of the ruler to the common people, while, on the other hand, portraying the common people as expressing Heaven's will: Heaven "sees with the eyes of its people" and it "hears with the ears of its people." My interpretation of these two passages suggested that the common people simply acted as a gauge of the competence of the ruler (rather than as agents with independent choice), but I did not say anything about the role of *tian*. On the one hand, Mencius seems to suggest that Heaven can do whatever it wants when he says that if Heaven raises a worthy to power, then a worthy is raised to power, and if it raises a son, then a son is raised (*tian yu xian, ze yu xian; tian yu zi, ze yu zi* 天與賢，則與賢；天與子，則與子). On the other hand, he quickly dissolves the dichotomy between the worthy and the son in what follows: Explaining why it is that Heaven favored hereditary succession in the case of Yu's son, but not in the case of Yao's and Shun's, he says that Qi, Yu's son, was capable and worthy of succeeding his father, while Yao's and Shun's sons were useless. Moreover, while a worthy minister, Yi had assisted Yu only for a short period of time, whereas Shun had assisted Yao and Yu had assisted Shun over a long period of time, and had benefited the people.

and the nobility of humans (*tianjue renjue* 天爵人爵), and the ethical importance of knowing and serving *tian*, which is the source of the human heart-and-mind and its ethical predispositions." See Tan, *Confucian Democracy*, 138.

[31] *Mencius* 5B.3. Mencius makes a distinction between two sorts of pursuits: the pursuit of wealth, rank, even a ruling position, for their own sake, is something that is beyond humans' control to some extent, but also beyond what Heaven wishes for humans to pursue, while the pursuit of the virtues (including as a way to obtain rank) is both within humans' control and part of Heaven's plan or "mandate." See *Mencius* 6A.16, 7A.3, 7A.21, 7B.33. In *Analects* 12.5, on the other hand, wealth and honor are associated with Heaven.

[32] See, for example, *Mencius* 2A.5 and 2B.8. See also 7A.19 where Mencius speaks of "the subjects of Heaven" (*tianminzhe* 天民者).

He concludes, "Shun and Yu differed from Yi greatly in the length of time they assisted the Emperor, and their sons differed as radically in their moral character. All this was due to Heaven and could not have been brought about by man. When something is brought about though there is nothing that brings it about, then it is Heaven that does it. When something arrives though there is nothing that makes it arrive, then it is [the mandate] (*ming* 命)."[33] Mencius thus recasts Heaven's involvement in the choice of the ruler as bringing about that some candidates are more worthy than others, hence some candidates are deserving of promotion and others not. Heaven does not decide, according to standards fully fathomable only to it, the appropriate recipient of the throne and then signals him to the people. Rather, it simply causes some sons to be superior in some cases, and ministers to be superior in other cases, or, to put it in a more straightforward manner, Heaven is invoked as an expression of approval of the more worthy candidate.

Commenting on this passage, Michael Puett writes that Mencius "hardly answers the larger point . . . why did Heaven ordain hereditary monarchy to be the norm?"[34] The first remark that is in order in response to Puett's point is that Mencius does not specifically say that Heaven ordained hereditary monarchy: Heaven is mentioned only to justify the specific cases of Yao, Shun, and Yu and their sons (precisely because they required special justification). And, as I just showed, Heaven's choice, according to Mencius, tracks competence (or, more accurately, readiness for the job) in these three cases. I agree, however, with Puett, as I argued in Chapter 1, that hereditary succession is indeed the norm favored by the early Confucians (and that Shun and Yu are the exceptions here), and while Mencius does not explicitly state that Heaven favors hereditary succession, he does say that Heaven only puts aside (*fei* 廢) one who inherits the throne if he is tyrant-like. Heaven is thus deployed in order to signal disapproval of tyrants. As I argued in Chapter 1, a tyrant is a ruler who cannot win his people's support and thus cannot achieve political order. He is not a legitimate ruler, and it is therefore no surprise that Heaven is invoked to cast doubt on his legitimacy. As for the typical cases of hereditary succession, that is, cases where a heir is not the most competent of all candidates but is not bad enough to be removed, then they are neither here nor there: there is no need to refer to Heaven to signal either disap-

---

[33] *Mencius* 5A.6.
[34] Puett, *To Become a God*, 138.

proval (since the heirs are in fact legitimate) or approval (since there is no difficulty in ascertaining their legitimacy).

Uncertainty and Political Involvement

In the preceding section, I showed how Heaven is used as a symbol of legitimacy for the Confucian political project with regards to the distribution of political authority, especially in the hard cases where there is a case to be made about the rightful recipient of the throne. The section started with a distinction between what is decreed, and what is within human control. The latter includes virtue and the achievement of merit. As for fate, I related it to biological life: whether people are stricken by disease, whether they die young or old, and so on. The Confucians also offer, however, a more political idea of "fate," namely fate relating to participation in political life. It is this idea of fate that this section is concerned with.

I argued in the previous chapter that the Confucians approve of the participation of their disciples in government, even under corrupt rulers and during turbulent times. What I want to show here is the way in which *tian* provides legitimacy for this participation through the twofold role I described above: on the one hand, in the same way that *tian* is used to support the pursuit of political virtue and the promotion of the worthy, it also encourages well-motivated political engagement. On the other hand, and crucially, by delimiting areas beyond human control, it justifies certain political failures, shielding the political agent from responsibility for unforeseen or uncontrollable events.

Heaven's encouragement of political action is clearest in the story of Yi Yin discussed in the previous chapter. After many attempts by the virtuous prince Tang to have him join his court, Yi Yin is persuaded upon rehearsing the following thought, quoted earlier but worth repeating here: "Heaven, in producing the people, has given to those who first attain understanding the duty of awakening those who are slow to understand; and to those who are the first to awaken the duty of awakening those who are slow to awaken. I am among the first of Heaven's people to awaken. I shall awaken this people by means of this Way. If I do not awaken them, who will?"[35] Yi Yin is thus described

---

[35] *Mencius* 5A.7.

as moved by the recognition of a Heaven-ordained duty to become politically active to help the people.

Yet Heaven plays an even more distinctive role in encouraging political engagement: just as the mandate separates aspects of human life that are within our control from those beyond it, similarly, on the political level, it separates events that the gentleman worries about from those that he should not worry about. For example, Mencius attributes the Duke of Lu's reluctance to meet with him not to the Duke's advisor Zang Cang, but rather to Heaven: "When a man goes forward, there is something which urges him on; when he halts, there is something which holds him back. It is not in his power either to go forward or to halt. It is due to Heaven that I failed to meet the Duke of Lu. How can this fellow Zang be responsible for my failure?"[36]

For Mencius to say that it is not in people's power to go forward or to halt is surprising, since he insists otherwise that people can, or at least should try to, be good and undertake good actions. The passage can thus more plausibly be read as suggesting not so much that the Duke of Lu's actions are overdetermined, but that Mencius's own failure is: that there is nothing more he could have done to have an audience with the Duke, that this meeting was beyond his ability to control, because he cannot control how the Duke will act. Similarly, when faced with a threat from a military minister from Song, Confucius says, "Heaven is the author of the virtue that is in me. What can Huan Tui do to me?"[37] Here, Confucius's reference to Heaven allows him to shield himself from a concern with Huan Tui and to keep focused on his own mission instead, the mission that presumably caused Huan Tui's enmity in the first place. Another similar passage finds Confucius under siege in Kuang, to which he responds by emphasizing the nature of his mission, centered on the preservation of Zhou culture, and by referencing Heaven to explain why the threat he faces is beyond his control and thus not worth his worry: "With King Wen dead, is not culture (*wen* 文) invested here in me? If Heaven intends culture to be destroyed, those who come after me will not be able to have any part of it. If Heaven does not intend this culture to be destroyed, then what can the men of Kuang do to me?"[38] Heaven is thus both the source of Confucius's project and the source of its potential failures: it presses him forward both

[36] *Mencius* 1B.16.
[37] *Analects* 7.23.
[38] *Analects* 9.5.

through a goal to be pursued and through minimizing the disappoint-
ments that beset the way toward it.

In the same line of thought, when Zifu Jingbo warns of killing
Gongbo Liao for speaking ill of Zilu, Confucius discourages him from
doing so by saying, "It is [the mandate] (*ming*) if the Way prevails; it is
equally [the mandate] if the Way falls into disuse. What can Gongbo
Liao do in defiance of [the mandate]?"[39] Eno reads in Confucius's response a rejection of political intrigue, and relates this rejection to the
idea of ethical purism that he finds in early Confucianism (see Chapter
5).[40] Yet it is not obvious why Confucius would need to appeal to the
mandate to defend the idea that killing a person for speaking ill of another is wrong. On my interpretation, the work that the mandate is
doing here is to signal that there are political events, including the actions of distant others like Gongbo Liao, that one cannot control and
thus should not worry about responding to.

It is true that, in some instances, a great deal is attributed to Heaven
(and thus seen as beyond human control). For example, Mencius says
that whether the less virtuous serve the more virtuous or the more virtuous serve the less virtuous is due to Heaven.[41] The first remark to
make about this passage is that it is meant to justify why Duke Jing of
Qi gave his daughter in marriage to a "barbarian" tribe, thus absolving
him by attributing his action to the vagaries of his time. The second is
that the statement does not imply that one should not work toward a
world where it is the less virtuous who serve the more virtuous; instead, it is meant to temper disillusionment when such a situation does
not obtain, which means both that the former goal is to be maintained,
but also that the appropriate response to existing circumstances might
be to accept them, at least temporarily. This is made clear in a similar
passage where Mencius says that "he who submits to a state smaller
than his own delights in Heaven; he who submits to a state bigger than
his own is in awe of Heaven."[42] Heaven's symbolic force is invoked
here to legitimize two scenarios, as Bryan Van Norden argues: the normatively preferred scenario in which "the powerful are generous
enough to serve the weak" but also the "prudential" scenario in which
"the weak are wise enough to serve the strong."[43]

[39] *Analects* 14.36.
[40] Eno, *Confucian Creation of Heaven*, 92.
[41] *Mencius* 4A.7.
[42] *Mencius* 1B.3.
[43] See Van Norden, trans., *Mengzi*, 18.

In any case, what is important to emphasize is that the attribution of unwieldy political events to Heaven is not meant to justify an attitude of fatalism, where one is not responsible for one's actions (which is what the Mohists accused the Confucians of, insistent as the former were, as I explained earlier, on the direct link between actions and consequences).[44] The Confucians in fact explicitly make a distinction between what is properly beyond one's control and what is not. As Mencius says, "Though nothing happens that is not due to [the mandate], one accepts willingly only what is one's proper [mandate]. That is why he who understands [the mandate] does not stand under a wall on the verge of collapse. He who dies after having done his best in following the Way dies according to his proper [mandate]. It is never anyone's proper [mandate] to die in fetters [i.e., as a criminal]."[45]

Following the Way, I argued in the previous chapter, does not always imply ethical purism as Eno submits. It also involves attempting, for example, to counsel an incompetent ruler. It is noteworthy that Confucius and Mencius do not attribute the failure of such counsel to Heaven in the way that they do with regard to actors and events relayed in the preceding. One has much more leverage in counseling a ruler under whom one serves than in securing a meeting with a ruler of a different state, and in influencing the former than in influencing a scheming enemy; this is presumably the sort of distinction that explains the difference between the political events that one should be responsible for and those not. I thus disagree with Eno that references to Heaven completely separate the development of one's virtues from "the actual outcome of events," thus "rationalizing" the Confucian "persistence in ethical conduct in the face of political futility."[46] On my interpretation of the preceding passages, the notion of the mandate is meant to shield the Confucians from being discouraged by the vagaries of the political world; their quest is not independent from outcomes per se, but simply from unforeseen and unpredictable outcomes.

[44] Mark Csikszentmihalyi argues that there are two potential explanations for why the Mohists attribute an "unequivocal fatalism" to the Confucians when the latter advocated "a limited notion of *ming*": either the passages from the *Analects* available when the *Mozi* was composed did not reflect the view of fate that our current version of the *Analects* offers, or the Mohists thought "the notion of limited fatalism logically inconsistent." See Csikszentmihalyi, *Material Virtue*, 40–42.

[45] *Mencius* 7A.2.

[46] Eno, *Confucian Creation of Heaven*, 126.

While not sharing Eno's view on the "political futility" of the Confucian project, Slingerland argues that the Confucian conception of *ming* allows for a "a realistic and mature redirection of human energy toward the sole area of life in which one does have control—the cultivation and moral improvement of one's own self."[47] My disagreement with Slingerland concerns what counts as a "realistic" project: on my interpretation, offered in the previous chapter, political engagement can be described as a realistic project too.

Thus, while drawing on the framework used by both Eno and Slingerland, my conclusions about the Confucian conception of Heaven's role in politics differ from theirs because my conception of Confucian politics is different. For example, in one passage in the *Analects*, Confucius complains that no one understands him—which might be taken as a complaint about his lack of employment—but he keeps away from despair and resentment by mentioning Heaven: "I am not bitter toward Heaven, nor do I blame others. I study what is below in order to comprehend what is above. If there is anyone who could understand me, perhaps it is Heaven."[48] Eno reads this passage as expressing the thought that Confucius is fulfilling Heaven's plan by focusing on studying.[49] On my interpretation, however, Confucius's reference to Heaven is merely meant to justify his project, which includes his political mission, despite its failures: Heaven alone understands this project and the obstacles that beset it, and the fact that Heaven understands it suggests that it is not, and never was, a misguided project.[50] Or, consider the following passage from the *Mencius*:

[47] Slingerland, "Conception of *Ming*," 568.

[48] *Analects* 14.35, quoted from Slingerland.

[49] Eno, *Confucian Creation of Heaven*, 92.

[50] Also consider *Analects* 3.24: the border official in the state of Yi tells Confucius's followers that they should not worry about Confucius's loss of office, because "the Empire has long been without the Way," which means that Heaven, which would not let this situation continue for too long, is "about to use your Master as the wooden tongue for a bell." According to Slingerland, the bell is "the kind used by itinerant collectors and transmitters of folk songs or functionaries who circulated around the countryside promulgating official announcements." See Slingerland, trans., *Confucius: Analects*, 28. In other words, Confucius was going to be the transmitter of the Way. Both Slingerland and Eno read this passage as suggesting that Heaven purposefully made Confucius's quest for employment fail so that he could focus on spreading his teachings. See Eno, *Confucian Creation of Heaven*, 89. Yet the passage might also be interpreted simply to suggest that the border official believed that Confucius was soon going to be employed and thus be in a position to put the Way into practice. In *Analects* 9.9, however, Confucius sounds a more desperate note: "The Phoenix does not appear nor does the River offer up its Chart. I am done for." Slingerland comments that "both the phoenix and chart were auspicious

When Mencius left Qi, on the way Chong Yu asked, "Master, you look somewhat unhappy. I heard from you the other day that a gentleman reproaches neither Heaven nor man."

"This is one time; that was another time. Every five hundred years a true King should arise, and in the interval there should arise one from whom an age takes its name. From Zhou to the present, it is over seven hundred years. The five hundred mark is passed; the time seems ripe. It must be that Heaven does not as yet wish to bring peace and order (*pingzhi* 平治) to the Empire. If it did, who is there in the present time other than myself? Why should I be unhappy?"[51]

Philip Ivanhoe offers many alternatives for interpreting the seeming contradiction between Mencius's initial unhappy countenance, and his final statement that he is not in fact unhappy.[52] The alternatives that fit best with my interpretation are the ones that do not get rid of the contradiction (by suggesting, for example, that Mencius only looks unhappy but is in fact not). For, on my reading, it is to be expected that Mencius would be unhappy, and slightly inclining toward resentment, given all his efforts toward obtaining a political position (see Chapter 5). But Mencius also understands that there are limits to what he can hope to achieve in this world, and that these limits do not raise doubts about the validity of his mission; the mission is, ultimately, both ordained and guided by Heaven.

As Xunzi says, "those who know [the mandate] do not resent Heaven" (*zhimingzhe bu yuan tian* 知命者不怨天) for those who resent Heaven cannot accomplish their aims (*yuantianzhe wu zhi* 怨天者無志).[53] Confucius similarly says that one who does not understand the mandate "has no way of becoming a gentleman."[54] A proper understanding of Heaven entails a reconciliation with the limits of the political world,[55] a reconciliation that is neither passive resignation nor idealistic faith,

---

omens sent by Heaven in the past to indicate that a sagely ruler was arising to bring peace to the world." See Slingerland, trans., *Confucius: Analects*, 89. Confucius thus seems hopeless here about the possibility of being employed by a wise ruler.

[51] *Mencius* 2B.13. See also 3B.9 and 7B.38.

[52] Philip Ivanhoe, "A Question of Faith: A New Interpretation of Mencius 2B.13," *Early China* 13 (1988): 153–65.

[53] *Xunzi* 4.5.

[54] *Analects* 20.3.

[55] Eno takes the limit to human action to be "entailed with existence as a determinate entity." I agree that there is something to this existentialist reading, but I wish to empha-

but, to use Slingerland's words, a "mature" and "realistic" sense of where one should direct one's energies, what one should pursue, and what one should feel responsible for.

Heaven's Patterns

Of our three texts, the *Xunzi* actually has the most to say about Heaven: devoted to the topic is a whole chapter whose most obvious aim is to argue against divination and other superstitious practices of the times.[56] The following passage from the chapter is exemplary and worth quoting in its entirety:

> If you pray for rain and there is rain, what of that? I say there is no special relationship—as when you do not pray for rain and there is rain. When the sun and moon are eclipsed, we attempt to save them; when Heaven sends drought, we pray for rain; and before we decide any important undertaking, we divine with both bone and milfoil. We do these things not because we believe that such ceremonies will produce the results we seek, but because we want to embellish (*wen* 文) such occasions with ceremony. Thus, the gentleman considers such ceremonies as embellishments, but the Hundred Clans consider them supernatural (*shen* 神). To consider them embellishments is fortunate; to consider them supernatural is unfortunate.[57]

This passage underscores humans' inability to control the powers of nature. It also shifts the emphasis from nature-centered practices to their human ends. As Eno argues, the intellectual milieu of Xunzi's time was dominated by what he calls "naturalism," an amalgam of trends that "shared a conviction that human values must be founded upon the pre-human entity of Nature." For Eno, "the *Xunzi* should be viewed as first and foremost a response to that threat."[58]

---

size here the political dimension of the limit to action. See Eno, *Confucian Creation of Heaven*, 127.

[56] Knoblock translates the title of the chapter (*tianlun* 天論) as "Discourse on Nature," while Watson prefers "A Discussion of Heaven." For a discussion of whether Xunzi's *tian* is best rendered as Nature or not, see Machle, *Nature and Heaven in the Xunzi* and Janghee Lee, *Xunzi and Early Chinese Naturalism* (New York: State University of New York Press, 2005).

[57] *Xunzi* 17.8.

[58] Eno, *Confucian Creation of Heaven*, 143. Interpreters generally agree that however Xunzi's *tian* is understood, it does not command the course of human events. See Lee,

The twofold role of Heaven is to some extent at play here as well. On the one hand, Heaven brings about the natural events which are beyond humans' power to affect: as Xunzi says, we do not perceive the process through which *tian* works (allowing for the sun and moon to shine, for the four seasons to unfold, for wind and rain to occur, etc.); this is why we describe it as supernatural (*shen* 神). Moreover, the sage "acts not seeking to know *tian*."[59] On the other hand, the events that are in fact within our control and that we should focus on are also the product of Heaven: "How can glorifying *tian* and contemplating it, be as good as tending its creatures and regulating them? How can obeying *tian* and singing its hymns of praise be better than regulating what *tian* has mandated (*ming*) and using it?"[60]

Thus, in the same way that, for Mencius, both biology and morality are provided for by Heaven, but it is only the latter that Heaven encourages us to pursue, so the distinction for Xunzi is between a natural order and a social order, both made possible by Heaven, but it is only the latter that humans are supposed to focus on. Xunzi thus asks that humans concentrate on avoiding "monstrosities among men": crop damaged by bad plowing, harvest lost through poor weeding, and people confused by ill-conceived government regulations and hungry because of expensive grain.[61]

The main difference here though is that Xunzi does not emphasize the normative role of Heaven as much as Mencius and Confucius do; in other words, he does not explicitly say that to focus on human monstrosities and embellishments is to fulfill Heaven's wishes.[62] On the other hand, Xunzi's distinguishing thought, not to be found either in the *Analects* or in the *Mencius*, is the idea that the social order achieved by humans is a complement to the natural order achieved by Heaven.[63] As he puts its, "*tian* has its seasons; earth its resources, and man his

---

Xunzi and Early Chinese Naturalism, 21; Chan, *Source Book in Chinese Philosophy*, 117; Creel, *Chinese Thought*, 130–31; Graham, *Disputers of the Tao*, 239; Xu, *Zhongguo renxing lunshi*, 257.

[59] *Xunzi* 17.2b. As he also puts it, "If you understand the division between *tian* and humankind, then you can properly be called a 'Perfect Man' (*zhiren* 至人)" (17.1).

[60] *Xunzi* 17.10.

[61] *Xunzi* 17.7.

[62] I thank Aaron Stalnaker for alerting me to this difference.

[63] In Eno's words, "The grandeur and perfection of Tian as Nature . . . serves as a positive model, and represents the goal of human aspiration. . . . Nature is what man must transcend to become ethical, yet the greatest of goals toward which man strives is to become Nature's equal." See Eno, *Confucian Creation of Heaven*, 165.

government (*zhi* 治)," adding that they form a "Triad."[64] This Triad points to what I mentioned in Chapter 3 as an underlying "Coherence" in the world, involving both natural and human aspects, and signaled by the use of the term *li* 理 in the *Xunzi*, which becomes central only with later Neo-Confucians, but which arguably suggests the seeds of such a metaphysical view in the *Xunzi*. The "Coherence" of the world— its patterning—involves both hierarchical relations in Nature (between Heaven and Earth) and hierarchical human relations mirroring the former (ruler/minister, father/son). Thus the sages pattern society just like Heaven patterns the Natural world.[65]

This said, Xunzi, like Confucius and Mencius before him,[66] is primarily interested in the human, not the Natural, order: "The Way of the Ancient Kings . . . is not the Way of Heaven or the Way of Earth, but rather the Way that guides the actions of mankind and is embodied in the conduct of the gentleman."[67] Xunzi contends that while Heaven is the source of the "myriad things," these remain undifferentiated before the sage comes in to make distinctions and assign everyone their position (see Chapter 3).[68]

Because Xunzi distinguishes the world of Heaven and the world of humans so sharply, Heaven is not invoked to legitimize in any direct way the Confucians' political ideas, either in terms of the succession to the throne or in terms of political engagement. This explains why I have relegated a discussion of his view to the end of this chapter. I do not necessarily agree, however, with Hsiao that Xunzi's repudiation of an active Heaven "represented an attack on one of the important theoretical means by which the ancients had limited the ruler."[69] In both the *Analects* and the *Mencius*, Heaven is deployed to legitimize ideas that are justified on the "secular" grounds of achieving political order, and this goal itself (i.e., political order) can be described as a "theoretical means" to restrain rulers. This is not to deny, however, the persuasive (as opposed to theoretical) force of Heaven, adding symbolic clout to the sociological argument for the Confucian political vision.

[64] *Xunzi* 17.2a. See also 9.15 and 13.9.
[65] *Xunzi* 17.5.
[66] Mencius says, "Heaven's weather is less important than earth's advantageous terrain, and earth's advantageous terrain is less important than human unity" (2B.1).
[67] *Xunzi* 8.3.
[68] *Xunzi* 19.6.
[69] Hsiao, *History of Chinese Political Thought*, 211.

Conclusion

In a famous passage in the *Analects*, Confucius describes his life journey thus: "At fifteen I set my heart on learning; at thirty I took my stand; at forty I came to be free from doubts; at fifty I understood [the Mandate] of Heaven; at sixty my ear was attuned; at seventy I followed my heart's desire without overstepping the line."[70] Eno takes the reference to the Mandate of Heaven in this passage to be a reference to Heaven favoring the failure of Confucius's political attempts as a way to encourage his focus on teaching. According to Eno, the "culmination" of Confucius's sagehood lies in his "reconciliation of ethical imperatives with descriptive limitations," that is, limitations imposed by Heaven and the world.[71] My aim in this chapter was also to show the way in which *tian* and its decree provide such limitations on human action; yet the reconciliation I have elicited does not require the Confucians to withdraw from the political world, but simply to accept that their political engagement is ridden with risk, and that there is never a guarantee of success. As T'ang Chün-i puts it, "For a superior man, thus, circumstances do not matter; for him, there is no distinction between 'success' and 'failure'; or, rather, both 'success' and 'failure' are for him 'success' [for he has done his duty]."[72] Again it is important to emphasize here that the duty is not only ethical, but also through and through political. The duty is to bring about a peaceful, orderly society, over and against the world's turmoil.

Finally, I have also argued in this chapter that Heaven is not so much the "source of political authority"[73] in this orderly society, but rather its cloak. The source of political authority is the ability to establish political order. If Heaven is, as Pines puts is, "an active and sentient being, which, albeit not speaking directly with its appointees, intervenes in human affairs,"[74] it intervenes in alignment with, and not independently of, the Confucian conception of political order.

---

[70] *Analects* 2.4.

[71] Eno, *Confucian Creation of Heaven*, 91.

[72] T'ang Chün-i, "The *T'ien Ming* [Heavenly Ordinance] in Pre-Ch'in China," *Philosophy East and West* 11, no. 4 (January 1962): 216.

[73] See, for example, Tiwald, "Right of Rebellion," 275.

[74] Pines, *Envisioning Eternal Empire*, 74. See also Hsiao, *History of Chinese Political Thought*, 161.

Epilogue

As the early Greeks were propounding their views on ethics and politics that became the foundation for the Western philosophical tradition, the Confucians were, at almost the same time, offering their own views on the good life and the good society, paving the way for China's two-thousand-year-long tradition of thought.

For a long time, and for complex historical reasons, the Chinese intellectual tradition did not receive academic interest in its own right similar to that received by the Western tradition, especially outside of China. While the urgency of the renewed interest in it, alluded to in the prologue, is both timely and welcome, it has meant that the Confucian texts are now mined with a view to contemporary concerns. Many of the political discussions in the early texts have thus been ignored for being irrelevant today. In this book, I have bracketed the question of contemporary relevance and turned instead to reconstructing the political vision offered in the three Classical Confucian texts. This has allowed me to focus on the discussions they provide of political personages, rules, and events, however antiquated these might seem. This focus has in turn led me to the argument that these discussions cannot simply be explained by resorting to the Confucian ethical precepts. I have thus elicited an independent "realm of the political,"[1] to use Schwartz's phrase, that is concerned with what I have called "political order."

My interpretation of early Confucianism meshes with the recent trend in the discipline of political theory critiquing the post-Kantian approach to political theorizing that takes ethics as a basis.[2] A central

[1] Schwartz, *World of Thought in Ancient China*, 102.
[2] See, for example, Williams, *In the Beginning Was the Deed*; Raymond Geuss, *Philoso-*

part of the critique of the post-Kantian approach is a critique of the
way in which this approach sidesteps the centrality of violence and
conflict in politics.[3] It might thus be relevant to note here that the Confucians do not have much place for conflict in their political theory either, despite the fact that theirs is not an ethics-based political theory.
Perhaps the best way to see this is to draw again the comparison to
Hobbes, whose political theory starts with the inevitability of conflict in
the state of nature. Hobbes favors the political order brought about by
a unitary sovereign as a solution to the chaos of the state of nature. The
early Confucians, on the other hand, do not start from the premise of
discrete individuals faced with the challenge of how to organize collective life. This partly has to do with the issue I raised in Chapter 1 about
the absence of a strong notion of consenting and deliberating individuals. Related to this, the early Confucians never consider individuals
separately from their social grouping: for them, humans are inherently
social and sociable beings and, left to their own devices, are more likely
to come together rather than draw apart. The question of order then
is not this: under what conditions can discrete self-interested individuals come together to live in peace and security in society? Rather, the
question is this: under what conditions can people fulfill their social
dispositions? Or, how can we remove obstacles to people's natural propensity to come together? In other words, the starting assumption is
society, not war, and the question is not how to escape war, but how to
maintain peace.

Confucian optimism about humans and their social tendencies has
led to the criticism that Confucians put too much faith in the rule of
persons, as opposed to institutions. Many Chinese intellectuals today
thus seek to replace Confucianism's emphasis on "rule by man" (*renzhi*
人治) with the concept of "rule by law" (*fazhi* 法治).[4] But the evidence
presented in this book suggests that the idea that the Confucian political vision stands or falls with the presence or absence of a few good
men on top is exaggerated. I have indeed shown how government relies on institutional mechanisms, rather than virtue per se, for the regu-

---

phy and Real Politics (Princeton: Princeton University Press, 2008); Eckard Bolsinger, *The
Autonomy of the Political: Carl Schmitt's and Lenin's Political Realism* (Westport, CT: Green-
wood, 2001); and Bonnie Honig, *Political Theory and the Displacement of Politics* (Ithaca,
NY: Cornell University Press, 1993).

[3] Bolsinger, *Autonomy of the Political*, xii. See also Honig, *Political Theory and the Displacement of Politics*.

[4] Leigh Jenco, *Making the Political: Founding and Action in the Political Theory of Zhang
Shizhao* (New York: Cambridge University Press, 2010), 72–102.

lation of society. These mechanisms include welfare measures, punishments even if only as a last resort, rituals, and education to promote filiality. The critics are of course right about the absence of guarantees that the ruler and his ministers will actually promote and maintain these institutions and policies. But the point remains that these institutions exist in early Confucian political thought.

In any case, a normative evaluation of Confucianism, at least with regard to its applicability to the modern world, is a separate project from the one that this book is concerned with. Philosophers and political theorists have long studied the early Greeks without expecting them to necessarily solve modern problems. In fact, Plato and Aristotle often provide a foil to modern thought, in terms of an account of possible philosophical paths that were in fact rejected in the modern world.[5] Similarly, the importance of early Confucian political thought should not depend on its modern applicability. My aim in this book has been to re-create the political world as imagined by the early Confucians, by proposing a new interpretation of Classical Confucian political thought.

---

[5] See, for example, Quentin Skinner, *Visions of Politics Volume 1: Regarding Method* (Cambridge: Cambridge University Press, 2002).

Bibliography

Ackerly, Brooke. "Is Liberalism the Only Way toward Democracy? Confucianism and Democracy." *Political Theory* 33, no. 4 (August 2005): 547–76.

Ames, Roger T. "Mencius and a Process Notion of Human Nature." In Chan, *Mencius: Contexts and Interpretations*, 79–90.

Ames, Roger T. and Henry and Rosemont, trans. *The Analects of Confucius: A Philosophical Translation*. New York: Ballantine Books, 1998.

Angle, Stephen C. *Contemporary Confucian Political Philosophy: Toward Progressive Confucianism*. Cambridge: Polity, 2012.

———. *Sagehood: The Contemporary Significance of Neo-Confucian Philosophy*. Oxford: Oxford University Press, 2009.

Aristotle. *Politics*. Translated by C.D.C Reeve. Cambridge: Hackett, 1998.

Bai, Tongdong. "A Mencian Version of Limited Demcoracy." *Res Publica* 14 (2008): 19–34.

———. "The Political Philosophy of China." In *The Routledge Companion to Social and Political Philosophy*, edited by Gerald F. Gaus and Fred D'Agostino, 181–91. New York: Routledge, 2013.

Bauer, Joanne R. and Daniel A. Bell. *The East Asian Challenge for Human Rights*. Cambridge: Cambridge University Press, 1999.

Bell, Daniel. *Beyond Liberal Democracy: Political Thinking for an East Asian Context*. Princeton: Princeton University Press, 2006.

———. *China's New Confucianism: Politics and Everyday Life in a Changing Society*. Princeton: Princeton University Press, 2008.

Bloom, Irene. "Biology and Culture in the Mencian View of Human Nature." In Chan, *Mencius: Contexts and Interpretations*, 91–102.

———. "Mengzian Arguments on Human Nature." In Liu and Ivanhoe, *Essays on the Moral Philosophy of Mengzi*, 64–100.

Bolsinger, Eckard. *The Autonomy of the Political: Carl Schmitt's and Lenin's Political Realism*. Westport, CT: Greenwood, 2001.

Brooks, E. Bruce and A. Taeko Brooks. *The Original Analects: Sayings of Confucius and His Successors*. New York: Columbia University Press, 1998.

Chan, Alan. "Does *Xiao* Come Before *Ren*?" In Chan and Tan, *Filial Piety in Chinese Thought and History*, 154–75.

———, ed. *Mencius: Contexts and Interpretations*. Honolulu: University of Hawaii Press, 2002.

Chan, Alan and Sor-hoon Tan, eds. *Filial Piety in Chinese Thought and History.* New York: Routledge, 2004.

Chan, Joseph. *Confucian Perfectionism: A Political Philosophy for Modern Times.* Princeton: Princeton University Press, 2014.

———. "Democracy and Meritocracy: Toward a Confucian Perspective." *Journal of Chinese Philosophy* 34, no. 2 (2007): 179–93.

Chan, Sin Yee. "Filial Piety, Commiseration, and the Virtue of *Ren.*" In Chan and Tan, *Filial Piety in Chinese Thought and History*, 176–88.

Chan, Wing-tsit. *Source Book in Chinese Philosophy.* Princeton: Princeton University Press, 1963.

Chang, Carsun. *The Development of Neo-Confucian Thought.* New York: Bookman Associates, 1962.

Chen, Ning. "The Concept of Fate in Mencius." *Philosophy East and West* 47, no. 4 (1997): 495–520.

Chen Huan-chang. *The Economic Principles of Confucius and His School.* New York, 1911.

Clark, Kelly James and Justin T. Winslett. "The Evolutionary Psychology of Chinese Religion: Pre-Qin High Gods as Punishers and Rewarders." *Journal of the American Academy of Religion* 79, no. 4 (2011): 928–60.

Cline, Erin. *Confucius, Rawls, and the Sense of Justice.* New York: Fordham University Press, 2013.

———. "Religious Thought and Practice in the *Analects.*" In *Dao Companion to the Analects*, edited by Amy Olberding, 273–74. Dordrecht: Springer, 2014.

Company, Robert F. "Xunzi and Durkheim as Theorists of Ritual Practice." In *Structure and Function in Primitive Society*, edited by A. R. Radcliffe-Brown, 157–58. New York: Free Press, 1965.

Confucius. *The Analects.* Translated by D. C. Lau. London: Penguin, 1979.

———. *The Analects of Confucius: A Philosophical Translation.* Translated by Roger T. Ames and Henry Rosemont. New York: Ballantine Books, 1998.

———. *A Concordance to the Lunyu.* Edited by D.C.Lau and Chen Fong Ching. ICS Series. Hong Kong: Commercial Press, 1995.

———. *Confucius: Analects with Selections from Traditional Commentaries.* Translated by Edward Slingerland. Indianapolis: Hackett, 2003.

Creel, Herrlee Glessner. *Chinese Thought, from Confucius to Mao Tsê-Tung.* Chicago: University of Chicago Press, 1953.

Csikszentmihalyi, Mark. *Material Virtue: Ethics and the Body in Early China.* Leiden: Brill, 2004.

Cua, Antonio. *Human Nature, Ritual, and History.* Washington, DC: Catholic University of America Press, 2005.

de Bary, William Theodore. *The Liberal Tradition in China.* New York: Columbia University Press, 1983.

———, ed. *Sources of Chinese Tradition.* New York: Columbia University Press, 2000.

———. *The Trouble with Confucianism.* Cambridge, MA: Harvard University Press, 1996.

de Bary, William Theodore and Tu Weiming, eds. *Confucianism and Human Rights.* New York: Columbia University Press, 1998.

Ebrey, Patricia. "Imperial Filial Piety as a Political Problem." In Chan and Tan, *Filial Piety in Chinese Thought and History*, 122–40.

Elstein, David. *Democracy in Contemporary Confucian Philosophy*. New York: Routledge, 2015.

———. "Why Early Confucianism Cannot Generate Democracy." *Dao* 9 (2010): 427–43.

Eno, Robert. "Casuistry and Character in the *Mencius*." In Chan, *Mencius: Contexts and Interpretations*, 198.

———. *The Confucian Creation of Heaven: Philosophy and the Defense of Ritual Mastery*. New York: State University of New York Press, 1990.

Fingarette, Herbert. *Confucius: The Secular as Sacred*. Long Grove, IL: Waveland Press, 1972.

Frank, Jill. "Citizens, Slaves, and Foreigners: Aristotle on Human Nature." *American Political Science Review* 98, no. 1 (February 2004): 91–104.

Fraser, Chris. "Happiness in Classical Confucianism: Xunzi." *Philosophical Topics* 41, no. 1 (2013): 53–79.

———. "Mohism." In *The Stanford Encyclopedia of Philosophy (Summer 2010 Edition)*, edited by Edward N. Zalta. http://plato.stanford.edu/archives/sum2010/entries/mohism/.

Fung Yu-lan. *History of Chinese Philosophy*. Translated by Derk Bodde. Princeton: Princeton University Press, 1952.

Geertz, Clifford. *Negara: The Theatre State in Nineteenth-Century Bali*. Princeton: Princeton University Press, 1980.

Geuss, Raymond. *Philosophy and Real Politics*. Princeton: Princeton University Press, 2008.

Goldin, Paul. *Confucianism*. Berkeley: University of California Press, 2011.

———. *Rituals of the Way: The Philosophy of Xunzi*. Chicago: Open Court, 1999.

Graham, A. C. "The Background of the Mencian Theory of Human Nature." In Liu and Ivanhoe, *Essays on the Moral Philosophy of Mengzi*, 1–63.

———. *Disputers of the Tao: Philosophical Argument in Ancient China*. Chicago: Open Court, 1989.

Hall, David and Roger Ames. *Democracy of the Dead: Dewey, Confucius, and the Hope for Democracy in China*. Chicago: Open Court, 1999.

———. *Thinking through Confucius*. New York: State University of New York Press, 1987.

Han Feizi. *The Complete Works of Han Fei Tzŭ: A Classic of Chinese Legalism*. Volume 1. Translated by W.K. Liao. London: Arthur Probsthain, 1939.

———. *Han Feizi: Basic Writings*. Translated by Burton Watson. New York: Columbia University Press, 2003.

Hansen, Chad. *A Daoist Theory of Chinese Thought: A Philosophical Interpretation*. Oxford: Oxford University Press, 1992.

Harris, Eirik Lang. "Constraining the Ruler: On Escaping Han Fei's Criticism of Confucian Virtue Politics." *Asian Philosophy* 23, no. 1 (2013): 43–61.

———. "The Role of Virtue in Xunzi's Political Philosophy." *Dao* 12 (2013): 93–110.

Herr, Ranjoo Seodu. "Confucian Democracy and Equality." *Asian Philosophy* 20, no. 3 (2010): 261–82.

Honig, Bonnie. *Political Theory and the Displacement of Politics*. Ithaca, NY: Cornell University Press, 1993.

Hsiao Kung-chuan. *History of Chinese Political Thought*. Translated by Frederick Mote. Princeton: Princeton University Press, 1979.

Hsu, Cho-yun. *Ancient China in Transition: An Analysis of Social Mobility, 722–222 B.C.* Stanford: Stanford University Press, 1965.

———. "The Spring and Autumn Period." In Loewe and Shaughnessy, *Cambridge History of Ancient China*, 545–87.

Hsu, Cho-yun and Katheryn M. Linduff. *Western Chou Civilization*. New Haven: Yale University Press, 1988.

Hu, Shaohua. "Confucianism and Western Democracy." In Zhao, *China and Democracy*, 55–72.

Hui, Victoria Tin-bor. *War and State Formation in Ancient China and Early Modern Europe*. Cambridge: Cambridge University Press, 2005.

Hunter, Mick. "Sayings of Confucius: Deselected." PhD dissertation, Princeton University, 2012.

Hutton, Eric. "Does Xunzi Have a Consistent Theory of Human Nature?" In Kline and Ivanhoe, *Virtue, Nature, and Moral Agency in the Xunzi*, 220–36.

———. "Han Feizi's Criticism of Confucianism and Its Implications for Virtue Ethics." *Journal of Moral Philosophy* 5 (2008): 423–53.

Ing, Michael. *The Dysfunction of Ritual in Early Confucianism*. Oxford: Oxford University Press, 2012.

Ivanhoe, Philip. "Confucian Self Cultivation and Mengzi's Notion of Extension." In Liu and Ivanhoe, *Essays on the Moral Philosophy of Mengzi*, 221–41.

———. "A Happy Symmetry: Xunzi's Ethical Thought." *Journal of the American Academy of Religion* 59, no. 2 (Summer 1991): 311–12.

———. "Heaven as a Source of Ethical Warrant in Early Confucianism." *Dao* 6 (2007): 211–20.

———. "A Question of Faith: A New Interpretation of Mencius 2B.13." *Early China* 13 (1988): 153–65.

Jiang Qing. *A Confucian Constitutional Order: How China's Ancient Past Can Shape Its Political Future*. Princeton: Princeton University Press, 2013.

Jiang, Xinyan. "Mengzi on Human Nature and Courage." In Liu and Ivanhoe, *Essays on the Moral Philosophy of Mengzi*, 143–62.

Jenco, Leigh. *Making the Political: Founding and Action in the Political Theory of Zhang Shizhao*. New York: Cambridge University Press, 2010.

Keay, John. *China: A History*. London: Harper, 2008.

Kern, Martin, ed. *Text and Ritual in Early China*. Seattle: University of Washington Press, 2005.

Kim, Sungmoon. "Between Good and Evil: Xunzi's Reinterpretation of the Hegemonic Rule as Decent Governance." *Dao* 12 (2013): 73–92.

———. "Confucian Constitutionalism: Mencius and Xunzi on Virtue, Ritual, and Royal Transmission." *Review of Politics*, no. 73 (2011): 371–99.

———. "From Desire to Civility: Is Xunzi a Hobbesian?" *Dao* 10 (2011): 291–309.

———. "Virtue Politics and Political Leadership: A Confucian Rejoinder to Han Feizi." *Asian Philosophy* 22, no. 2 (2012): 177–97.

Kline, T. C., III and Philip Ivanhoe, eds. *Virtue, Nature, and Moral Agency in the Xunzi.* Indianapolis: Hackett, 2000.

Kline, T. C., III and Justin Tiwald, eds. *Ritual and Religion in the Xunzi.* New York: State University of New York Press, 2014.

Kraut, Richard. *Aristotle: Political Philosophy.* Oxford: Oxford University Press, 2002.

Lau, D. C. "Theories of Human Nature in *Mencius* and *Xunzi.*" In Kline and Ivanhoe, *Virtue, Nature, and Moral Agency in the Xunzi,* 188–219.

Lee, Janghee. *Xunzi and Early Chinese Naturalism.* New York: State University of New York Press, 2005.

Lewis, Mark Edward. "Ritual Origins of the Warring States." *Bulletin de l'Ecole française d'Extrême-Orient* 84 (1997): 73–98.

———. "Warring States Political History." In Loewe and Shaughnessy, *Cambridge History of Ancient China,* 588–652.

———. *Writing and Authority in Early China.* New York: State University of New York Press, 1999.

Li, Chenyang. *The Confucian Philosophy of Harmony.* New York: Routledge, 2014.

———. "Confucian Value and Democratic Value." *Journal of Value Inquiry* 31, no. 2 (1997): 183–93.

Li, Feng. *Landscape and Power in Early China.* New York: Cambridge University Press, 2006.

Liu, Honghe. *Confucianism in the Eyes of a Confucian Liberal: Hsu Fu-Kuan's Critical Examination of the Confucian Political Tradition.* New York: Peter Lang, 2001.

Liu, Jeeloo. *An Introduction to Chinese Philosophy: From Ancient Philosophy to Chinese Buddhism.* Oxford: Wiley-Blackwell, 2006.

Liu, Xiusheng and Philip J. Ivanhoe, eds. *Essays on the Moral Philosophy of Mengzi.* Indianapolis: Hackett, 2002.

Loewe, Michael and Edward Shaughnessy, eds. *The Cambridge History of Ancient China: From the Origins of Civilization to 221 BC.* Cambridge: Cambridge University Press, 1999.

Louie, Kam. *Critiques of Confucius in Contemporary China.* New York: St. Martin's, 1980.

Machle, Edward. *Nature and Heaven in the Xunzi: A Study of the Tian Lun.* New York: State University of New York Press, 1993.

Makeham, John. *Transmitters and Creators: Chinese Commentators and Commentaries on the Analects.* Cambridge, MA: Harvard University Press, 2003.

Mencius. *A Concordance to the Mengzi.* Edited by D.C.Lau and Chen Fong Ching. ICS Series. Hong Kong: Commercial Press, 1995.

———. *The Essential Mengzi: Selected Passages with Traditional Commentary.* Translated by Bryan Van Norden. Indianapolis: Hackett, 2009.

———. *Mencius.* Translated by Irene Bloom. New York: Columbia University Press, 2009.

———. *Mencius.* Translated by D. C. Lau. Rev. ed. London: Penguin, 2003.

———. *Mengzi: With Selections from Traditional Commentaries.* Translated by Bryan Van Norden. Indianapolis: Hackett, 2008.

Metzger, Thomas. *A Cloud across the Pacific: Essays on the Clash between Chinese and Western Political Theories Today*. Beijing: Chinese University Press, 2006.

———. *Escape from Predicament: Neo-Confucianism and China's Evolving Political Culture*. New York: Columbia University Press, 1986.

Mote, Frederick. *Intellectual Foundations of China*. New York: Knopf, 1971.

Mozi. *The Ethical and Political Works of Motse*. Translated by Yi-Pao Mei. London: Arthur Probsthain, 1929.

———. *Mozi: Basic Writings*. Translated by Burton Watson. New York: Columbia University Press, 2003.

———. *The Mozi: A Complete Translation*. Translated and annotated by Ian Johnston. New York: Columbia University Press, 2010.

Munro, Donald. *The Concept of Man in Early China*. Stanford: Stanford University Press, 1969.

Murthy, Viren. "The Democratic Potential of Confucian *Minben* Thought." *Asian Philosophy* 10, no. 1 (2000): 33–47.

Needham, Joseph. *Science and Civilization in China*. Vol. 2. Cambridge: Cambridge University Press, 1956.

Nivison, David. "Mengzi: Just Not Doing It." In Liu and Ivanhoe, *Essays on the Moral Philosophy of Mengzi*, 132–42.

———. "Motivation and Moral Action in Mencius." In Van Norden, *Ways of Confucianism*, 91–119.

———. "Two Roots or One?" In Van Norden, *Ways of Confucianism*, 133–48.

———. "Xunzi and Zhuangzi." In Kline and Ivanhoe, *Virtue, Nature, and Moral Agency in the Xunzi*, 176–87.

Nivison, David and Arthur F. Wright, eds. *Confucianism in Action*. Stanford: Stanford University Press, 1959.

Nylan, Michael. *The Five "Confucian" Classics*. New Haven: Yale University Press, 2001.

———. "The Politics of Pleasure." *Asia Major* 14, no. 1 (2001): 73–124.

———. "Toward an Archaeology of Writing: Text, Ritual, and the Culture of Public Display in the Classical Period (475 B.C.E.–220 C.E.)." In Kern, *Text and Ritual in Early China*, 3–49.

Nylan, Michael and Harrison Huang. "Mencius on Pleasure." In *Polishing the Chinese Mirror: Essays in Honor of Henry Rosemont*, edited by Marthe Chandler and Ronnie Littlejohn, 245–70. La Salle, IL: Association of Chinese Philosophers of America and Open Court, 2007.

Pankenier, David. *Astrology and Cosmology in Early China: Conforming Earth to Heaven*. Cambridge: Cambridge University Press, 2013.

Peterson, Willard. "Another Look at Li." *Bulletin of Sung-Yuan Studies* 18 (1986): 13–32.

Pines, Yuri. "Changing Views of *Tianxia* in Pre-imperial Discourse." *Oriens Extremus* 43, nos. 1–2 (2002): 101–16.

———. "Disputers of Abdication: Zhanguo Egalitarianism and the Sovereign's Power." *T'oung Pao* 91, no. 4 (2005): 243–300.

———. *Envisioning Eternal Empire: Chinese Political Thought of the Warring States Era*. Honolulu: University of Hawaii Press, 2009.

Plato. *The Republic*. Edited by G.R.F. Ferrari. Cambridge: Cambridge University Press, 2011.

Puett, Michael J. "Following the Commands of Heaven: The Notion of *Ming* in Early China." In *The Magnitude of Ming: Command, Allotment, and Fate in Chinese Culture*, edited by Christopher Lupke, 49–69. Honolulu: University of Hawaii Press, 2005.

———. *To Become a God: Cosmology, Sacrifice, and Self-Divinization in Early China*. Cambridge, MA: Harvard University Press, 2002.

Rawls, John. *A Theory of Justice*. Rev. ed. Cambridge, MA: Harvard University Press, 1999.

Robins, Dan. "Xunzi." In *The Stanford Encyclopedia of Philosophy*, edited by Edward N. Zelta. http://plato.stanford.edu/archives/fall2008/entries/xunzi/.

Roetz, Heiner. *Confucian Ethics of the Axial Age: A Reconstruction under the Aspect of the Breakthrough toward Postconventional Thinking*. New York: State University of New York Press, 1993.

Rosemont, Henry, Jr. "State and Society in the *Xunzi*: A Philosophical Commentary." In Kline and Ivanhoe, *Virtue, Nature, and Moral Agency in the Xunzi*, 1–38.

Rosen, Sydney. "In Search of the Historical Kuan Chung." *Journal of Asian Studies* 35, no. 3 (May 1976): 431–40.

Rowe, William T. *Saving the World: Chen Hongmou and Elite Consciousness in Eighteenth-Century China*. Stanford: Stanford University Press, 2001.

Sa Mengwu. *Zhongguo zhengzhi sixiang shi* 中國政治思想史 [The history of Chinese political thought]. Taibei: Sanmin shuju, 1969.

Sato, Masayuki. *The Confucian Quest for Order: The Origin and Formation of the Political Thought of Xun Zi*. Leiden: Brill, 2003.

Schaberg, David. *A Patterned Past: Form and Thought in Early Chinese Historiography*. Cambridge, MA: Harvard University Asia Center, 2001.

Schwartz, Benjamin. "Some Polarities in Confucian Thought." In Nivison and Wright, *Confucianism in Action*, 50–62.

———. *The World of Thought in Ancient China*. Cambridge, MA: Harvard University Press, 1985.

Shaughnessy, Edward. "The Duke of Zhou's Retirement in the East and the Beginnings of the Minister-Monarch Debate in Chinese Political Philosophy." *Early China* 18 (1993): 41–72.

———. "Western Zhou History." In Loewe and Shaughnessy, *Cambridge History of Ancient China*, 293–352.

Shun, Kwong-loi. "Mencius." In *The Stanford Encyclopedia of Philosophy (Winter 2010 Edition)*, edited by Edward N. Zalta. http://plato.stanford.edu/archives/win2010/entries/mencius/.

———. "Moral Reasons in Confucian Ethics." *Journal of Chinese Philosophy* 18 (1991): 353–70.

Shun, Kwong-loi and David B. Wong, eds. *Confucian Ethics: A Comparative Study of Self, Autonomy, and Community*. Cambridge: Cambridge University Press, 2004.

Sim, May. *Remastering Morals with Aristotle and Confucius*. Cambridge: Cambridge University Press, 2007.

Skinner, Quentin. *Visions of Politics Volume 1: Regarding Method*. Cambridge: Cambridge University Press, 2002.

Slingerland, Edward. "The Conception of *Ming* in Early Confucian Thought." *Philosophy East and West* 46, no. 4 (1996): 567–81.

———. *Effortless Action: Wu Wei as Conceptual Metaphor and Spiritual Ideal in Early China*. Oxford: Oxford University Press, 2003.

Stalnaker, Aaron. "Xunzi's Moral Analysis of War and Some of Its Contemporary Implications." *Journal of Military Ethics* 11, no. 2 (August 2012): 97–113.

Sterckx, Roel. "The Economics of Religion in Warring States and Early Imperial China." In *Early Chinese Religion: Part One: Shang through Han (1250 BC–220 AD)*, edited by John Lagerwey and Marc Kalinowski, 839–80. Leiden: Brill, 2009.

Tan, Sor-hoon. "Between Family and State: Relational Tensions in Confucian Ethics." In Chan, *Mencius: Contexts and Interpretations*, 169–88.

———. *Confucian Democracy: A Deweyan Reconstruction*. New York: State University of New York Press, 2004.

———. "Democracy in Confucianism." *Philosophy Compass* 7, no. 5 (2012): 293–303.

T'ang Chün-i. "The *T'ien Ming* [Heavenly Ordinance] in Pre-Ch'in China." *Philosophy East and West* 11, no. 4 (January 1962): 195–218.

Tillman, Hoyt Cleveland. *Confucian Discourse and Chu Hsi's Ascendancy*. Honolulu: University of Hawaii Press, 1992.

———. "The Development of Tension between Virtue and Achievement in Early Confucianism: Attitudes toward Kuan Chung and Hegemon (*pa*), as Conceptual Symbols." *Philosophy East and West* 31, no. 1 (January 1981): 17–28.

———. *Utilitarian Confucianism: Ch'en Liang's Challenge to Chu Hsi*. Cambridge, MA: Harvard University Press, 1982.

Tiwald, Justin. "A Right of Rebellion in the *Mengzi*?" *Dao* 7, no. 3 (Fall 2008): 269–82.

———. "Xunzi on Moral Expertise." *Dao* 11 (2012): 275–93.

Tu Wei-ming. *Confucian Thought: Selfhood as Creative Transformation*. Albany: State University of New York Press, 1985.

Twiss, Sumner B. and Jonathan Chan. "Classical Confucianism, Punitive Expeditions, and Humanitarian Intervention." *Journal of Military Ethics* 11, no. 2 (August 2012): 81–96.

———. "The Classical Confucian Position on the Legitimate Use of Military Force." *Journal of Religious Ethics* 40, no. 3 (2012): 447–72.

Valentini, Laura. "Ideal vs. Non-ideal Theory: A Conceptual Map." *Philosophy Compass* 7, no. 9 (2012): 654–64.

Van Norden, Bryan, trans. *The Essential Mengzi: Selected Passages with Traditional Commentary*. Indianapolis: Hackett, 2009.

———. "Mengzi and Xunzi: Two Views of Human Nature." In Kline and Ivanhoe, *Virtue, Nature, and Moral Agency in the Xunzi*, 103–34.

———, ed. *The Ways of Confucianism: Investigations in Chinese Philosophy*. Chicago: Open Court, 1996.

Veyne, Paul. *Les Grecs ont-ils cru à leurs mythes? Essai sur l'imagination constituante*. Paris: Editions du Seuil, 1983.

Waley, Arthur, trans. *The Analects*. New York: Knopf, 1938.

Wang, Enbao and Regina F. Titunik. "Democracy in China: The Theory and Practice of *Minben*." In Zhao, *China and Democracy*, 73–88.

Williams, Bernard. *In the Beginning Was the Deed: Realism and Moralism in Political Argument*. Edited by Geoffrey Hawthorn. Princeton: Princeton University Press, 2008.

Wolin, Sheldon. *Politics and Vision: Continuity and Innovation in Western Political Thought*. Expanded ed. Princeton: Princeton University Press, 2004.

Wong, David. "Is There a Distinction between Reason and Emotion in Mencius?" *Philosophy East and West* 41, no. 1 (1991): 31–44.

———. "Reasons and Analogical Reasoning in *Mengzi*." In Liu and Ivanhoe, *Essays on the Moral Philosophy of Mengzi*, 187–220.

———. "Xunzi on Moral Motivation." In Kline and Ivanhoe, *Virtue, Nature, and Moral Agency in the Xunzi*, 135–54.

Xu Fuguan. *Xueshu yu zhengzhi zhi jian* 學術與政治之間 [Between academia and politics]. Taizhong: Zhongyang shuju, 1957.

———. *Zhongguo renxing lunshi: xian Qin pian* 中國人性論史：先秦篇 [The history of the Chinese philosophy of human nature: The pre-Qin period]. Taizhong: Sili Donghai daxue, 1963.

———. *Zhongguo sixiang shi lunji* 中國思想史論集 [Collected essays on the history of Chinese thought]. 1974. Reprint, Taibei: Taiwan xuesheng shuju, 1975.

Xunzi. *Xunzi: Basic Writings*. Translated by Burton Watson. New York: Columbia University Press, 2003.

———. *A Concordance to the Xunzi*. Edited by D.C.Lau and Chen Fong Ching. ICS Series. Hong Kong: Commercial Press, 1996.

———. *Xunzi: A Translation and Study of the Complete Works*. 3 vols. Translated by John Knoblock. Stanford: Stanford University Press, 1988–94.

Yang Guorong. "Mengzi and Democracy: Dual Implications." *Journal of Chinese Philosophy* 31, no. 1 (2004): 83–102.

Zhao, Suisheng, ed. *China and Democracy: The Prospect for a Democratic China*. New York: Routledge, 2000.

Index

꿍

agriculture, 71–72; and land ownership by peasants, 72; taxes on agriculture, 72n53; the well-field system, 71

Ames, Roger T., 103n98; depiction of the common people (*min*), 35; on the individuation of the *min*, 36n35; translation of *Analects* 14.16, 53–54n106; on the translation of essential Confucian tenets into a communitarian form of democratic society, 5–6; translation of *ren* (as "authoritative conduct"), 3n5

Analects: anecdotes about government in, 2; anecdotes about a person's conduct in society in, 2; attack on expertise in, 77–78; attribution of to Confucius ("The Master said . . ."), 22, 23; on the common people and the cardinal Confucian virtues, 32n15; composition of, 22–23; Confucius on the qualities expected of the common people in, 34; Confucius's advice to Ji Kangzi in, 31–32; Confucius's advice to Zhong Gong in, 79; Confucius's advice to Zilu in, 32; Confucius's description of his life journey in, 193; Confucius's example of proper attire in, 98n63; Confucius's identification with the underdog, 75; Confucius's preference for the hereditary principle in, 40n49; on Confucius and rituals, 92; Confucius's version of the Golden Rule, 136n85; Confucius's view of the common people's intellectual abilities in, 33; consistency and dating of, 23; contro-versy surrounding its composition, 22–23; on courage, 60, 60n140; editing of by officials of the Han dynasty, 23, 24–25; on fairness or evenhanded treatment, 50, 50n94; on filiality, 107–8, 108n128; the first entry in, 2; on the gentleman's self-cultivation, 147–48; on Heaven as a model of effortless rule, 131n56; on Heaven's allotments, 180–84, 181nn24–25, 188–89n50; lack of mention of *ren*, rightness, and wisdom in relation to the ruler in, 136n78; on merit, 74, 79, 97; on modesty in ritual, 85; on ornamentation in public functions, 85; on political involvement, 148; on the population size in the state of Wei, 70; portrayal of Bo Yi, 166; portrayal of Chen Wenzi, 166–67; portrayal of Duke Huan, 54n108; portrayal of Duke Wen, 54n108; portrayal of Guan Zhong, 53–55, 59, 63, 137n87; portrayal of Shun, 131–32; portrayal of Yao, 131–32; on proper demeanor, 96, 96n58; on public display, 97; on punishments, 66, 67; on remuneration, 153, 155; on resoluteness, 60n139; on taxes on land output, 72; on uncertainty and political involvement, 184–90; use of harmony in, 99, 99n70; on the use of music in rituals, 99–100; on the use of punishments, 66; on the welfare injunction, 68. See also *Analects*, on political involvement, ethical versus political pursuits; *Analects*, on rulers and ministers